CLASSROOM PUBLISHING

A PRACTICAL GUIDE TO ENHANCING STUDENT LITERACY

CLASSROOM PUBLISHING

A PRACTICAL GUIDE TO ENHANCING STUDENT LITERACY

LAURIE KING & DENNIS STOVALL

BLUE HERON PUBLISHING, INC.
HILLSBORO, OREGON

CLASSROOM PUBLISHING
A Practical Guide to Enhancing Student Literacy

Copyright © 1992 by Laurie King & Dennis Stovall

Published by
Blue Heron Publishing, Inc.
24450 NW Hansen Road
Hillsboro, Oregon 97124
503.621.3911

King, Laurie.
    Classroom publishing : a practical guide to enhancing student literacy / Laurie King & Dennis Stovall. — Hillsboro, Or. : Blue Heron Publishing, c1992.
        p. : ill. ; cm.
    Includes bibliographical references and index.
    ISBN 0-936085-52-5

    1. Language arts—United States. 2. Children's writing—Publishing. 3. Youth's writings—Publishing. 4. College student's writings—Publishing. 5. Interdisciplinary approach in education—United States—Case studies.   I. Stovall, Dennis.   II. Title.

LB1570.K   371.3'32 dc20

ISBN 0-936085-52-5
Library of Congress Catalog Card Number: 92-085501

Cover by Marcia Barrentine
Interior design by Dennis Stovall
Printed in the United States of America on paper that is acid-free and recycled

Acknowledgments

The authors have a lot of people to thank. This was an amazingly labor intensive project, too much for the two of us to do in any sensible number of months without an outstanding support group at Blue Heron Publishing.

Many interviews were done by Linny Stovall, who along with Mary Jo Schimelpfenig provided project coordination. They were joined by publishing interns Scott Jones, Anna Reynolds, Holly Santos, Christian Seapy, and Martha Wagner who typed, edited, proofed, researched, checked, double-checked, got permissions, bought rights, and argued fine points of grammar and usage.

Thanks go to all the students whose work we got to study and show. Sorry we can't list them all. But we'd like to invite them to join us in applauding their teachers. Many times we were moved to tears by their reports — as well as by some of the student writing.

We had more material than we could possibly include, and sometimes the decisions about what to use — and where — were tough, the arguments occasionally heated. Whether we finally mentioned a project — or showed a sample — we used everything to create this book.

To the right are the names of those teachers, librarians, publishers, and others who participated. Thank you all.

Geraldine Albert
Bob Argentieri
Gary Bacon
Julia Bates
Michael Bergen
Verity & Gayle Bryant
Ami Bumgardner
Sheila Cantlebary
Bruce Chapman
Janet Charles
Linda Clifton
Donna Clovis
Bill Coate
Janis Cramer
Michael Crosby
Forrest Cuch
Chris Duthie
Sharon Dorsey
Pat Egenberger
Nan Elsasser
Tom Engleman
Carolyn Erwin
Mick Fedullo
Kathy Fiedler
Fran Filer
Patricia Foote
Mary Lu Foreman
Tim Gallagher
Marilyn Gantz
Debbie Garman
The Gingold Family
Diane Goddard
Jennifer Goldman
Nancy Gorrell
Pat Graff
H.L. Hall
Carol Hallenbeck
Keith Hefner
Grady Hillman
Arlene Hirschfelder
Mel Jones
Sheryl Lain
Daniel Lake
Carol Lange
Jerry Large
Nancy Mack
Andrea Mayer
Bruce Maylath
Margaret McLaughlin

Sherry McVeigh
Jerry Mintz
Patricia Muggleston
Emily Norton
Steve O'Donoghue
Michelann Ortloff
Linda Parrish
Robert Pedroncelli
Jerry Phillips
Patricia Price
Joan Purton
The Richman Family
Marcia Roberts
Bain Robinson
Phyllis Rude
Cheryl Sackmann
Lin Sanders
Rich Sanders
David Schaafsma
Ken Schmidt
Cheryl Shackleton
Karen Shepard
Beverly Singer
Lea Smith
Gabrielle Stauf
Bill Stenson
Celeste Stivers
Patti Stock
Dennis Stovall
Anne Sullivan
Michelle Takenishi
Robert Thomas
Carolyn Tragesser
Takiyah Watkins
Chris Weber
Eliot Wigginton
Don Willamson
Connie Woebke
Ellie Zimet

CONTENTS

CHAPTER 4 / EXPANDED AUDIENCES / 87

Section 2
Publishing: who, what, when, where, why, & how

Section 3
Resources

INTRODUCTION

One of our editors remarked that this could be several books. That's right. Think of this as a compact library on classroom publishing and its relationship to the world and the history of all publishing. It's both how-to and here's-how-they-did-it. Then throw in information on careers, a detailed glossary, an annotated bibliography, an index, and several useful resource lists. For the case studies, we considered wonderful projects from all across the country. We've included as many as possible. There are riches to be found here. We were constantly amazed by the ingenuity, the energy, and the indefatigability of the teachers we interviewed and met in the course of this book. And we were just as amazed at the exceptional publications their students produce.

Let no one bad mouth teachers. From a wide range of pedagogical approaches come an equally impressive range of successes. If anything, this book says: "Don't worry. Don't even hesitate. You can experiment with publishing and make it an exciting part of your teaching style and method, no matter what it is."

The book originated in a series of workshops done by the publisher in the schools over the past five years. It became clear that, like writers, most teachers — not to mention librarians — know too little about the actual process of publishing after the writing is done. Not only were both students and teachers responsive to the workshops, but the demystification of the process helped put the writing itself in perspective. There was an obvious opportunity to take students to the next step. But there was something else. Classroom publishing captured the imaginations of students who weren't comfortable writing or editing — kids who had little natural access to the world of words other than reading, if they even did that well. Suddenly they found ways to participate in the world of books because the natural division of labor in the complete publishing process requires so many disparate talents and skills.

Obviously, here was an important tool for educators. Teachers asked if there were texts on the subject, and we could recommend only a few resources, none of which truly addressed their needs. Meanwhile, our travels and conversations added to a growing list of projects that used publishing in a host of ways — from modest to complex, from the expected to the innovative, from single student publications to cross-curricular projects. We knew there was more than enough for a book that could be used by teachers at all levels, and we figured we'd better get busy and publish it. Thus was born CLASSROOM PUBLISHING.

Once we began serious research, the wealth of material became obvious. In fact, it poured in from teachers around the country. We noticed that there were informal networks, but no consistent contact and sharing among the teachers who were breaking new ground in classroom publishing. But over and over, we heard incredible stories of educational success. For instance, Patricia Muggleston of Academy Elementary School in Madison, Connecticut, wrote: "When I was a 5th-grade teacher, I had a special needs student who had published two books before he came into 5th-grade. He was one of these kids who just couldn't ever sit still or stop talking. Constant movement. One day I said something to him about getting started on his work, paying attention. It must have been the tone of voice I used, because he looked me right in the eye and said, 'I don't care what you think of me. I'm an author. And you'll never be able to take that away from me.'"

Enthusiastic hardly describes how teachers who use the publishing process view its impact. High school English teacher Carol Hallenbeck of Sunny Hills High School in Fullerton, California, put it succinctly. "Classroom publishing," she wrote, "fits into my philosophy of education because it develops individual skills in a group situation in which everyone is interdependent. There is room for creativity and initiative and individual glory in an atmosphere where the greatest cooperation is absolutely essential. There is room for growth in any and all directions — people management, technical skills in darkroom or on computer, artistic skills, writing skills, editing skills, critical thinking skills — all involved in every story and every page and every issue. Nothing is ever the same and no problem is exactly like the last one. It's never dull."

We wanted to share this excitement as widely as possible. Illiteracy continues to be a major problem in our society, and here is a means to get even reluctant students involved. Moreover, using the publishing process in the curriculum involves much more than simply learning to read. To take full advantage of it, a variety of resources are necessary. And those needs dictated the content and organization of this book.

We divided the book as follows. There are two major sections: First, we introduce and discuss the case studies, interviews, curricula, testimonials, admonitions, essays, and teacherly discussions. Second, we tackle both theory and practice at once, in adjacent columns. This is a detailed description of the complete publishing process, from manuscript on, including copious examples of student projects. We believe the table of contents will do a good job of directing you to appropriate chapters. And you can use the index to home in more closely on a subject of interest.

A project like this has no distinct beginning or end, only landmarks. This book is one such. We expect there will be others. Certainly, there are many wonderful publishing projects we didn't learn of in time to include. There will be many more. As you use this volume, add your notes to the margins. Better yet, type them up and send us a copy. We'll try to keep in touch. The generous support of those of you in the trenches has made CLASSROOM PUBLISHING possible.

Dennis Stovall &
Laurie King
Portland, Oregon
August 1992

THE AUTHORS

Laurie King has taught philosophy at Reed College and at Portland State University. She also taught high school English in southern California and humanities in a middle school in Portland. Laurie is the author of *Hear My Voice: An Anthology of Multicultural Literature from the United States* to be published in the spring of 1993 by Addison Wesley.

Dennis Stovall is co-publisher of Blue Heron Publishing. He is a writer and a teacher of writing and publishing who has regularly encouraged the inclusion of publishing in the curriculum at all levels. He is a frequent presenter at conferences of writers, teachers, and librarians. Dennis, by the way, is no known relation to the Dennis Stovall of Anchorage interviewed for this book, though he looks forward to meeting him.

Tales from the classroom

How to Use Section 1

The purpose of SECTION 1, TALES FROM THE CLASSROOM is to present publishing ideas developed by educators we interviewed. In each segment, we tried to capture the educator's pedagogical approach and style.

Because we used over 50 sources, and because there is so much information presented by the teachers, we thought that a short tour of SECTION 1 would be helpful.

1. Variety in format — Some segments include step-by-step lesson or unit plans. You will find, for instance, detailed sequential plans on how to produce a children's book in *Chapter 1,* which contains many step-by-step plans, but you will find such plans throughout the book. Other segments present kernels of ideas for classroom publishing projects. In *Chapter 4,* for example, a reporter from *The Seattle Times,* who works in the "Adopt a School" program, relates how she conducts her assigned interviews in front of a class in order to teach interviewing techniques by example. This kernel can be infused into a variety of lessons or units.

Look for "Additional Ideas" at the end of some segments. Other projects that arose organically from the original project are found here, as well as our suggestions.

2. Chapter organization — SECTION 1 is has four chapters, each with a short introduction. *Chapter 1, Publishing and the Language Arts Classroom,* includes lesson ideas from English teachers for whom pub-

lishing is a natural way to integrate language arts skills. *Chapter 2, Publishing Across the Curriculum,* looks at publishing projects that draw from more than one subject area. The projects in *Chapter 3, New Voices,* publish the voices of teenagers who are among the least heard from members of our society. In *Chapter 4, Expanded Audiences,* the focus is on projects which bring student writing to audiences that are unusually sophisticated for young authors.

Teachers we interviewed told us rich, unique stories that do not fit into four neat categories. We grouped them in chapters to bring out what we felt were the most salient features of each project. You may well see additional aspects of the projects that are important to you.

How can teachers in different subject areas, as well as homeschool instructors or teachers in self-contained classrooms, use these chapters?

a. English, foreign language, and ESL teachers will be able to use the lessons developed by English teachers in *Chapter 1,* the cross-curricular projects in *Chapter 2,* the multicultural projects in *Chapter 3,* and journalism lessons and techniques in *Chapter 4.*

b. Social science, natural science, mathematics, vocational, and art teachers should turn to *Chapter 2,* which contains multi-curricular projects. There you will find, for example, ideas on publishing technical manuals and guides that can illuminate topics in any discipline.

However, *Chapter 2* should not be an end point for teachers in the various content areas. Publishing projects originally developed for language arts classes in *Chapter 1* may be adapted to all these other subjects. For instance, you may have your class write children's books on math problems or on scientific concepts and experiments using the step-by-step lesson on writing children's books in *Chapter 1.*

A number of projects in *Chapter 3* can be used in all content areas. For instance, a social studies teacher may wish to practice social science techniques by publishing ethnographies as described in *Chapter 3.*

c. Journalism teachers will want to turn to *Chapter 4,* which includes discussions by journalism teachers and journalists in the schools.

d. Magazine advisors can find literary arts magazines discussed in *Chapter 1,* while cross-curricular magazines are explored in *Chapter 2.* Multicultural projects in *Chapter 3* would be welcome additions to many school magazines. Also, magazine advisors are likely to be interested in innovative journalistic techniques, as well as ways to expand the audience for student publishing. These can be found in *Chapter 4.*

A last note on grade levels: Teachers have developed their lessons for the grades they teach, but ideas can be adapted for other age groups. In fact, both a high school teacher and a 1st grade teacher have presented units on student-produced anthologies of readings.

Chapter 1

PUBLISHING AND THE LANGUAGE ARTS CLASSROOM

Our exploration of publishing ideas and formats begins in the traditional English classroom, where students write poetry, stories, essays, and read literature. Publishing can find a home in a number of areas in the school, both academic and vocational, but perhaps the most hospitable niche for publishing is the primary place of language learning — the English class.

For some teachers, publishing is the keystone of a content, or meaning based, approach to teaching English. When reading and writing are presented as part of a process of thinking and communicating (rather than as discrete skills to be mastered), it is indeed a logical extension to publish student work. English teachers who help their students publish, *demonstrate* to their students that language functions to communicate. Publishing, like performing a play, is a tangible form of communication.

We believe the facts show that when publishing is part of language arts activities, the quality of reading and writing are significantly enhanced. The activities in this section show how the prospect of publishing helps raise students' motivation and dedication. Instead of just writing stories, essays, or poetry, students write books for an appreciative audience of young children, compile a class set of provocative essays for community distribution, and create personal anthologies of exceptional depth and beauty.

BOOKS OF ESSAYS ON A COMMON THEME

Dennis Stovall

Anchorage, Alaska

Clark Junior High School

7th & 8th-grades

4

"Publishing isn't really a part of my program — it is my program."

"My students write about a wide range of topics. They write about Vietnam veterans. They evaluate the process by which they were taught to read. They write about truth and lies in our society. And they write about why the American educational system is in a state of collapse. Is there a special slant to their published work? Whenever necessary, whenever possible, whenever the time is right."

Dennis Stovall's 7th and 8th-graders in Anchorage, Alaska, produce books of essays, books of poetry, newspapers, and TV scripts. They also submit individual works of fiction and non-fiction to publishers. When asked how publishing fits into his program, he replied, "Publishing isn't really a part of my program — it is my program. What's the alternative? Students turning in work to me for a quick grade, and then having the same work returned to them? It's like the old Peggy Lee song, 'Is that all there is?' My goal is to bring students' work to the world." In this section we will look at the books of essays that Dennis helps his students bring to the world.

The books that Dennis' students produce once or twice a year are about provocative topics, and they are widely distributed. These students know that their audience is far broader than is typical for middle school writers. About 250 copies of each book of essays on a common theme are distributed in the outside community.

Coming Into Focus — the Vietnam Years was distributed to many who went through that era. *How I Learned To Read*, an evaluation of the factors that make learning successful or unsuccessful, was distributed to student teachers and university students planning to become teachers. *Truth and Lies Through 14-year-old Eyes*, a collection of personal essays on the importance of honesty in our society, found its audience in local lawmakers, school administrators, and criminal justice system personnel. The book for 1991, *Is There No Hope for America's Schools?*, is a series of essays explaining the premise: "The American education system is in a state of collapse." The students' audience included school administrators and state and community leaders.

Because the students write about topics they care about, and because Dennis makes them aware that they have important things to say and that people are interested in what they have to say, these students are motivated to do their best writing and revising. The students write in a clear voice from their own viewpoints. It is obvious that they are not just writing to do the assignment.

The essays are reflective and are carefully constructed to be persuasive. Students provide ample evidence to explain and illustrate their points.

Who puts together these handsome books? Dennis explains, "At one time or another, every student does every step. I require all students to write, word process, edit, proofread, and re-edit their own writing. In addition, I rotate different students on an editorial team that reviews student writing. That editorial team is responsible for editing, proofreading, design and layout, as well as printing on the laser printer. The editorial team also assists with distribution. Binding assistance comes from a different class at our school, a Special Education class of handicapped students who likes to help us. These students get recognition in our publications as 'support staff.'

"What classroom management techniques have I developed to keep the publishing process flowing relatively smoothly? I hate the term 'flowing smoothly.' I've never seen teaching flow smoothly. With each of my twelve years I've actually seen it get tougher and tougher. Oddly, with each successive year, I've learned to get kids to write more, write better, and write with more success. What I've learned is that the key to successful writing is motivation, and leaving students alone to write. I talk to them about purpose, I fully explain their audience, and I try to make the room quiet enough for them to write. I had to learn to let go of my earlier rigid control. I wish I could say that the whole class is always involved, but that would be a lie. The students are not always on task. Writing doesn't work that way — sometimes we work, sometimes we play. I just look to the end product."

"Community support is overwhelming," Dennis reports. "All our books and newspapers are sold out, local newspapers and TV stations cover our projects, students receive hundreds of letters of support for their work, and businesses, community groups, and public officials donate money to us for equipment. Students don't always enjoy the work, but they enjoy the success!"

COMMUNITY RECOGNITION

OLDER STUDENTS PUBLISH BOOKS FOR A YOUNGER AUDIENCE

Pat Graff

Albuquerque, New Mexico

La Cueva High School

English

"I think she said she's going to read to us!"

"The students write alphabet books, books about cats and magic French bread, animal books, and stories about young men who grow forests in their urban apartment."

Pat Graff of La Cueva High School in Albuquerque, New Mexico, has developed a comprehensive publishing project that integrates reading, listening, speaking, and writing, as well as art. In this project older students create books for a younger audience. The most striking aspect of this activity is how virtually all student writers are motivated to do their very best writing and revising. Pat's guidelines are quite structured, although students help develop the criteria for grading their books.

A number of other teachers have developed projects similar to this one. For instance, we will see later in this chapter how Janis Cramer prepares her students to enter the Landmark children's book contest. We have included Pat's plans in detail because they form a complete model that includes all facets of language arts. Teachers will want to revise and embellish these plans for their own use.

The following was excerpted by permission from Pat Graff's booklet *Forging Links to Literacy: High School Students Promote Reading and Writing.*

A hush falls over the classroom full of super-cool sophomores as they struggle to understand what the teacher has just said.

"I **think** she said she's going to **read** to us!" one student whispers, aghast. "A kiddy book, even!"

As they shift nervously in their chairs, the teacher nods with a smile. "Let's make a circle with our chairs," she instructs. "Gather around me and listen. I'm going to read a children's story to you. It's one of my favorites: *Alexander and the Terrible, Horrible, No Good, Very Bad Day.*"

The students comply skeptically, then they start to listen. They *really* listen! This is a good book, and they don't have to take notes. Then there are *more* children's books to read! Excitement builds as they recognize some familiar favorites. They begin to read to each other!

This is the kind of enthusiasm generated with a unit I teach in my Communication Skills classes on writing, speaking, and reading. At the end of the unit, students have written their own children's book, learned to read books to others, and developed storytelling skills. The unit is culminated with a day-long trip to several area elementary schools where these same "super-cool sophomores" share their love of reading and writing with younger students. All the elements of a successful program are in this unit:

writing to a real audience, dealing with the community, and developing creativity and self-esteem while working with one's peers. Yet the unit is easily adapted to suit many different grade levels, situations, locales, and student ability levels. Here is a description of the project:

Learning to love reading and writing, and sharing that love, is the primary purpose of this classroom unit. During the program, students familiarize themselves with a variety of children's books, write their own book, learn storytelling techniques, generate their own stylized stories, and then present 30–45 minute group programs to various elementary schools in the area. In 1990, 70 students reached 55 classrooms in three different schools on our one-day field trip.

The books are produced by the students themselves; they either draw the pictures or find other ways to illustrate: photography, magazine cut-outs, or another artist. Once the books are finished, we listen to good storytellers — local people and tapes of Bill Cosby and Joe Hayes. After each student develops his/her own special story to tell, they practice with each other.

To culminate the learning process, we travel to three elementary schools during a school day as a school-related absence. Students are divided into teams of 4–5, based upon the reading level of their respective books. They plan their 30–45 minute programs for their audiences. They "arm" themselves with extra books and stories, in case they need more material. Flexibility must be remembered, since each teacher will want things done slightly differently. In planning our itinerary, schools are chosen for the variety of socio-economic backgrounds they offer to our "middle class" student population. Arrangements are made with each school's principal. We talk about appropriate dress, serving as models of behavior, and how to handle emergency situations.

The travel day arrives. Students spend the first hour going over their programs one more time. Then we board the bus and arrive at our first school. The "super-cool sophomores" are awfully nervous; they don't yet realize that their audience is going to love them because of their age, their enthusiasm, and their "product." Students go into their first room, hesitant and unsure; they emerge, beaming and enthusiastic! Little ones hang on their every word, they are invited to play basketball at recess, teachers gush praise, and a feeling of confidence develops. This is replayed twice more during the day.

Each year I have them fill out evaluations of the project; many feel it is the best thing they have done in high school so far.

1. I introduce this unit by reading to the students one of my favorites: *Alexander and the Terrible, Horrible, No Good, Very Bad Day*, by Judith Viorst. It's a book to which students can relate, and its humor is appreciated. As I read, I stop and show them the pictures, modeling for them the way one should read books to a large group of children We also usually have cookies that day to set the "fun" tone of the unit.

2. After opening the class with *Alexander*, I pass out stacks of children's books for them to read to each other. (My students are grouped at tables, so this activity is easily arranged.) I ask them to read to each other as I have done, and I challenge them to sample as many books as possible. I get the books from my own children's collections as well as the local public library; usually I bring in 50–100 books.

3. We continue the sharing for two class periods. Students then generate lists of the "Top Ten Books," which they share with the class. From this discussion, we talk about what makes a good children's book.

4. Next, students take notes on the various types of children's books that can be written. These categories are somewhat arbitrary, but help give the students ideas about types of books they might want to write: primary (alphabet, numbers, shapes), animals/science, fairy tale, adventure, fantasy/science fiction, teaching/moral/fable, cultural/historical, careers, circle book. As we talk about these types, students name examples they have read in class. I also instruct them on some key elements in all children's books: art, story or plot, use of feelings, easy to read type, and a catchy, colorful cover and title.

5. Finally, students develop their own grading criteria for the books they will create. These criteria serve as my guideline for grading their books. Here is a sample of criteria developed by students in the past:

- 10 pages minimum
- creative
- includes artwork
- neatly done
- cover includes the title and author's name
- age-appropriate vocabulary
- entertaining

- use of color
- easy-to-read for intended audience
- neat lettering/big type
- title page
- story/plot
- original
- topic appropriate for young audience

By developing their own grading criteria as a group, students feel more comfortable with the grading to be done on their books and know clearly what is expected of them. There is virtually no grumbling about length and requirements, since they developed these themselves and agreed on them.

1. It helps to have students hear from a guest speaker as they begin to create their own books. In the past, Eleanor Schick, a nationally-published author who lives in Albuquerque, has come to speak to my students regarding the entire process of authorship: from developing the concept to writing to illustrating to checking printer proofs. As an alternative to an actual author, teachers might invite a local children's bookstore owner or a librarian. It's important for the students to hear from outside resources regarding their impending project.

2. Grading criteria for their books have already been developed, so students know what is expected. With regard to illustration, I encourage them to be creative. They can use photographs, simple line drawings, cut-outs, magazine pictures, stickers, or whatever! They may also "commission" their art and collaborate with an illustrator to develop the book; the only requirement is that they must give credit for the art to the artist. Once the assignment is made, I generally give them 3–4 weeks to do the actual writing.

3. Production days at school are important in helping the students with the final touches in binding and finishing. We borrow a spiral binder and a laminating machine. Students get handouts on different ways to bind. Two to three class periods are planned for this work shortly before the deadline for turning in the books.

4. When the books are finished, we spend a day reading each other's work in small groups. Sometimes we use Post-it notes to write positive comments on the books; other times we use reader's logs to comment on 5–10 of our favorite books.

5. As I grade the books, using the students' developed criteria, I also do a quick analysis of readability on each book in order to group the book for our future field trip. I group the books in one of three categories: primary (grades K–1), middle (grades 2–3), and advanced (grades 4–5). This helps greatly when I am grouping the students for their sharing later in the school year. I do not use any set formula; instead I group by vocabulary, story line, topics, and sentence structure. When in doubt, I group a book in the higher category.

Teaching Tips: Storytelling

1. Now that the books are written, it's time to develop the oral storytelling skills which students will use in their field trip. We start by listening to recorded storytellers. Be sure that the recorded artists you use are appropriate for your classroom, as some can be extremely obscene! We listen to Bill Cosby's "Greatest Hits," Arlo Guthrie's "Alice's Restaurant," and several stories by Southwestern storyteller Joe Hayes. ("La Llorona" and "The Day It Snowed Tortillas" are favorites.) All of these are available on cassette. We then talk about what makes a good storyteller and come up with elements such as a good story, characterization through voices, description, setting created, and humor.

2. This is a good time to bring in a local storyteller so students can observe storytelling techniques in person. It might be good to share this experience with a younger group of students; at my school we have a preschool that meets three times a week and which makes a good audience. By having the younger children there, students can see what storytelling techniques work with children; it also helps modify any derogatory behavior that might develop.

3. Students then prepare and deliver a story that is age-appropriate for younger children. Stories can be original or traditional, regional or international, humorous, scary, or moralistic. Stories should be 3–5 minutes in length and incorporate gestures, characterization, and good speaking skills. They tell their stories to the class, which takes several days.

Michelann Ortloff, of Portland, Oregon, devotes three or four class periods to the study of plot and character in published books. This measurably helps her 8th-graders at Sellwood Middle School improve the quality of their own books.

Michelann reads an exciting children's book to the students and then announces that they are going to graph the plot. First the class lists the main parts of the plot or storyline, and these events or episodes are listed on the X-axis drawn on graph paper on the overhead or blackboard. Then for each event, she asks the class what "excitement" value it should receive, and she plots a numerical Y-value to denote the excitement level. In pairs, the students practice graphing the plots of a couple of other published children's books. The class discusses what makes an interesting plot. Action should build and excitement should vary. The story should not be given away too early.

Michelann reads another children's book to the class after priming students to think about the personalities of the characters. After the reading, students discuss the main characters, analyzing their personality traits and the specific ways the author has developed these traits. Students analyze characters using other books that are displayed around the room. The class then discusses the various ways character can be developed.

Michelann asks students to pre-write or brainstorm about their books. She asks students to make some preliminary decisions about the age of their intended audience, the type of book they will write, the title of the book, the personalities and names of their characters, and the overall storyline.

The next two lesson ideas can be incorporated into all or part of Pat Graff's unit on publishing children's books.

Nancy Mack says, "My students wrote children's books that had certain specified grammatical forms. Each page had to have three states of meaning verbs with different complements, like an adjective phrase, noun phrase, or place phrase."

Nancy Mack was preparing herself to begin grammar instruction to her 8th-grade students in Urbana, Illinois, when she suddenly had some new thoughts on the topic. "On my long drive to school, gearing up to teaching grammar eight periods a day, I thought that I just couldn't teach those baby sentences that are linguistically beneath the kids. And then it became clear. BABY SENTENCES! I'll have them write children's books using a variety of specific grammatical forms." Students could use new

ADDITIONAL PROJECTS

DEVELOPING PLOT
AND CHARACTER

PRE-WRITING

SPECIAL KINDS OF
CHILDREN'S BOOKS TO
PUBLISH

TEACHING GRAMMAR
BY WRITING
CHILDREN'S BOOKS

sentence forms as well as punctuation that they do not normally use, like colons and semi-colons."

Nancy's students loved the books they made and had a difficult time giving them away to elementary kids. "When the books were completed it was close to Christmas, so a few kids, dressed as elves, went to the elementary school to give away some of our books. We received thank you notes on huge elementary school paper with big lines, and there wasn't a dry eye in the house. They thought this was so wonderful."

Nancy subsequently used this project with high school students. She is currently teaching composition courses for education majors at Wright State University. They, too, learn how to make children's books, so that they will be able to take their students through the process.

MAKING CHILDREN'S BOOKS HELPS WITH DIFFICULT READING

Anne Sullivan, whose high school publishing project comes later in this chapter, offers an unusual idea. "On several occasions I've had my students publish children's books as a way of helping them read some very difficult books. When I was teaching 9th-grade gifted students, they were having a lot of trouble just following the plot line of *The Odyssey*. One of the ideas I came up with was having them break a chapter from *The Odyssey* into basic events and create a children's book from those events."

This method can be used to help read Shakespearean plays and other difficult works.

"Tomorrow we're going to the elementary school, and my students are going to each do three critiques of children's books. The critiques cover the art, the author's style, plot, characters, the layout, book jacket, everything."

THE EXCITEMENT OF CONTESTS

Janis Cramer

Bethany, Oklahoma

Mustang High School

English

Entering writing contests can be a good vehicle for motivating students to do their best writing and revising. There are many kinds of writing competitions, and perhaps the most fruitful ones are those that actually publish students' work.

Janis Cramer leads her 10th–12th grade creative writing students in Bethany, Oklahoma through a process of writing children's books, beginning with a critique of children's books, and culminating with students entering the Landmark Contest (see Resources). The Landmark organization publishes the books of winning students each year. Janis uses *Written & Illustrated by…* the guide to writing for this contest written by David Melton. Janis finds this guide to be helpful, although she thinks it underestimates the amount of time the different stages will take.

Her students do an excellent job. One year, with 7,500 entries across the nation, she had one student place in the top ten in the oldest age group category and five placed in the top one hundred. "My kids are very competitive with each other, and they also motivate each other in a lot of ways. They cannot stand for someone else to do a better job. On the other hand, they are extremely proud of each other's product."

Janis' interpretation of the Landmark process strikes a careful balance of collaborative and individual work. It is interesting to compare this version of a children's book writing unit to the one created by Pat Graff in order to use elements of both — whether or not students eventually enter the Landmark contest.

JANIS' PROCESS

1. Critique — Students critique three children's books. Students use the elementary school library to look for a good, average and poor book to write about. They look at the art, style, plot, character development, and the book jacket. They do this to sharpen their own writing as well as to develop an eye for what book companies are looking for.

2. Pre-writing: Telling The Story — In their writing groups, the students first tell each other their stories. "It becomes a collaborative effort," Janis explains, "because they just come up with the basic ideas, and then they get so many new ways to change and add to their stories from their groups."

3. The Rough Draft — Janis agrees with David Melton that if students have to write their stories in a short amount of time, they will be more creative. In fact, she has her students write rough drafts in one period! You may wish to keep to this time frame with your students, or

you may want to allow them to have more time. When students write their rough drafts, they also draw sketches of their main characters and these are displayed so students can discuss them.

4. Revising — Students work on drafts with their writing groups. They then use the word processor, and revise and edit again, this time with the aid of new editing groups. The next stage is printing the story, cutting, and doing the layout on big sheets of paper. "They read each other's books and write rave reviews for each other that go on the actual book cover."

5. Artwork and Binding — "Students must do their own art work, which," says Janis, "is a problem for some of the kids. This year I'm going to have the art teacher work with them. The books are hardbound, and they use the cardboard that comes off the backs of art tablets. After covering the cardboard with construction paper, they sew their books together with needle and thread.

6. Older Students Read to the Younger Ones — In contrast to other projects involving writing books for children, including Pat Graff's, Janis only has some students go to the elementary school to read their books. The elementary teachers select the books they want read, and it is a special honor for students to be chosen.

7. Celebration — "We have a cookie and punch reception in the library which is filled with family, friends, high school teachers, and elementary school teachers. We make a poster of each kid, taking information and reviews off their book jackets. All the books are spread out on the tables for everyone to look through. The students gain a certain amount of fame, which is good, because my creative writing kids don't usually get a lot of recognition."

Some of these Mustang High School students achieve further recognition in the community. The Oklahoma Council of Teachers of English February 1992 newsletter announced that the students were available to go to other schools to read their books and explain how they made them.

"I had a lot of fun creating my book. It would be enjoyable and rewarding as a career." — Amy A. Lindberg

Chad Patton's book was selected as one of the top 100 in the country in its age category out of 7,500 entries in the 1991 "Written and Illustrated by..." contest.

Additional Ideas for Contest Projects

Here is another example in which preparing for contests is an integral part of the curriculum.

Carol Lange, a high school teacher in Alexandria, Virginia, teaches an advanced placement Intensive Journalism course in which everyone who wants a B or an A must explore essay writing and enter a competition in the second quarter of the year-long class. Some contests are sponsored by universities. If students do not choose one of these, they may choose a contest from a list that Carol posts. The list comes from two sources. The guidance counselor gives her all the contest information that comes into the school. Carol has also developed ties with several magazines that have developed theme or writing contests. "Last year," Carol says "My students entered a health issues theme contest that the Children's Hospital sponsored. They won the feature writing aspect of that, and their essays were then published through the hospital."

CLASSROOM PUBLISHING AND THE WRITING CONNECTION

Nancy Gorrell

Morristown, New Jersey

Morristown High School

English

TEACHER'S GOALS VS. STUDENTS' GOALS

"Unless you write a book, you never think of your work fitting together. You think of all the isolated exercises. We worked on individual poems; we worked on order; we worked on theme; we worked on organization. And then finally, they had to make those hard decisions on how to put their books together."

Nancy Gorrell's students at Morristown High School in New Jersey wrote regularly and kept writing portfolios. She thought that having her students produce chapbooks of their own poetry, 16 to 24 pages long, would motivate them to do their best work. In addition, she believed that the task of organizing a book logically would encourage them to find and create thematic connections in their poetry, and would thus help them find a focus for their work.

Students dealt with complex problems in putting their books together. "After they had many poems to choose from, I asked them to categorize the themes that might be there. I asked them what they were spending most of their time writing about. I directed them to look for transitions from chapter to chapter, and to look for beginning and ending poems. Sometimes I recommended that they generate new work to fill in gaps. Students learned about how to write better poetry, but this method could work with so many other genres, like family stories.

"There was great success in the projects they did and great personal growth. But I had a goal that the students did not really get behind. I wanted them to make two books, one to take home and one to be catalogued in the school library. My feeling is that kids today don't graduate from high school with any sense of permanence or accomplishment. I wanted them to graduate with a legacy that they could leave behind. I told them, 'I want you to have a book that your family can read, your fellow students, and community members can find and read at the school.' But the students just did not feel this way. They loved the books, but most did not care about the library. I was so disappointed, but finally decided that requiring that they leave one book in the library to get an 'A' was invading their space."

"They have no idea until they do this what it takes to make a book. They have to make a table of contents that is organized in some meaningful way. They must write a preface in which they tell the story of their reading and editing process. How did they choose what to include? What are the connections between the pieces in the anthology? How did the works connect with them as human beings?"

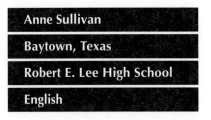

PERSONAL READING ANTHOLOGY

Anne Sullivan

Baytown, Texas

Robert E. Lee High School

English

Anne Sullivan's high school students in Baytown, Texas, compiled personal anthologies of literature. Taking on the role of literary editor puts students in the frame of mind to read closely, thoughtfully, and with personal commitment.

By requiring that they select works from a wide range of categories, Anne made sure her students went beyond familiar fare in their reading and, thus, she encouraged them to expand their horizons. Here is an example of the guidelines students were required to use in the fall of 1988:

Works by living Texas authors:
1 poem
1 work of short fiction
1 essay or article
1 work from genre of your choice

Works by Southern writers:
1 poem
3 works from genre of your choice

Works by fellow students:
3 works from genre of your choice

Samples from one or more published journals or diaries:
3 (a sample consists of at least 200 words, not necessarily consecutive.)

A work of science fiction

In addition to the above, 10 poems of your choice by poets who are still living or who have died within your lifetime

(Note — Texas and Southern writers are the regional writers for the students.)

Suzi Cox, anthology reading day, Robert E. Lee High School, 1988

Anne encouraged her students to use their full latitude of choice within the guidelines. Judging from the selections they chose for their anthologies and the stories in their prefaces, students looked for works that spoke for them. One senior, for instance, wrote that she found

PUBLISHING HELPS DEVELOP THOUGHTFUL READERS

works that helped her affirm the value of the lives of black people, especially black women. She related how she could identify with an author who felt that education tried to negate his blackness. The student called her anthology *My Name is Black*.

Another student purposely sought works that took a stand against human rights oppression and was happy to even find a science fiction selection that fit his theme. His anthology was titled, *every day a dreamer dies*. On the cover was a picture of the motel in Memphis where Dr. Martin Luther King Jr. was killed.

CLASS CAN BE REPEATED

The guidelines for content varied from semester to semester, allowing students to take the class a number of times. "The process was under more control the second time around. For instance, the students got started earlier on the table of contents. One student compiled selections from works of Milton and the Bible for his anthology. This anthology assignment is variable. You can keep kids growing; they can do it over and over and not be doing the same thing."

ADDITIONAL PROJECTS

Other guidelines may require students to include literature from your region of the United States or from a variety of regions of the country. You might assign specific authors or require that students read a range of authors from different cultural or ethnic groups. You may require students to include literature from different historical periods or literature treating certain themes in their anthologies.

Staci Mitchell (L) and Kalyani Naik (R) work on their anthologies for Anne Sullivan's class, 1988.

Two personal anthologies from Fall 1989: Nubs *by Kristi Foreman,* Learning to Fly *by Jeff Thomas*

"I chose the skinniest poetry book I could find. I sat in the hall with the book in my face pretending to be reading. Then my curiosity or boredom, I can't remember which, got to me. I took a glance at a randomly picked poem and began reading....The poem was very different from any I had ever read. I enjoyed the poem so much I began laughing....It opened a whole new world for me."— excerpt from one of Anne's students

1ST-GRADERS CREATE POETRY ANTHOLOGIES

Chris Duthie and Ellie Zimet

Trumansburg, New York

Trumansburg Elementary S.

1st-grade

LEADING UP TO THE POETRY WORKSHOP

EXPERIENCE WITH A READING AND WRITING PROGRAM

THE BULLETIN BOARD

POSTER POEM

"Each child wrote several poems during the three-week poetry emphasis, and then selected one of these poems to be placed in a class anthology of original poems. Each child individually conferenced with the teacher about how the poem would appear on the page. We discussed lining and use of white space. The children began to realize how hard poets work!"

Chris Duthie and Ellie Zimet, teachers in Trumansburg, New York, work with 1st-graders. Their classes spend three weeks on a poetry workshop that culminates in the publication of two anthologies. Each child contributes to a class anthology of original poetry, and each compiles a personal anthology of favorite poetry, much as Anne Sullivan's high school students created personal anthologies of favorite readings.

To prepare for the workshop, Chris and Ellie collected poetry books from various sources: the school library, public library, and personal collections. "We gathered close to 200 books for our students to use during our poetry emphasis. We divided the books into four categories: thematic anthologies, anthologies by a single poet, general anthologies, and single poems. The poetry workshop took place in February. In the three preceding months, our classes read and discussed a different poem every day. This exposure to so many poems provided a foundation on which to proceed."

"The poetry emphasis fit into the routines and procedures of our reading and writing program which had been in place since September. We had a daily reading and writing mini-lesson, so the children were used to editing."

Tyler, one of the students, comments: "I know about editing. I make sure the 'I' is a capital letter and make sure that there is a capital letter at the beginning of the sentence. That stuff helps my reader to read my writing better." Matt, another student adds, "When I do a rough draft, I go through a lot of work so I feel like an author."

There were several special classroom activities during the poetry workshop. "We developed a bulletin board with three irregularly shaped blobs labeled, 'feelings,' 'things around us,' and 'images.' We felt that all poetry fit into these categories. The children discovered — and taught us — that the individual reader's interpretation defined where the poem belonged."

"Each child selected a poem out of an anthology and it was copied onto 24" x 36" paper. The child interpreted and illustrated the poem, creating a poster that was displayed in the hall. This activity gave credibility to the creativity entailed in selecting a poem written by someone else. It was a valuable introduction to the kind of thinking the children would be doing when they published their personal poetry anthologies."

POEMS ON TAPE

"We enlisted the help of parents to make our own poems on tape. The children practiced reading poems of their choice. A parent did the taping and typed the poems with the names of the author and reader. The poems were fastened into a cover. Each tape and accompanying book contained approximately six poems."

MINI-LESSONS ON POETRY

"During the poetry emphasis, we taught lessons, using published poems as models, on topics that the children needed to be exposed to in order to grow as readers and writers of poetry. Lessons were on alliteration, repetition, lining, the shape of poems, and word choice."

Nathaniel: "It's really hard to write poems. You have to think about a lot of stuff...like if I was going to write a poem about Peter, I'd use a lot of 'P' words."

Rachel: "When I write poetry, I line it in patterns. Sometimes, I make it go up and down and even sideways."

CLASS ANTHOLOGY OF ORIGINAL POETRY

For *Lake of Poems*, the classroom anthology, Chris and Ellie, followed their usual writing process. "The children started with drafts, conferenced with peers and teacher, made revisions, and edited their own writing.

"The anthology was divided into the same three categories that were on the bulletin board. During the final individual conferences with the teacher, children decided on the final lining and presentation of their poems, and also decided into which categories to place their poem. We then typed up the poems, made copies, and stapled them into book covers. It was a magical morning when each child received a copy of *Lake of Poems*. A popular feature of the anthology was an author index. The kids wanted to use the index to find their poems and those of their classmates. Extra copies of the anthology became the most popular books in the classroom library."

PERSONAL ANTHOLOGIES OF FAVORITE POETRY

"We taught mini-lessons on ways to compile selected anthologies, using published anthologies as models. Each child had to decide what type of anthology to create. Should it be thematic, with poems on cats or dinosaurs, funny poems, or outdoor poems? Should it be a general anthology of poems? Each child chose four to ten poems to include. "In a mini-lesson on titles of the anthologies, we pointed out that the title can be the name of one of the poems in the collection, it can relate to a theme, or it can be general, for instance, 'Poems I Like,' or 'Beautiful Poems.' These personal anthologies, like *Lake of Poems*, were read and re-read by the children."

Eddy Hodgson reading for Anne Sullivan's anthology publication project, Robert E. Lee High School, Baytown, Texas, 1988

Before teachers talked about "the writing process" and before different types of classroom publishing began to flourish, many schools had at least one form of publication — the literary arts magazine. This avenue for student expression has through the years been a source of pride for many schools. In more recent years, whole language instruction, including literature-based courses and an emphasis on writing for an audience, has given more students and teachers the tools and confidence to create and build literary arts magazines. In the next two segments, we'll read about teachers who are magazine advisors.

Cheryl Sackmann, Nancy Gorrell, and Anne Sullivan have taught high school and have been magazine advisors for many years. If they are lucky, these good friends and colleagues from different corners of the country meet at the National Council of Teachers of English conference once a year.

Cheryl: "When I came to Flagstaff High School, I started a literary arts magazine. The philosophy of *Wingspan*, from its inception, has been to mirror the various voices in our school. It is not an elitist magazine. We include work from special education kids, jocks, and artists. We feature music, original recipes, anything that is an original creation of a kid. In the fall I have a volunteer staff — kids who come in before school, after school, lunchtime. These are the ones who help do the advertising, solicit materials, and determine which materials will go in the magazine. In the spring my Advanced Creative Writing students sift through these materials and determine themes and layout."

Anne: "In the 10 years I was a magazine advisor in Texas, we worked really hard to have all segments of our school population involved. We wanted pieces that represented our Hispanic and black populations. We didn't always get as much as we wanted, but we made a conscious effort."

Cheryl: "*Wingspan* is 100 percent student produced and edited. And I have put in some controversial things. Things about suicide, for instance. You need to realize that Flagstaff, Arizona is a small community of about 40,000 people in a very conservative state. So things that might not be controversial in Seattle or in New York are still continually controversial. Like sexual activity among teenagers — I mean we don't have a tradition of talking about that. In our yearbook we just published a story about a teen mother who was in our school. We have also published pieces about divorce and abuse in *Wingspan*. These kinds of things would not have been published when I first started the magazine."

Nancy: "One of the things we did this year, and I want to thank Cheryl Sackmann for this idea, was to have a poetry reading in our li-

HONORING THE LITERARY ARTS MAGAZINE

Cheryl Sackmann

Flagstaff, Arizona

Flagstaff High School

English

Nancy Gorrell

Morristown, New Jersey

Morristown High School

English

Anne Sullivan

Baytown, Texas

Robert E. Lee H.S.

English

LITERARY READINGS BUILD MAGAZINES

brary after our literary magazine [*Tricorn*] came out. Anyone who had contributed to the magazine or who had done a poetry chapbook was invited to read. Thirty students were part of the oral presentation — in

Wingspan 1990, *Flagstaff High School, Flagstaff, Arizona. Cover art by Amy Perry. Advisor, Cheryl Sackmann.*

Tricorn 91, *Morristown High School, Morristown, New Jersey. Cover art by Heather Parmiter. Advisor, Nancy Gorrell.*

the evening — with their parents and friends — and it was lovely. That is what writers do after something of theirs is published."

Cheryl: "In conjunction with Love of Reading Week, we invite published writers to the school. A couple of days during that week we have an open mike for students and teachers to read their works. The group that sponsors the open mike is the Advanced Creative Writing Club, which is called Shake and Popcorn Jive. It started four years ago and is named after a poem a student wrote that everybody loved."

Nancy: "Cheryl shared the Shake and Popcorn Jive idea with me. I've instituted it at Morristown High School, but we don't call it Shake and Popcorn Jive because we're not West Coast. We call our club Writers Forum. The kids come during lunchtime. It is just to listen, just to honor the writer. At Writers Forum we are always saying afterwards, 'Put that in the magazine.' Sometimes I say it privately to the kid afterwards, because I don't want to make it a competitive thing. One shy, little 9th-grade girl, who was in a middle stream English class came to Writer's Forum. Her English teacher encouraged her to come. It was a few days after our country entered the Persian Gulf War. She read a piece on how she felt about going to war. When she finished, my seniors said, 'I can't read what I wrote, Mrs. Gorrell, after hearing that.' It was printed in our magazine that year."

PRODUCTION PROCESS: THE JOYS AND TRIBULATIONS

Anne: "For the actual printing we had the cooperation of the administration. There was a print shop for district use in the administration building, and when we had everything camera ready, we moved into the administration building. I mean, moved in — potato chips, tape decks, everything. We lived there for the weekend. From Friday, when the administrators left, to the wee hours of Sunday morning we were printing and binding *Mind Flight*. It was high quality Xerox that we used. If we could not finish, because of machines jamming or whatever, we would go back the next weekend and print again. There were always trials and tribulations. It was terrible and it was wonderful.

"The administrative people taught me to use the machines, then I taught the kids. But once I taught the kids, they took over. I wanted them to do everything, to the extent that it was humanly possible. And essentially I was just there to consult, to monitor, and to cheer them on. We set up shifts. Most of the kids were involved in the printing. The ones who weren't had weekend jobs, or other demands.

Although this magazine was established as a quality product, we always kind of reinvented it at the beginning of every year. The kids knew what the traditions were, but I also wanted them to know what their options for change were. We always discussed the possibility of going to professional printing, but they did not want to do it. They wanted that experience, and they wanted the magazine to be theirs from beginning to end. Some of our editors have written about that first copy off the press — how it felt like a baby, like a child. I've seen kids in tears when the first ones come out. It's really been incredible."

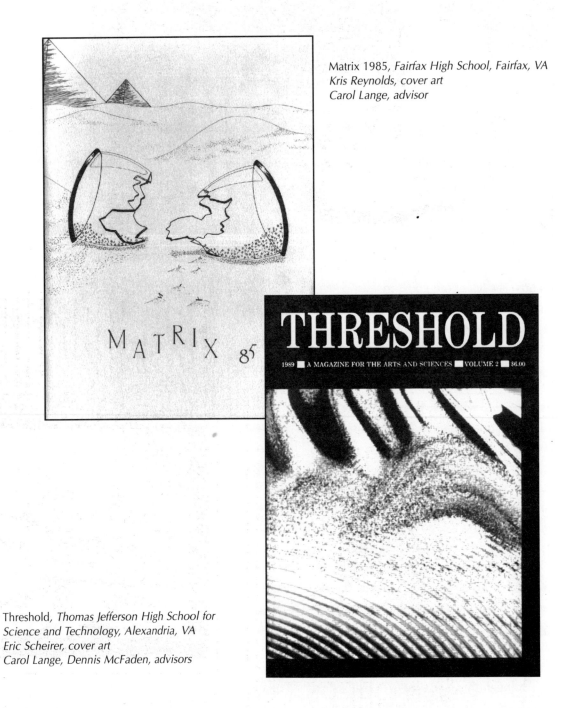

Matrix 1985, *Fairfax High School, Fairfax, VA*
Kris Reynolds, cover art
Carol Lange, advisor

Threshold, *Thomas Jefferson High School for Science and Technology, Alexandria, VA*
Eric Scheirer, cover art
Carol Lange, Dennis McFaden, advisors

Jeff Thomas, Mind Flight 1989

Mental Graffiti 1991, *Mustang High School, Mustang, OK*
Jimmy Sanders, cover art
Janis Cramer, advisor

Mind Flight 1990, *Robert E. Lee H.S., Baytown, TX*
Juan "Pumpkin" Hernandez, cover art
Anne Sullivan, advisor

From Junior High: A Foxfire Style Literary Magazine

Carolyn Tragesser

Moscow, Idaho

Moscow Junior High School

English

Decisions, Decisions

"Everything that was involved in publishing Ursa Major, *our literary magazine, we decided on as a group."*

Carolyn Tragesser, one of the advisors of the literary arts magazine at Moscow Junior High School in Moscow, Idaho, can be described as a team leader. Even when she had strong opinions about the production of the premier issue of the magazine, she was careful to limit her role to primarily facilitate student discussion and decision making. The members of the writing club, who eventually published the magazine, created their own guidelines. This process contrasts with the approach used by Anne Sullivan in her reading and writing anthologies. Although Anne's students felt that they had freedom of choice within her guidelines, they were required to follow them.

Carolyn's original belief in the importance of student decision making and ownership was further augmented by the fact that the writing club applied for a Foxfire grant for $500 to do the magazine. Foxfire insists on student leadership from the start, beginning with the writing of the grant. Students must clarify goals, structure, and evaluation.

After *Ursa Major* was published, the students told Carolyn that the entire project made them feel very grown-up and had given them a special learning opportunity. That is no wonder. The students had been through many soul-searching decisions. Carolyn explains, "The kids had to figure out if they wanted a magazine, and what kind of magazine. Originally, they agreed that their purpose was to celebrate writing. Then they decided that they also wanted the magazine to be a hot seller, and so the question arose: 'Do we want to make the magazine glitzy and glamorous? Do we want it to be filled with gossip and song dedications that would make it sell?'

"The kids kept discussing this, and they finally came back to their original purpose, which was to celebrate writing. So they said, 'We'll have stories and poems, without the gossip.' But in order to make the literary magazine appealing to the entire school population, they wanted to publish a classy-looking product that didn't 'look as though a teacher photocopied it.' They decided to devote a large portion of grant funding from both Foxfire and the National Writing Project to the cover. To save money, we stapled all the magazines ourselves.

"More decisions had to be made. Which four titles would be featured on the cover as teasers? How many times a week would the magazine staff meet? Would only the regulars, who attended virtually all meetings, get credit for being on the staff? Should the magazine be sold and how much should it cost? One last question to be considered concerned distribution.

"Two downtown bookstores offered to carry the magazine. To promote the magazine and stimulate sales, we put a cub paw stamp in two of the books in the bookstores, entitling each recipient to a $10 gift certificate. The question was whether the certificate should only be for a bookstore, since we stood for literacy, or if it could also be for a music store."

The advisors wanted the students to have a clearly defined division of labor, but the students wanted to be more casual about job descriptions. Carolyn says, "This year I told them, 'I realize you guys are still in charge of it, but let me tell you what my bottom line is: I want one of you to be responsible for each area, because when time becomes critical, I end up typing at least half of this myself.'

"These are very involved students. We have cheerleaders and basketball players. So this year we have divided up the labor. The kids decided what committees we needed, and they had elections for the chair of each committee. They can still do everything, but we have some people in charge."

Ursa Major was well received. "Literary magazines are common in high schools, but not in junior high schools," Carolyn explains. "Junior high kids put each other down an awful lot and our kids were prepared for that — we discussed that too. They were surprised that there were so few put-downs. They thought it was because the cover looked so good. 'Cool.' That was what everybody said, 'Cool.'"

WHAT WE LEARNED ABOUT DIVISION OF LABOR

THE BEST KIND OF EVALUATION

An Ethnography of 8th-grade Culture

Sheila Cantlebary

Sharon Dorsey

Columbus, Ohio

Wedgewood Middle School

8th-grade Language Arts

"We wanted the students to do some sort of ethnography. Some of the samples that we brought in to show the kids were publications like the Foxfire *books. We had* The Preppy Handbook, The Yuppie Handbook, *and* The Valley Girl's Guide To Life. *After a lot of class discussion, the kids decided to do a book on their own 8th-grade culture."*

Dedication to Fresh Talk: *"We would like to dedicate this book to Mrs. Sheila Cantlebary, our language arts teacher, for giving us the time and help to write this book. Her interest in us made us look at ourselves in new and different ways."*

Sheila Cantlebary a language arts teacher at Wedgewood Middle School in Columbus, Ohio, and Sharon Dorsey, the reading resource teacher, decided to substitute a publishing project for the regular language arts/reading curriculum in one of Sheila's double-period 8th-grade classes. "We thought that if we were going to have publication as a goal, we should first discuss with the kids what they wanted to write about."

Sheila suggested doing an ethnography and brought in several student-produced models for her class to look at. The students then decided to research and write about their own 8th-grade culture. "We first brainstormed for categories that would help focus their research. They came up with eight categories: spare time, clothes and jewelry, books and movies, the slang of that particular school year, note writing, what middle schoolers eat, school rules, and music." The table of contents hints at the detailed pictures of a distinct culture that await the reader.

Publishing Replaces Language Arts Curriculum

Sheila and Sharon made it clear to the students that the book they were writing was theirs, yet they did create a structure, a process, to help the students create their book. The following description of this process is excerpted from a paper that Sheila and Sharon wrote for an Ohio State University course they were taking.

Stage 1. Choosing a topic for the project
If interest is to be sustained, the topic needs to have student appeal and approval. Motivation is all-important at the middle school level. The topic should be sufficiently broad to generate enough sub-categories or spin-off sections to provide work for the entire class. Bring in models of other student publications.

Stage 2. Identifying categories of the topic
Through class discussion, divide the topic into workable categories for individual students or groups of students to develop.

Stage 3. Making a commitment to a category

In order to foster the development of student ownership, students must commit themselves to working on one of the categories of the topic. Students were asked to give a first and second choice for the categories they wanted to develop. At the same time they were asked to choose the student(s) with whom they wanted to work. This was done in writing after a period of consultation among the students. Sharon and I then took the student choices and formed working groups of two to five students. An effort was made to place each student with a friend of his or her choice. Groups were balanced so that a possible leader or organizer was present in each.

Stage 4. Pre-writing discussion

Pre-writing activities provide motivation for students as well as begin their actual thinking about the topic. Our classroom discussions provided language about the topic. Our whole class brainstormed "jot lists" under each of the categories on the chalkboard. File folders were given out to each group. In the groups each student took individual research and writing assignments. Each group had to present its plan for writing to the teacher for final approval.

Stage 5. Researching the categories

Working in groups or individually, students developed a set of questions they wanted answered about their category or sub-category. They determined how to get their answers. Some wrote and administered surveys. Some did interviews outside of school or by phone during class hours. For certain categories, student observation and field notes were the best source of information. The verbal language (slang) group had the teacher help design a form for recording field observations that was regularly used by the whole class to record the unique words or phrases of middle schoolers. The forms were collected each Friday and the findings were verified by the whole class for accuracy of meaning and appropriate contextual information.

Stage 6. Writing the first drafts

Individual students flowed back and forth between writing alone and getting direction or support from their groups to do their drafting. The teacher must serve as facilitator, orchestrating the movement. Sometimes at this stage, it is necessary to teach the whole class to give the students examples or models of what they can do. Classroom lessons in percentages and fractions were necessary for interpreting the surveys. Editing of grammatical and usage features was generally overlooked until the next stage.

Stage 7. Rewriting, revising, and editing

Many students do not comprehend what revision means or entails. So, in teaching about revising, the language arts teacher is developing a whole new concept and a new pattern of behavior for students. The following is a list of suggested techniques to get students to see their writing as something that is "in process."

a. Use a peer partner or a group of readers.

b. Have students write three beginnings to their pieces. After writing three beginnings in three timed writing periods, a peer partner or group can help the student author select the best one. Students should discuss what makes one beginning better than the others.

c. Take a section of writing from the middle of the piece and make it the beginning. Students must then rewrite the article as if the middle chunk was the beginning. This procedure works best if the peer partner selects the chunk of writing for the new beginning.

d. Invite guest speakers who will motivate and inform the students. These speakers might talk about their excitement over the writing project and/or provide new information. Some examples of potential guest speakers include: the education writer for the local newspaper, the language arts supervisor for the school system, a representative from a local publishing company, parents, and local experts on the project.

e. While students are revising their work on the computer, share your writing to show how you revise. Students are amazed that teachers and authors have to revise.

Stage 8. Create a proofing mock-up

Only when they see the mock-up does the realization set in that this product will be read by a real audience of peers. They become aware of how their writing will represent them to the readers, and they become tremendously motivated to locate all the grammatical and usage errors. They recognize the need for additional artwork, catchier titles, and more vivid descriptions. Students see the need for changing the layout in order to emphasize text or artwork. This might be called the final editing phase.

EXCERPT FROM "JEANS" BY VICKI MOORE

...Several girls have wounds on their index fingers from trying to pull up the zipper on their tightest pair of jeans. One student said that she lies on her bed and her mother sticks a coat hanger through the hook in the zipper to pull the zipper up. One student was observed with the seam marks of her tightest Jordache jeans engraved in her legs in gym class. On some occasions, students have been known to put their jeans in the bathtub to get them saturated. This allows them to stretch out and then they are easier to put on. After the wet jeans have been put on, they will dry them with the hair dryer, which makes them shrink back to fit the body.

USING MATH, ART & SOCIAL SCIENCES

Producing the ethnography worked as an interdisciplinary project. Sheila explains, "They were using math as they computed the results of their survey; they used techniques of the social sciences as they created

Fresh Talk, Middle Schoolers Write About Themselves, *Wedgewood Middle School, Columbus, Ohio*

Robert Maccabee, cover art

forms for field notes and surveys, and they learned about the importance of details in writing." They became experts at detecting boring writing and learned how to spice it with examples from real life, like the student who rewrote her "Jeans" article to include the story of a mother using a coat hanger to zip her daughter's overly tight jeans.

The students also increased their design and computer skills as indicated in the preface to *Fresh Talk*: "The student authors did almost all of the composing, layout, and art work...In the final stages of production, groups of students rotated use of the eleven computers in the school. They used *The Bank Street Writer* word processing program to do much of the writing. Some banners, clip art, and layouts for the various pages were designed with *The Newsroom* computer program."

EVALUATION

Sheila says, "While doing a project like this isn't a panacea for all the ills of the language arts classroom, motivation was much higher in this class than in my other 8th-grade classes. Eventually, when it came down to final publication time, we put in some marathon nights at the school, when the custodian kicked us out at nine or ten. Our best testament to increased interest occurred on the second to the last day of school — the traditional 8th-grade cut day. The typical class on this day had only eight students. But this was the day that *Fresh Talk* was to be distributed. Our class was in full attendance except for two excused students who came back later to get their copies."

It is no wonder that this project excited students. They got to use computers regularly, the project validated their culture to the entire community, and students to a large degree took the initiative and worked in partnership with their teachers.

Chapter 2

PUBLISHING ACROSS THE CURRICULUM

Published works that we see in bookstores and libraries often do not fall into the neat categories that stamp the school day. Even within the departmentalized structure of school, we have seen a significant amount of published student work that crosses the curriculum.

In this section we will look at some wonderful projects, including history books that use creative techniques usually associated with language arts, an arts *and* science magazine that exhibits vocational arts, and art books that embrace poetry.

In our survey of student publishing, we have seen how content and skills that are usually developed in separate subject areas can be woven together to produce exceptionally lively published works. Before looking in detail at some examples, let's explore briefly why cross-curricular works are so exciting for both author and reader.

It is not difficult to see that the intrinsic interest many of us have in psychology, society, science, history, visual art, math, and other subjects can draw us into the writing and revising necessary in most publishing. Cross-curricular projects *draw* writers and audience into the content of the work. They are a hook into literacy.

In some cases, cross-curricular publishing projects involve more than one class, and many even involve groups in the school that do not normally have much to do with each other. In these instances, the fusion of the creative energies and perspectives of different faculty members and students leads to highly original projects. Important examples of such projects break down the traditional distinction between academic and vocational subjects.

We believe that you will find the following publishing projects blend exciting subjects and are also adaptable to your school and locale.

"In our History-Media class the content is always multi-disciplinary. We examine the periods of American history through the lens of the media. One of our main goals is for students to learn to discover slant and bias in publications. Students also use current journalism styles to produce newspapers and television shows about different periods of American history."

HISTORY-MEDIA PROJECTS

Michael W. Bergen

Appleton, Wisconsin

Appleton East High School

English

35

Many students at Appleton East High School in Appleton, Wisconsin, elect to fulfill their 11th-grade American Literature and U.S. History requirements by taking the History-Media class. This course has an 18-year history of its own and is currently taught by Michael Bergen and two colleagues. The students learn about American history through media: pamphlets, newspapers, and other written sources, as well as newscasts and Hollywood movies. At the same time they learn how information is shaped by the media. The course has been successful, according to Michael, when students see that to understand history or current events, they have to take an active, critical role. They need to figure out how an author of a newspaper article, an editor of a newspaper, or a movie director may be shaping their values and beliefs. He teaches his students to detect the slant in historical sources that purport to be totally "neutral" and unbiased.

A major part of Bergen's History-Media class is student production of media. Students produce newspapers and television newscasts which deal with different periods of American history. One newspaper is called the *Columbus Clarion-Republican* and is written from an abolitionist point of view. The *Clarion*, for instance, contains stories describing the hardships of slavery. The tone of articles about the underground railroad approves of its mission and notes the bravery of the conductors.

Another newspaper is called *The Richmond Chronicle*, and it is written as if it were published in Richmond, Virginia, in January 1866. This southern newspaper is written from the point of view of slave owners. One of the articles in this newspaper criticizes *Uncle Tom's Cabin*. Other stories portray slavery as a benign institution that was better for the slaves than life in Africa. Instead of a positive or open-minded article about John Brown, one piece begins: "John Brown was hanged today in Charleston for his many abolitionist murders." Students learn from their hands-on experience in journalism how world events are shaped by the language and images of the media.

Bergen sees some problems arising in student publishing. "Classroom publishing fits into my philosophy of education: it involves critical thinking, writing, and cooperative learning. But classroom publishing needs

WORLD EVENTS SHAPED BY LANGUAGE

EVALUATING PUBLISHING

to be made more accessible to teachers by making more computers available and by devising less complicated software. Without this support, teachers can end up doing too much work themselves.

"Another problem that faces teachers is that as publishing becomes more common in classes K–12, it can lose some of its novelty and possibly lose some of its effectiveness with the kids. Teachers need to prevent this blunting effect by expanding their publishing curriculum, by getting new ideas."

The Continental Times

Appleton, W.I.   Sunday, December 15, 1991   A History/Media Production

Slave Free, Slave Not Free
By Michael Meulemans

Washington D.C. March 6, 1857.
Supreme Court Chief Justice Roger Brooke Taney voiced the majority vote on the Dred Scott v. Sanford case. Dred Scott's 7-2 vote issued him still a slave.

On April 6, 1846 Dred and Harriet Scott field charges of trespassing for false imprisonment. The St. Louis Court house put charges on Irene Emerson. On June 30, 1847, the first trail was held in the Circuit Court of St. Louis County. Due to an error in presentation on January 12, 1850 a second trail was held. Dred and Harriet Scott , plus, Eliza and Lizzie, were freed .

On March 22, 1852 , lawyers appealed the decision in the Missouri Supreme Court. When the court ruled against him, they decided to enter the Supreme Court .

In 1856, the case was presented in the Supreme Court. Finally, today, the verdict was issued.

In the North, the people were mad because when he moved north he moved into the Northern Territories. Acording to the Northwest Ordinance of 1787, no slavery was allowed in this region.

Supreme Court Chief Justice read the verdict of the Dred Scott v. Sanford case. In the end, Dred Scott did not turn out a free man.

Source provided by Mr. Bergan

Inside
- People in the Court
- Roe v. Wade
- Editorials
- The 15th Amendment

Black Child Does Not Have To Walk
By Michael Meulemans

Washington D.C. May 17, 1954.
Today the Supreme Court of the United States made a 9-0 desicion on the case of Brown v. the Board of Education of Topeka. Chief Justice Earl Warren read the decision.

Oliver Brown represented his daughter Linda. Every morning Linda Brown had to walk 20 blocks to school. Down the street from her house was a white school. She wanted to go there so she did not have to walk across town.

According to Judge Warren he had to look at the "effect of segregation itself on public education." He also said that the Court must "consider public education in the light of its full development." In the end the Court found that education was "perhaps the most important function." Also the decision was a short 13 paragraphs long.

Linda Brown got her dream wish. She no longer has to walk 20 long blocks across town to school.

Sources: "Brown vs. Board", Supreme Court and Individual Rights, New York Times

Civil Rights Amendment 14 (1868)

Section 1. All persons born or naturalized in the United States, and subject to the jurisdiction thereof, are citizens of the United States and of the state wherein they reside. No state shall make or enforce any law which shall abridge the privileges or immunities of citizens of the United States,nor shall any state deprive any person of life, liberty, or property without due process of law, nor deny to any person within jurisdiction the equal protection of the laws.

Section 2. Representatives shall be appointed among the several states according to their respective numbers, counting the whole number of persons in each state, excluding Indians not taxed. But when the right to vote at any election for the choice of electors for the President and Vice-President of the United States, Representatives of Congress, the excutive and judicial officers of a state, or the members of the legislative thereof, is denied to any of the male inhabitants of such state, being twenty-one years of age, and citizens of the United States, or in any way abridged, except for participation in rebellion, or other crime, the basis of representation therein shall be reduced in the proportion which the number of such male citizens twenty-one years of age.

Section 3. No person shall be a Senator or Representatives in Congress, or elector of President and Vice-President, or hold any office, civil or military, under the United States or under any state, who, having previously taken an oath as a member of Congress, or as an officer of the United States, or as a member of any state legislative, or as an executive or judicial officer of any state, to support the Constution of the United States, shall have engaged in insurrection or rebellion against the same or given aid or comfort to the enemies thereof. But Congress may by a vote of two-thirds of each house remove such disability.

Section 4. The validity of the public debt of the United States, authorized by law, including debts incurred for

Continued on Page 4

"I hook my middle school students into writing history books from primary source materials. We might research somebody who has been dead for a hundred years and whose story is lost, who was important at one time to a lot of people. This person lived, loved, died, and this lack of recognition is not fair. Fairness is an important value to the kids. 'So this is not fair,' I say, 'Let's correct it. Let's write a book about it.'"

Bill Coate is a middle school teacher in Madera, California who is passionate about the study of California's past. In his classroom, he combines his interest in history with a love of storytelling. His students publish history books that link historical research with language arts techniques in a process that's now known as the Madera Method.

How did Bill come to work with his students on publishing books? How are these books produced and distributed? And how can these projects be adapted to your area of the country?

Bill's classroom publishing ventures began at a local cemetery. He recalls: "I was informed of the existence of a trio of graves with the name 'Mintern' on the banks of the Chocola River. It turned out that no one knew anything about these old graves. I wondered if my 6th-grade class could recover the paper trail that these nineteenth-century people had left: death certificates, land deeds, probate records, and so forth. Could we resurrect this nineteenth-century family? When I brought my students to see the graves, needless to say, they were excited and bought into the project. We started pulling in primary source materials by the handful, including wills, inventories, obituaries, that sort of thing.

"Within about four months we had the story of the Mintern family, and it began to attract attention around the county. Associated Press picked up the story and Irving Stone read about it down in Beverly Hills. He wrote me and suggested that we use this information, much as he used his own information, to write a biographical novel. Mr. Stone asked, 'Why don't you have the kids write a diary, a fictionalized diary, but one based upon the actual research? Every entry will be documented. Give the kids a little literary license, but it all has to be grounded in research.'"

FICTIONALIZED DIARY

"So that's what we did. We took the matriarch of the family, Abby Mintern, and we wrote her diary, with each kid becoming Abby for a year, 1870, 1888, and so on. In the year they were responsible for, they had to use all of the relevant research about the family that we uncovered. In addition, they had to incorporate facts about what was going on in that year locally, statewide, and nationally. We were very proud to

> *"It's to the point now where people come to us and say, 'Well, who's the next pioneer?'"*

RESEARCH AND WRITING PROCESS IN BILL'S ROOM

publish a hardcover book called, *The Mintern Chronicles*. It was the first book published by the Classroom Chronicles Press.

"From that first book we went on to produce one every year. In fact, these projects now form the basis of my social studies curriculum. Generally, we choose a pioneer of Madera County and we begin research on this person's life history, using the county courthouse, the museum, the library, and Mormon records. We always trace these people back — we have yet to fail — to their entry into America. And we find their descendants. And then to put the final period on the sentence, we have a graveside ceremony. We start at the tombstone, we end at the tombstone. We present the book to the dignitaries, who flock in by the hundreds. We hold a little memorial service, with an oral litany, an oral tribute and music. In this way we say 'good-bye' to the person we have studied.

"The kids are producing local history. I call it 'local history nationalized,' or 'national history localized.' They learn to appreciate the rocks and the rills of their own community, while the community learns about itself. Both the students and the local people develop an awareness of the greatness of the nation as a whole. It's to the point now where people come to us and say, 'Well, who's the next pioneer?'"

How does Bill help the students organize their writing about the past? He explains: "First we visit a grave or we read a document like a diary or a letter. Then I appeal to their sense of fairness, which encourages them to uncover the lives of forgotten people. Once they're hooked, we move into the cooperative learning mode. They're divided into groups. As every document comes in, we make a big 'to do' about it. Every group does an analysis of every document by following this format:

1. List the facts
2. Write down one question that document raises in your mind but does not answer
3. Draw a hypothesis
4. Ask how are we going to test it?
5. Where are we going to go to find the answer? And that moves us from document to document.

"Quite frequently, after we've done a document analysis we'll do a quick write. I'll ask for each group to give the class a summary of everything we know about, say, George Mordecai. Or I might ask students to pretend that they are George Mordecai writing home about California at this point. We don't wait until the end of the year to write. All the students have project folders to keep all their writings in."

Classroom Chronicles Press cultivates an audience and distributes its books just as any publisher would. Gala occasions are part of publishing in Bill's classes.

"Under the auspices of the local historical society we have a young authors' reception. We invite the children into the auditorium, we seat them there, and the public comes in and buys their books. And then community members run up to these young children and say, 'You're an author, you helped write these books. Would you sign this one?'"

Bill and his students contact and work with the media which further helps with publicity and distribution. He reports that media interest in student publishing is phenomenal. The local newspapers always carry stories about new publications and the *Los Angeles Times* sent a reporter up to Madera to do a feature story. The AP has sent the story of Bill's students' books around the country three different times.

The local historical society, which helps to promote and distribute Classroom Chronicles Press publications, also fronts the money for publication. Part of the proceeds from book sales is used to reimburse the historical society.

"Every time a book is sold, the check is made out to the Historical Society Madera Method Fund. If we have a 350-page book, which uses about 175 sheets of paper, and about 20 photographs, and if we have a nice dust jacket with a hardcover, it is going to cost about $13 to produce. The Historical Society sells a book for $25. Even though every author receives a free book, the books always generate more money than they cost, so that extra money goes into field trips and research costs."

How are these books physically put together? Who does the typing, layout, printing, and binding of the books? A few of the students do the final word processing, parents help with the typing, and Bill does the final layout.

"We take our final copy down to a job printer. The printing company also designs the dust jacket for us. The kids come up with the title and they choose the photos for the jacket. Then we buy dissrtation covers. Once the strip bound pages are inside that hardcover with the flyleaves and the adhesive and once the jacket comes around it, you can't tell it from a thread bound book."

The students help with the binding. The school district purchased a Gestetner binder that affixes strip bindings at the rate of about 10 or 12 per hour. This is a delicate process, so Bill wants adult help at this point. "We allow the kids to bind a few books, simply to say they've had their hand in that process also. The whole run is done by parent volunteers. And they feel important too.

AUDIENCE, PUBLICITY AND DISTRIBUTION

"Classroom Chronicles Press cultivates an audience and distributes its books just as any publisher would."

FUNDING SUPPORT

NUTS AND BOLTS OF PRODUCTION

"We build up a fine reputation for integrity in research and composition. We want our end product to look good, so when people walk away with the book, they have a coffee table book."

McAllister Family: From Slavery to the Twentieth Century

The method of combining primary source research with literary forms, like a fictionalized diary, can be applied to different historical settings and periods. Here are a few more of Bill's projects.

"We did an interview in our classroom of a local African-American family. The oldest member of the family suddenly said 'You know, my grandfather's name was Ben and I think he came from Gray's County, Kentucky.' We got on the phone and called the county historical society and they led us to Murray State University. Historians at the college checked their records for us, and sure enough, there was a Ben McAllister. By going through the census record and reports of land transactions, I found that this Ben McAllister was in the Civil War.

"Following one lead after another, I wrote for Ben's Civil War records and I found out who his master was. His master was a Wade McAllister, whose descendants live, to this day, on the very farm that Ben McAllister labored on as a slave.

"After putting together our research we published the book, again a hardcover edition, called, *The McAllister Family: From Slavery to the Twentieth Century*. We invited the McAllisters, who came to Madera for a reunion, to a presentation and we gave this book to them. There were more than 500 people. It was an emotional scene with tears flowing."

Networking Between Schools

"Another element of the Madera Method involves networking between schools. We always trace our pioneers to their American origins. For instance, Abby Mintern came from Rhode Island; the next three pioneers came from Texas, Mississippi, and Virginia. Once we learn where our subjects came from, we always contact a school back there to get at least one class to collaborate with us on research, writing, and publishing. We always take some students (we draw names out of a hat) to meet our colleagues. Similarly, we invite our colleagues from afar to Madera."

Involving Parents

"We found a tombstone of a Mexican forty-niner in California, and we traced him down to his origins in Mexico. Our class collaborated with students in Mexico to do research about his origins and life history. Together we produced a book called *Shadows of the Past*. It was fantastic! I took some kids to Mexico on the train to meet some of our colleagues there."

In addition to the history and language arts skills that Bill's students were developing, this cross-cultural project gave his class the opportunity to be exposed to the Spanish language and Mexican and Chicano cultures.

"The migrant families in the Madera community had a chance to shine. We had letters in nineteenth-century Spanish that the family had loaned us. The Mexican-American children in our school asked their fieldworker parents to help them translate these letters. These families all of a sudden became important, and we had a meeting in which the parents gave their input."

Looking back, Bill says the main mistake that he made in the beginning, and the one he must continually guard against, is trying to do too much for his students, "not giving them the credit for having the intelligence and the curiosity to carry forth. If I don't keep in mind that this is a kids' project, that I'm on the outside looking in, then it's easy for them to get shoved to the side. Once that happens, they know it immediately. They know when they're in charge, and when the teacher is in charge. And so I follow this philosophy, and it's very simple: if one takes the meaning of *teach* back to its Greek origins, the word 'dudusco' meant to teach and to learn. I try to remind myself every day that I am a learner and a teacher. The teacher doesn't know any more, or much more, than the students, and so we discover — together, and in truth become colleagues."

EVALUATION

41

"I try to remind myself every day that I am a learner and a teacher."

ORIGINAL HISTORY BOOKS

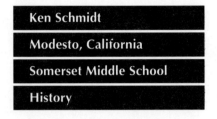

Ken Schmidt

Modesto, California

Somerset Middle School

History

TWO SCHOOLS WORK TOGETHER

"Our first book, which we did with Bill Coate, was about a Civil War regiment. Each student assumed the personality of one of the soldiers and wrote three letters home describing events that had occurred on or before that day. The book turned out to be a collection of letters that were fictional, but thoroughly based on fact."

Ken Schmidt, a middle school history teacher in Modesto, California, is a close friend and colleague of Bill Coate. Ken's students collaborate with Bill's students to publish original history books that grace the coffee tables of many Californians. Bill has shared his process of research and publishing with Ken, and in turn, Ken has developed his own projects combining primary source historical research with literary techniques.

In Ken's first experience with the Madera Method, his class joined with Bill's in studying the Second Massachusetts Cavalry Company A, known as the California Hundred. This group of men, mustered into the Union Army in 1862, fought with a Massachusetts regiment through the entire Civil War.

Ken explained that Bill Coate had been able to locate some diaries of men in the California Hundred.

"Bill started with the diary of Frederick Quant, and then we discovered other diaries in the archives of the Bancroft Library at the University of California-Berkeley. Projects like this take on a wonderful life of their own. We were on television news in Sacramento, talking about our research, when I received a phone call from one of the people watching the news. It turned out that the caller's great-grandfather was a member of the Cal Hundred and she offered us his diary. One after another, we've gathered up a number of diaries.

"Now that we had located much of our primary source material, I wanted to combine historical research with a language arts experience. We stretched paper across the front of the room, and made timelines. Bill had his timeline down in Madera, and I had my timeline up here in Modesto. We used them to mark down each of the years, divide them into months, and then into days. As the students read through the diaries, they marked various events on the timeline. Each student wrote three letters that incorporated facts collectively gleaned from the diaries. We produced a work of fiction that was based on fact."

FICTIONALIZED DIARY

Ken used Bill's process to do a project on his own. "Our class wanted to study the life and times of George McCabe, the first secretary of the Board of Trade of Stanislaus County (our county), and one of the last Wells Fargo agents, but we were having trouble locating primary sources.

MY VALLEY, MY HOME

Recollection of
George T. McCabe

Three entries from My Valley, My Home — Recollection of George T. McCabe.

May 29, 1915   Michael Donaldson

Today I arrived in Madera County ready to enlist the cooperation of the Madera Chamber of Commerce in the fight against the Hetch Hetchy plan. Mr. Church is the only powerful supporter of the Hetch Hetchy plan. He doesn't, however, have a very persuasive speech. I had dinner in Madera and spent the night.

June 30, 1915   Zach Hillman

Today I left for a meeting in San Francisco on behalf of the interests of Stanislaus County. I hope that my speech did not fall on deaf ears! If the Hetch-Hetchy plan succeeds, the valley will be hurt beyond our wildest dreams. Water, our state's most important resource, will be lost to the demands of a greedy population in the San Francisco area. Water is needed here for agriculture. If I can gain the support of the other valley communities, we may be able to fight this plan and, ultimately, save our valley's agricultural industry.

depot. I arrived before 8:00 to supply the excursionists with Stanislaus County descriptive books. Fresno County and Stanislaus County had a competition to see who could get the most people on their train. Fresno was expected to win; however, Stanislaus County came through! Among the prominent people who rode on our train were C. H. Reimenschneider (County President and leader of our train), Rev. H. H. Pitman, W. J. Brown and his wife, Mrs. W. E. Lewin, J. A. Selber, and Miss Mima Steinman (Secretary of the Stanislaus-Merced Union). It was a very pleasant day! How my dear wife, Kitty, would have enjoyed an outing such as that. I miss her terribly.

July 16, 1915   Audrey Glaser

I have been very busy today. I have been soliciting displays for the olive oil, grains, grape, beans, nuts, honey, and preserved figs as well as other fruits, and various other items from our county. These will go on display in the Ferry Building in San Francisco. I understand that the Ferry Building has recently gone through some minor changes. Two coats of white enamel and a new trimming

in bronze have resulted in a very attractive place for such exhibits as mine. This afternoon, I had a dreadfully long train ride to Sacramento. I was scheduled to speak to the Chamber of Commerce regarding Stanislaus County concerns. On the way up, I thought about Kitty. How I miss her! Time, it is said, heals all wounds. My heart still aches for my Kitty. My years in Knight's Ferry will always be remembered.

July 11, 1915   Christin Kuo

I feel confident that we will win the fight against the Hetch Hetchy project. I wrote a letter to the Fresno Chamber of Commerce and thanked them for all of their assistance. If all goes well, we should be able to protect our water rights from the demands of San Francisco. I went out to dinner this evening and ate a fine meal of tenderloin of pork, corn, and a nice bowl of ice cream. At 3.48 it was a great buy!

McCabe's granddaughter heard about us and came forward with his scrapbook containing newspaper articles about him.

"The collection of 300 news articles gave students a clear picture of George McCabe and Stanislaus County between 1913 and 1926. We used information from these articles to write fictionalized diary entries from the point of view of George McCabe."

Students used secondary sources to corroborate their entries. According to the Editorial Committee of *My Valley, My Home,* "The researchers of this project have been very careful to maintain accuracy. All names, dates, events, and facts such as prices of items, have been researched and evaluated."

Because their first book on the Cal Hundred was such a success and because there was so much historical material in the diaries that were donated, Ken and Bill are working on a sequel to the first book. Three schools are involved this time and will all contribute to the book.

"What we are doing here in Modesto," reports Ken, "is searching through all of the pension records, genealogical records, census records — anything we can pull out — on each man in the regiment, to reconstruct some sort of a biographical sketch. Originally, we thought that we would end up with about a paragraph on each, but we have about two pages per man. Bill Coate's classes in Madera are creating a 'harmonized diary,' combining entries from the same day from different diaries. Although we have a good number of diaries, some only cover 1863, or 1864. Finally, a school in San Francisco has gone through all of the diaries to identify all the proper nouns and major events in order to footnote the diary entries."

ARCHEOLOGICAL DIG AT KNIGHT'S FERRY

One of Ken's projects is an archeological dig that pulls natural science into its cross-disciplinary mixture of social studies and language arts. Ken tells how his class became involved in an archeological dig at Knight's Ferry, a California Gold Rush town that had its heyday in 1850.

"I read an article in the newspaper about a hotel owner in Knight's Ferry who had discovered some Chinese artifacts while the hotel was being renovated. I obtained permission from the hotel owner to go up there to dig, and we started our excavation.

"It was incredible how much parent involvement we had. Parents drove the children to Knight's Ferry to participate in the dig and they took photographs of the children at the dig site. One child's parent who was a dentist donated used dental tools that were very helpful in excavating and cleaning objects.

"We discovered in talking to some of the old-timers in Knight's Ferry that behind the hotel there had been two orange trees. One had been relocated, and the other had been chopped down many years ago. Underneath these fruit trees there are the remains of outhouses. Every time an outhouse filled up, people would put rock and charcoal on the top, plant a fruit tree there, and then move the outhouse."

THE NATURAL SCIENCE CONNECTION

"In the outhouse itself, as we started digging through that soil, we not only found bottles, but we also found the remains of their waste materials. We talked to our science teacher at school and said, 'We want to find out what the people ate from analyzing the remains in the outhouse. How can we do that?' He recommended flotation. We put the soil into the water, stirred it, and to the surface then, would float all of these little shells and seeds and so forth. We were able to skim off the seeds and find out what fruit they belonged to. They were berry seeds, from all different types of berries. From that we found out exactly what season we were digging in. So we were able to date the bottles to almost the exact year as we went down layer by layer. The kids loved it."

Ken's class is continuing its multidisciplinary study of the forty-niners in Knight's Ferry by looking through census records of the 1850s, 1860s, and 1870s in order to answer the question: what happened to Gold Rush towns when the gold ran out? In these records the kids are finding people who had been listed as miners abruptly listed with other occupations. On the basis of this information, they can trace the growth of new jobs and industries.

THE CALIFORNIA JUNIOR HISTORICAL ASSOCIATION'S JOURNAL OF HISTORY

Ken is aware that not all teachers can or wish to devote a large amount of their class time to publishing history books. So he is now publishing The California Junior Historical Association's *Journal of History* with a group of student editors ranging from 5th to 12th grade. The journal publishes student writing on smaller historical projects using primary source materials.

Teachers can find a few pages in each issue of the Journal outlining developments in the Madera Method, including a description of current projects and a list of historical materials needed.

WHY HELP KIDS PUBLISH?

What draws Ken to help students publish history books and articles? "What we're doing by publishing history books is encouraging students to take possession of material that has been hidden. By reconstructing and analyzing that material, they are doing the writing of historians. The product, the book, is something of value that is recognized by their community and they are proud of their work."

1st & 2nd-graders Make Research Books

"I have worked with 1st and 2nd-graders in publishing different kinds of books. This time I wanted to try something new. My goal was to teach the kids how to do research. They succeeded in producing information books. It broadened my perception; I think we usually conceive of the younger child as just producing fictional narrative."

Lea Smith

Louisville, Kentucky

University of Louisville

Early Childhood Education

In a collaborative project, Lea Smith, an instructor in Early Childhood Education, at the University of Louisville in Kentucky, worked with primary grade teachers in using classroom publishing projects with very young children. In her interview with us, she focused on a multi-disciplinary project in which primary graders did research and published it in small books.

Lea has helped bring university language arts and education departments into partnership with school districts. "We had a collaborative grant between Jefferson County, Kentucky public schools and the University of Louisville. I taught with a classroom teacher one day a week, in a room of 1st and 2nd-graders.

BRAINSTORMING

"We began by giving the kids an 'interest inventory' at the beginning of the year. We used pictures, and the kids indicated which subject in the row they wanted to study. They decided on dinosaurs, space, and farms. From there we went to brainstorming about farms and what we knew about farms, and we broke the topic into categories. The kids put themselves into self-selected groups and studied together. Within the groups they subdivided so that each child would study a certain aspect of the group's topic. It was a self-driven, self-motivated project from the beginning. Our first unit last fall was farms and then, in the spring, we studied space. The kids asked questions and they studied the literature. It's amazing how they develop in being able to research and put out a final product — a little book on their research question."

PRODUCTION

"Within each group, the members contributed information pages, and then in addition, some contributed the table of contents, others did artwork, and others 'bound' the book by stapling or taping."

TEACHING TEACHERS

"I took the experiences with the 1st and 2nd-graders into my university classroom. In my graduate level Language Arts class, students participate in a writing workshop. They have to submit a piece of writing for publication, and I suggest that they shoot for something like the 'In the Classroom' section of *The Reading Teacher.*

"I'm not just putting them though the writing process to have a finished product, but I have them submit for publication so that they really begin to see the process.

"I find that many of us did not experience a writing process ourselves when we learned to write. So it's real hard for us to teach a process approach to writing. We need to experience it ourselves in a hands-on way and be taken through the process, to see it from a bird's eye perspective."

One can only imagine what insightful researchers and writers the 1st and 2nd-grade children Lea has told us about will be when they reach high school.

A page from Why Dinosaurs Died *by Virginia Jolley, Nicia Seabrooks, Anthony McKevier, and Kasie Holland*

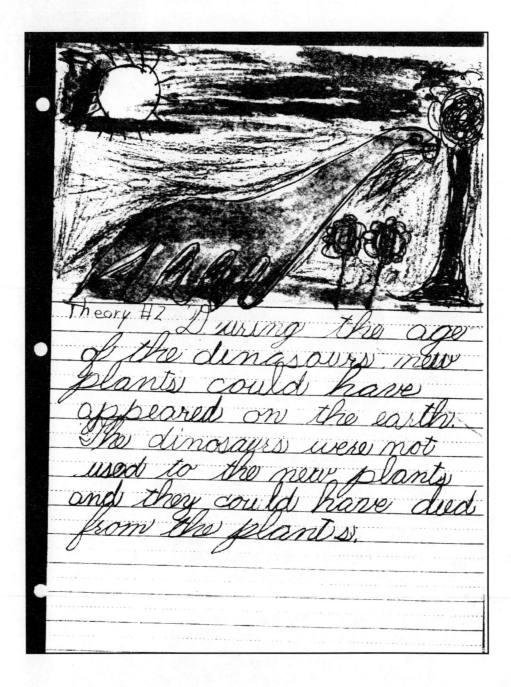

Theory #2 During the age of the dinosaurs new plants could have appeared on the earth. The dinosaurs were not used to the new plants and they could have died from the plants.

Michelle Takenishi has her 5th-graders at Red Hill Elementary School in Honolulu, Hawaii, incorporate social studies, art, and natural science in the storybooks they write.

She explains: "The students will infuse what they call 'database' into their stories. These are the details of setting and time period that tell the reader where the story is located globally."

"If the action takes place in Japan, the literary elements should reflect Japan, the architectural elements should be appropriate. If the story takes place in the southern U.S., the dialogue should show this.

If the story takes place in Vietnam, the animals or the foliage should reflect the place. When we have our authors' tea, we arrange the books by location."

Students can access information for their stories by using the full range of reference materials in the library, including books, vertical files, periodicals, and computer data bases.

Pat Egenberger's 7th and 8th-grade ESL students in Modesto, California, put together a book of "I-Search" reports.

"They wanted to write on topics, like animals or astronauts, that would ordinarily be covered in science classes. So not only were they learning English, they were learning a little science, and I was glad about that because we can't put them in the science classes. The 'I-Search' project is a way of doing research that I call 'user friendly.' I give them very specific questions to develop in their first paragraph: 'What do you want to learn about? Why do you want to learn it? What do you want to find out? What resources are you going to use?' That becomes the introductory paragraph. And the report is the narrative story of their search. As they read, they take notes on the information as well as write their ongoing comments and questions about their topic. This project involves real use of language, rather than being a simple exercise in copying the encyclopedia. I have them do a speech on their search at the end."

CULTURAL AUTOBIOGRAPHY

"Using paper, colored paste, paint, markers, colored pencils, memorabilia, and other personal items, we recreated our lives on the pages of books. What resulted was a dazzling mix of politics, art, and culture."

Cheryl Shackleton

New York, New York

Center for the Book Arts

BOOK ARTS FOR SCHOOLS

The Center for the Book Arts followed up Cheryl's work by designing a book arts curriculum for high schools of specialized workshops: cultural autobiography—past/present/future, personal family album, travel journals, dream journals, and eco-awareness.

Through the Center for the Book Arts in New York City, Cheryl Shackleton taught a workshop in bookmaking for high school students. Cheryl said that most courses at the Center concentrated on technique — bookmaking and bookbinding. In this case three kinds of book structures were taught (accordion, single section pamphlet, and concertina), "but the focus was on recreating one's self inside the covers of a book." The students constructed cultural autobiographies in which they wove together their traditions, languages, dreams, philosophies, and experiences. Some students were from Africa, Latin America, and Central America; the other students were first-generation Americans from Asia, Africa, Europe, and Latin America. The multicultural composition of the group gave students an excellent opportunity to reflect on their own lives as well as to appreciate their classmates' lives.

What could the students use in their books? Cheryl encouraged them to bring in photos, mementos, souvenirs, and writings, and incorporate them along with found objects into the books. Some books focused on war and poverty, and contained political poetry, images of female freedom fighters, and treasures from homelands. Other books centered on censorship, ancestors, abstract art, and personal journeys.

Although the books primarily contained visual imagery, some of the students added writing in their books. According to Cheryl, "One girl, who was from Honduras, wrote fiery political poetry as well as presidential speeches. She had seen poverty and war and wanted someday to be president of her country."

High school students at the Center for the Book Arts

Photo by Cheryl Shackelton

"We have a magazine for the arts and sciences, rather than a literary art magazine. We encourage the exploration of all forms of writing and all forms of the arts. In addition to the usual poetry and short stories, we also have reflective and scientific essays. We use what we call the Discover *magazine brand of science writing."*

SCIENCE & ART MAGAZINES

Carol Lange

Alexandria, Virginia

Thomas Jefferson H.S.

Intensive Journalism

Carol Lange teaches intensive journalism and is the magazine advisor at Thomas Jefferson High School for Science and Technology in Alexandria, Virginia. *Threshold*, the school magazine, combines literature, art, philosophy, social and natural science, mathematics, and music. It reminds one of the *Atlantic Monthly* or *The New York Times Magazine* in its breadth.

THRESHOLD

A special 11-page center section of the 1991 edition of *Threshold* exemplifies the magazine's cross-disciplinary approach — in this case, understanding AIDS. Carol explains: "We interviewed individuals who have AIDS. We also interviewed a man who worked on the repair of the Names Project quilt. We interviewed a doctor whose research on discerning the presence of AIDS in children is on the cutting edge. We interviewed a young man out in Colorado who began an organization in honor of his brother, who died of AIDS, which assists families of children with AIDS. We tried to educate our student body and make it aware of the diversity of support groups."

The same issue of *Threshold* includes other cross-curricular gems such as an article that is a series of mathematics puzzles in narrative form along with their solutions. "Walking a Fine Line" is an article exploring the science and ethics of genetic engineering. Also included are interviews with students from interesting backgrounds, reflective essays, and a display of computer-assisted drawing.

Threshold 1989 also sparkles with satire, interviews, reminiscences, and thought-provoking essays on economics, science, art, math, literature, and music.

MATRIX

Before working on *Threshold*, Carol taught at Fairfax High School, also in Virginia, where she initiated and was the advisor for *Matrix* magazine. Like *Threshold*, *Matrix* was, from its inception, a cross-disciplinary magazine. Carol said that the two schools were very different, although both magazines have the same purpose. "Whereas Thomas Jefferson is a governor's magnet school for science and technology, and students are admitted by application, Fairfax has vocational programs like home economics, auto shop, and drafting. There were work study students who were only in school half the day. It was just a very different school situation, yet I've seen in both schools a certain commonality through the written word and the exploring of that world around them."

Carol tells us about one of the early issues of *Matrix* and how it pulled together normally disparate parts of the school. The 1984 issue had a center section focusing on bridges, particularly the Brooklyn Bridge, since it was its 100th anniversary. Drafting students drew the bridge. Magazine and yearbook staff members took photos of the bridge.

"We had some of the students who are not the usual 'gifted' writers do research on the Brooklyn Bridge. In their readings, they discovered that the main engineer had his little puppy follow him most of the time. One of the pieces we published about how the Brooklyn Bridge was built was told from the perspective of a dog. It was called 'Birth of a Bridge — A Dog's Point of View.'

"For *Matrix 1985* my junior English class interviewed some people who had graduated from our high school 50 years ago. We learned through the interviews that a trolley line, which had once run near our school, connected Washington, DC with our area, and provided the milk for DC residents! I got together with the drafting teacher, his students began to do research, and they designed the trolley car and the route it took.

"Students of the fashion design teacher studied the time period and designed figures — in period clothing — that would be in proportion to the trolley that was drawn by the drafting students. Both the drafting and the fashion design students had to read and get involved. Though their writing didn't get into our publication, they had to write about their discoveries for the drafting and fashion design teachers. Until this year these kids had not really felt that much a part of the school. They felt that they were sort of a fringe group, especially the fashion design students. They bought copies of the magazine and felt an investment in it.

"Some of the magazine staff went to the library and searched through the old library files of photographs and found an early photograph of the trolley. It really turned out to be a very pleasing layout: the photo, the drawings of the trolley, and these little figures in period costume. What I liked about that year's publication is that not only did we get students participating who don't consider themselves to be writers or readers, we got them involved in research without their thinking they were doing research. Plus it brought different disciplines of the school together on a combined project. And I think that's part of the key to turning on some of the kids who feel a little bit alienated from the general school population."

VOCATIONAL AND ACADEMIC DEPARTMENTS COLLABORATE

Threshold 1991 *Table of Contents*

Another magazine that Carol began is *Teknos*, a publication of more formal writing on science, math, and technology, produced by seniors at Thomas Jefferson High School.

Whether the writing is technical or is aimed at a general audience, the magazines that Carol has helped publish encourage students to investigate and form intelligent opinions about the complex world around them.

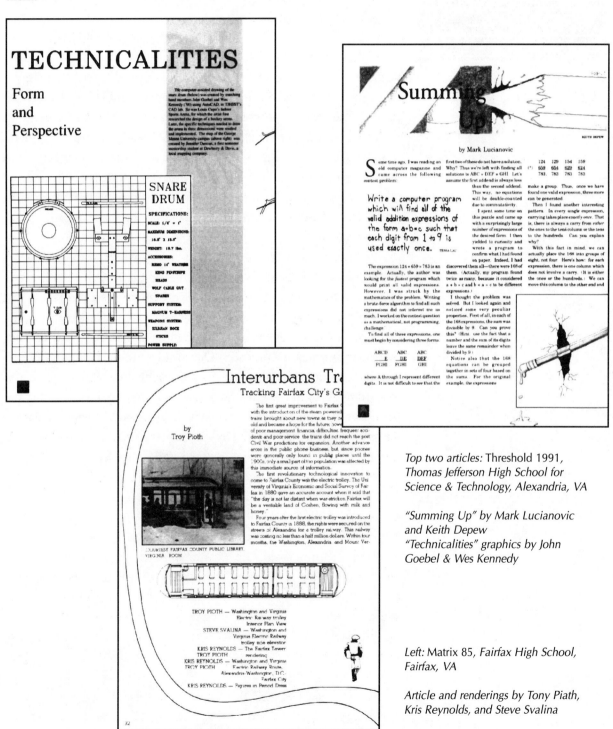

Top two articles: Threshold 1991, Thomas Jefferson High School for Science & Technology, Alexandria, VA

"Summing Up" by Mark Lucianovic and Keith Depew
"Technicalities" graphics by John Goebel & Wes Kennedy

Left: Matrix 85, Fairfax High School, Fairfax, VA

Article and renderings by Tony Piath, Kris Reynolds, and Steve Svalina

COMING OF AGE BOOKS

Patti Stock

Saginaw, Michigan

University of Michigan

English Department

"Students from two high schools in Saginaw, Michigan decided to publish a collection of their stories to show what it was like to grow up in their city. The Saginaw River separates the two high schools and their communities — physically and culturally. One school is about 55 percent white, 35 percent African-American, and 12 percent Latino. The other school is 99 percent African-American. The name the students chose for their book was The Bridge.*"*

Patti Stock, associate professor at Michigan State University, formerly taught at the University of Michigan where she helped set up a program called the Center for Educational Improvement Through Collaboration (CEIC). The Center's purpose is to support research jointly undertaken by school teachers and university teachers. Through this program Patti team taught with two high school teachers, one in each of the large high schools on either side of the Saginaw River. That co-teaching project led to the publication of *The Bridge*. As part of the process leading to publication, Patti drew from different disciplines to help her students enrich their writing.

"In Saginaw we were teaching 12th-grade students who were euphemistically labeled 'at risk.' We had persuaded the school administration to allow us to develop an experimental curriculum. It's a curriculum that I like to call 'dialogic,' in which the teachers have instruction plans, but the ways in which students pick up on those plans lead to the teachers' particular instructional practices. Our idea was to start out with a set of research questions that the students knew something about and needed to learn more about. The research questions we posed were: 'What has been your growing up experience here in Saginaw, Michigan? What are the stories you tell about it? How does that experience relate to other people's growing up experience and the stories they tell about it?'"

COLLECTING STORIES

"We started out by asking students to collect growing up stories from the people in their community, from the people who had shaped their culture. We asked them to collect growing up stories from their parents or guardians, from grandparents or grandparent-aged people, from siblings, from people in their neighborhood, and eventually from community leaders in Saginaw — for example, the mayor, the superintendent of schools. And then, in class, we studied the stories those people told, using ethnographic methods, looking at common themes in them and so forth."

STUDYING LITERATURE

At this point, Patti and the other teachers introduced a study of literature to give the students further jumping-off points and models for

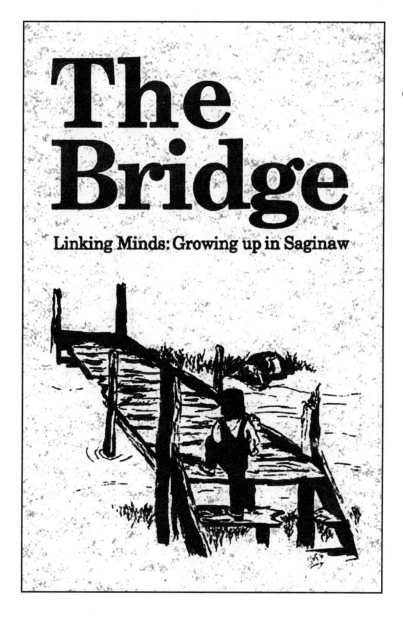

Gilberto T. Sanchez, cover art

The Bridge

A river runs through our city. We who live on either side look for ways to bridge it. One way we have done so is by composing these stories about our crossings from childhood toward adulthood.
Please walk with us.

(Excerpt from first page of *The Bridge*)

writing their own stories. They read growing up stories by Maya Angelou, Richard Rodriguez, and Maxine Hong-Kingston. The teachers also directed students to forms of literature or growing up themes that appealed to them. Some students chose great literature, and others chose young adult literature, but they all discussed what they read, and they wrote about it.

THREE MONTH READING/WRITING WORKSHOP

"Using writing in which they recollected personal growing up stories, we began to share stories. Students wrote a lot of stories in the first month or so. We didn't go back to develop them as pieces of writing. We were more concerned about the data they were providing us for study. Next, we did three months of a reading and writing workshop. Students wrote a story, and drafted it, and took it through several revisions, and to the final product. It took a whole month to do that. At the same time they were doing that, they were reading self-selected material — usually novels about growing up experiences like their own."

In addition to imaginative literature, the students were introduced to social science writing on adolescence that's usually read in university psychology and education courses. "They read excerpts from adolescent psychology, educational theory, sociology, and cultural history. We asked students to read from the point of view of experts. We said: 'You are experts now, so what do you think? Have these people got it right?' Some of our students had actually been labeled as reading at a 3rd-grade level, yet they were able to handle this material written for professionals, talk about it, and write about it."

EDITING GROUPS

"Some of our students had actually been labeled as reading at a 3rd-grade level, yet they were able to handle this material written for professionals, talk about it, and write about it."

After this three month workshop, students had in their writing portfolios many small pieces as well as three well developed stories. In January they formed editing groups.

"We Xeroxed about seven pieces of each student's work and then they met in groups of four or five to study each other's writing. The group would indicate to each student which pieces they thought were most interesting." It was in these groups that students received help with more revising.

"At that point in the school year we asked the students: 'What do you do with what you know, with all this research you've done?' We had always indicated to them that we wanted them to publish, somewhere along the line. It was their decision to publish a collection of their stories as a way of trying to demonstrate the growing up experience in Saginaw in the late seventies, early eighties. The kids from the two high schools decided that everyone involved would have one piece in the anthology."

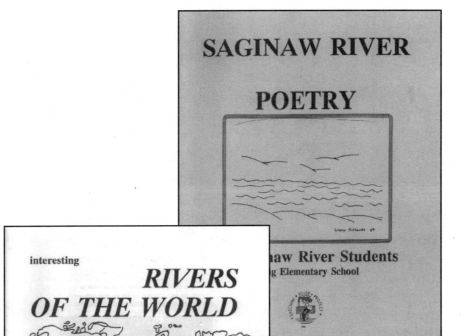

SAGINAW RIVER

POETRY

...naw River Students
...g Elementary School

Mrs. Joerke's Fifth Grade

interesting
RIVERS
OF THE WORLD

by: Kevin Sayer

authored by:
SAGINAW RIVER STUDENTS
Handley Elementary School
Third Grade

The
SAGINAW RIVER
A Coloring Book

AMY MURILLO
ZORAIDA VELUZQUEZ

After the production of The Bridge, *the river remained the focus for other projects at different schools and grade levels.*

Saginaw River Poetry, *Mrs. Joerke's 5th-grade, Herig Elementary School*
Lilene Richards, *cover art*

Rivers of the World, *Mary Lou Miller's 3rd-grade, Handley Elementary School*
Kevin Sayer, *cover art*

The Saginaw River, A Coloring Book, *South Intermediate School*
Amy Murillo and Zoraida Veluzquez, *cover art*

COMMUNITY SUPPORT AND THE FINAL STAGE OF PUBLICATION

"Most of our students worked outside of the school and a number of the students had children of their own, sometimes more than one child. So it was a complicated life they were leading. When we finally got to the publishing part of the project, we brought desktop publishing equipment into the classroom. The vice president for Minority Affairs at the University of Michigan gave us the money to do that.

"The CEIC hired a university student to teach the kids about word processing, and then, using a buddy system, students taught one another. We had one computer in each classroom all year, so the kids and I could 'talk' through electronic mail when I wasn't in Saginaw. So they had some familiarity with the technology. It was a big deal in both classes, playing around with the computer. Part of the requirement for the class became that you had to put your piece of writing on the computer."

For the kids most interested in computers, the classroom became a place to hang out after school.

The teachers asked the students to share their writing between the two classes and give feedback on the pieces. Then they decided it was time to bring the students together.

"We scheduled one Saturday at each of the high schools, near the end of the project, because we were running out of time. We invited graduate students in English and education from the University of Michigan to come up that day. And there were many high school English teachers there conferencing and helping students edit their work."

For the book's cover, one student produced a sketch of the bridge, and smaller thematic sketches were placed between sections of the book.

"Students named the sections of the book 'stepping on,' 'crossing,' and 'stepping onward.' They organized the selected pieces in chronological order. The first section covered stories about early childhood; the second one, the middle years; and the third, high school and anticipating life after high school. The themes range from a kid with a new bike to incest. It's all there."

CELEBRATION AND RECOGNITION

"We had a book publishing party at a very lovely inn in Saginaw. Local television, and radio, and newspaper people all came. Relatives of some of these young authors came from as far away as Alabama. I think the reality of what the students had done didn't hit them until then.

"Many of these students not only graduated, but went on to college. We only saw one or two who didn't finish. Most of them went on to Delta Community College in the area — I think many students went on to college because of the book.

"Over 2,000 copies of *The Bridge* have been printed. I am currently using it in a course at Michigan State. It has been used at George Mason University, the University of Michigan, the University of New York at

Albany, and other schools for classes in adolescent psychology, psychology of learning, and literature and the adolescent."

In the years that followed, the Saginaw school district and the University of Michigan have worked to interest other teachers in collaborative, interdisciplinary publishing projects. Interestingly, the river has remained a focus. Science, history, art, and even music classes have been involved, and kids have made reports to the local community. Elementary and middle schools have also become involved in these publication projects.

Footsteps, an anthology of student writing on growing up, published the year after *The Bridge*, is a beautiful, 400-page book. Its stories, poetry, and reflective essays are organized around these themes: "Reflections and Perceptions," "The Creative Image," "Death and Remembrance," "Affairs of the Heart — Family, Friends and Lovers."

The effects of the original publishing venture seem to be endless. As Patti Stock has said, "Student writers get to see their writing have an impact on the world. The next year their book was produced as a play. It doesn't stop there; it goes on and reverberates."

EVALUATION

"I am currently using it in a course at Michigan State. It has been used ...for classes in adolescent psychology, psychology of learning, and literature and the adolescent."

Footsteps *publishing party with students from Arthur Hill High School & Saginaw High School, Saginaw, Michigan*

REMEDIAL ENGLISH STUDENTS CREATE TEXTBOOKS ON ADOLESCENCE

Margaret McLaughlin

Patricia Price

Georgia Southern University

Statesboro, Georgia

Remedial English

"The students read, study, and analyze the book about adolescence that they have written. They each buy a book, so they each get a copy. This book is really another textbook in the classroom."

Margaret McLaughlin and Patricia Price involve their remedial English students at Georgia Southern University in a cross-disciplinary study of adolescence instead of drilling them to prepare for a standardized exam in English usage. Their students, who originally disliked reading and writing, not only end up enjoying this project, they also do much better on the standardized exam than the students who have been subject to a skill driven curriculum.

What are the common experiences of adolescence? What are the uncommon experiences? How do they shape a person? These are the questions that students think about as they read and write during the first part of the ten week class. They read published autobiographies about growing into adulthood as well as coming of age novels. They read about other adolescents while they write their own autobiographical essays about significant events in their adolescent years. The reading and writing enhance each other and help students express complex thoughts with style. The publication of their coming of age essays in one book is the mid-term activity for the class.

The students study their own book in the second half of the course along with academic essays and more scholarly work, like chapters on adolescence from psychology texts. Based on these readings, they write a research paper.

CHANGE IN ATTITUDE ABOUT READING

Margaret and Patricia give the class a questionnaire at the beginning of the course asking such questions as, "What is the best book you have ever read?" "They really hate the questionnaires," explains Margaret. "We give the same questionnaire at the end. From what they report, their attitudes about reading and writing have just taken a 180 degree turn. Furthermore, our studies show that not only do our students do better than those who take the standard remedial course, but they also stay in school longer. Until now, these students have not really had the sense that authors are real people who are attempting to communicate and who are open to question. I try to get it across in my class that they can communicate in the same way, that their opinions are worthwhile."

Lea Smith, who in a previous segment discussed 1st and 2nd-grade research books, makes the same point when she says publishing helps people feel like they are part of the "literacy club."

"Some of them wanted the 6th-graders to suffer just as they had, but, on the other hand, they were enthusiastic about a real live project that had an audience and a purpose and wasn't just something out of the book to do."

TECHNICAL MANUALS, HOW-TO BOOKS, AND GUIDES

Carolyn Tragesser

Moscow, Idaho

Moscow Junior H.S.

Language Arts

Most of us can remember dreading the move to a new, more grown-up school. In addition to the fears of forgetting locker numbers and getting lost are the myths about how everybody's going to get beaten up by the big kids. In Moscow, Idaho, the fears of 6th-graders persist even after junior high teachers go over to the elementary school to explain what can be expected in junior high. Carolyn Tragesser, an 8th-grade language arts teacher thought that a guide for incoming 7th-graders written by junior high students themselves would be a neat book to produce.

"I offered the germ of the idea to one of my 8th-grade English classes, and said, 'This is my idea, and if you don't like it that's fine. I'll offer it to another class. They liked the idea and really bought into it. That made it successful. Even though some of them initially wanted to see the younger kids suffer indignities as they did, the majority were thrilled to do this project."

The end product was a useful guide that drew from the disciplines of language arts, social studies, math, and art.

THE KIDS MAKE DECISIONS ABOUT CONTENT AND PROCESS

Carolyn is a firm believer in giving students ownership of projects in the style of the Foxfire method. (See discussion of the magazine, *Ursa Major*, in Carolyn's story in Chapter 1.) What makes this guide so usable for the incoming students is that the right people wrote it. It was not done in the voice of teachers or the administration. The tone of the 8th-graders was more friendly and inviting than that typically expressed by administrators. In addition, the authors decided what would be the most important information to have. "They decided to put on the first page a column called 'The First Day of School.' They knew that something like this would have helped them.

"They also made an elaborate map of our building and decided that it was really important to know the locker numbers. That's certainly not on any official school map. It was important for them to know where all the stairs were, as well as the pay phone. They said that as entering 7th-graders, they would have wanted to know what the halls looked like, what the teachers looked like, and where the hangouts were. So they took pictures and we reproduced them in the guide. I would never have thought of including pictures of empty halls and halls full of students. The title they decided on was 'Making Tracks to Moscow Junior High School,' and since we are 'the Cubs,' there is a connection with the tracks."

"If a group did not come to class prepared or did not meet a deadline, we had to work it out...they learned about setting goals, making decisions and working within a group."

EVALUATION OF THE PROJECT

WHAT DOES PUBLISHING MEAN TO THESE KIDS?

Students drew tracks on the page that continue into the photo of the school.

"As a group, the kids decided not only what to include in the guide, but they also decided how our process was to be structured. They brainstormed which committees were needed. They chose an editorial board that proofread everything. I was the final editor and I proofread as well. As a group we decided what our timeline was. It took longer than we expected. We started in March and picked it up from the printer the day before school was out."

The weakest part of the process, Carolyn recalls, "was keeping everyone busy when only some of the committees were meeting. I had students work on their own writing in their writing portfolios if their committees were not meeting. Something which I didn't think was a weakness, but which frustrated the students, was dealing with interpersonal relations within the class." If a group did not come to class prepared or did not meet a deadline, we had to work it out. The groups were at each other's throats a lot near the end, so we had to sit down and talk things through quite often. But that's real life, and they learned about setting goals, making decisions and working with a group."

Carolyn tells about how the map was done by two students who measured everything and then drew their map on a computer. "The assistant principal took a look at this and photocopied ours to use in place of the official school map. In fact my principal is now dependent on these guides." Perhaps the best evidence of success is the fact that the 6th-graders keep their guides all summer and they come prepared on the first day of school with their maps.

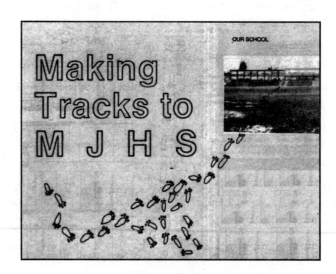

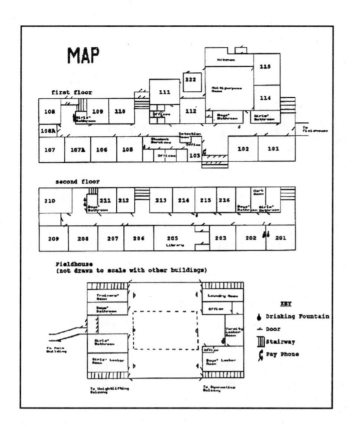

The nonfiction illustration/text format is as versatile in the classroom as it is in the world of professional publishing. Technical books can be produced by any age children, and they can range from the very simple to the complex. The illustrations can be photographs, drawings, or both. Students can write books describing and explaining processes in applied studies like auto mechanics, fashion design, agriculture, or publishing. Technical books can include descriptions of inventions, experiments or processes in physics, biology, chemistry, or the natural sciences.

Celeste Stivers, a 1st-grade teacher at Charlesmont School in Baltimore, Maryland, has presented several in-service programs on classroom publishing. Her quickest study was Deb Blimeline, the Chapter I assistant at her school.

"The first book with photos Deb showed me was about sewing teddy bears. She took photographs of them doing the process." The creative books Deb's very young children have produced confirm that very young children can produce nonfiction.

Celeste reports that after the picture book about sewing teddy bears, "the kids did a great book on cooking spaghetti. They went through the process of cooking, and again, Deb had pictures to go with each of the steps. There they were in their little chef's hats. They were just adorable. The kids then dictated to Deb the text that belonged with each picture, thereby producing a how-to book on making spaghetti."

ADDITIONAL IDEAS
FOR TECHNICAL
MANUALS

Chapter 3

NEW VOICES

Young people rarely have a voice in the mass media. They are spoken for, and they are frequently spoken about, but their own words are indeed rare. And the *most* silent of this already silenced group are the youth who have not been melted into the elusive mainstream. Included in this group are those who have been excluded from access to mainstream life as well as those who have chosen to remove themselves from it. Their stories are vital for us to hear, but they rarely get a chance to tell them. How often do we see in print the words of inner city youth or those of rural Southern children who have dropped out of school? What do we know of the thoughts of young people in the criminal justice system or of homeschoolers? We virtually never get their sustained visions. This silence is not healthy for these teenagers or for our society as a whole.

Educators and others who work with teenagers are beginning to fill this gap; the words of our diverse student population are being published as part of educational programs. This chapter will highlight some of the projects in which young people have expressed awareness of a culture or community in their work.

"Parents were invited in on the project. One of the ways they were involved was a family celebration day. We invited many parents to come and be interviewed. They brought in family artifacts, items that had been handed down for a long time — blankets, dishes, photographs, and art work."

David Schaafsma

Detroit, Michigan

Dewey Center for

Urban Education

David Schaafsma, assistant professor at the University of Wisconsin-Madison, formerly worked with inner city middle school and high school students in Detroit, helping them publish books that, like those produced by Patti Stock's students, weave interviews, autobiography, and fiction. Although Patti's students interviewed people in the community, their final pieces are autobiographical in nature. Students spoke with family and community members in order to help them understand their own growing up experiences. *The Bridge*, the first book published by Patti's students, was part of a cross-disciplinary study of coming of age.

For David's students, the interviews themselves are the focus of the books. As the students say in the preface to one of their books, *Struggles and Celebrations*: "We took inspiring stories from residents of Detroit and from Detroit itself as the roots of our stories and poems. Each piece is a unique celebration of Detroit."

The books written by David's students use Foxfire techniques that were pioneered by Eliot Wigginton. David explains: "Foxfire was an inspiration for us, as it has been for so many others. The two main things I learned from Foxfire were the importance of basing a writing project on a community and the importance of publication."

CORRIDORS: STORIES FROM INNER CITY DETROIT

The title, *Corridors*, refers to the Cass Corridor, an inner city section of Detroit. James Cook, an 8th-grade author, gives us an overview of Cass Corridor:

If I could write about any community in Detroit, it would be the Cass Corridor. Because of drugs and unemployment, many people moved away. But at one time, there were more people on Brainard between Second and Third than in most small towns in Michigan. Today, the Cass Corridor is mostly a bunch of burned down buildings. There are lots of drugs and prostitution, but I don't think it's as bad as its reputation.

David describes the demographics of the Cass Corridor region and the project: "The Dewey Center for Urban Education is an alternative, whole language, community-based public school in Detroit; the Dewey Center Community Writing Project takes place there each summer. The writing project is community-based and collaboratively designed by students, teachers, and some community members. It's a pretty troubled and yet, we think, healing part of inner city Detroit, near the Jeffries Homes, also known as 'The Projects.' This was the center of the 1968 riots. The scars from these riots are still there. Economically, the conditions are quite a bit worse than they were for people in the late sixties. Indications of this economic decline are the number of kids who are homeless, the number of teen mothers, and the dropout rate of 60 to 70 percent."

Corridors is full of the history and lives of people in this section of Detroit. How did David's students get their interviews for this book? In some cases, the children went to the people. For instance, the entire class went to the Cass Corridor Food Co-op to talk with the people who worked there. They went to Fred's Key Shop and Mack's Service Station. For most of their information gathering, students invited family and community members into the classroom. Billie Jo Roark, a 6th-grader, wrote a diary entry about a typical day in the life of the writing project.

> June 27, 1989
> 7:30 am
> Dear Diary,
> There were two people who came today and the class interviewed them. They were George McMahon and Rose Bell. We split up in two different groups and interviewed the person we wanted. We learned a lot about them. I really liked what we did. I really liked when Mr. McMahon was talking about jail. He went to jail because he tried to stick up for his neighborhood friends when they couldn't pay as much rent money as the owners of the buildings wanted them to pay. I think he was right to stick up for his friends. I would too.
> Yours truly,
> Billie Jo Roark

Variety in the style of presentation was important to the students. One of the selections by an 8th-grader, "George McMahon: A Man After His Own Kind," is a fairly faithful representation of the actual interview, whereas "The Other Side Of The Projects," also by an 8th-grader, is a short story about resident Rose Bell that distills the essence of an interview with her.

Although interviews with family and community members were the core of the selections in the books, David modified the oral history methods of Foxfire to allow students more opportunity for choice. "They did not have to do faithful renditions of the interviews. They could do interviews, fiction, short stories, combinations — blurring genres if they wanted to. We found that was the right way to go. To let them imagine new ways of using the interviews. We learned a lot from the kids.

"We printed 4,000 copies of *Corridors* and sold them all! We brought them to bookstores in Detroit and Ann Arbor and asked if we could sell them on consignment. They sold like crazy. There is a small, but excellent chain of bookstores called Borders located in various cities. On the basis of great sales in Ann Arbor, I proposed to their national distributor that they distribute the *Corridors* book nationwide. They did."

It stands to reason that these kids want the world to see that there are good things in their community, contrary to popular media images. Consequently, many of the selections in the three books David's students wrote express the positive, beautiful aspects of life in Cass Corridor. They tell about individuals, like Rose Bell, who have helped other people endure hard times. Focusing on these community people can motivate students to keep on working for their goals.

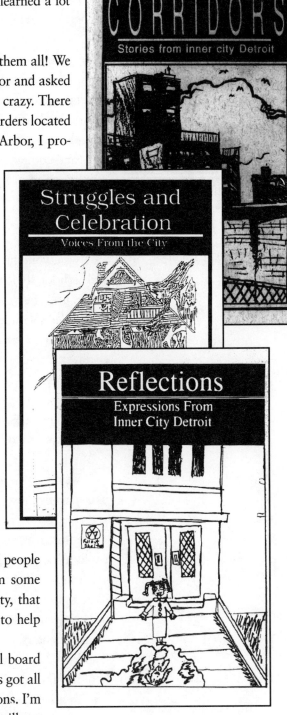

Dora, a 6th-grader, wrote a story based on an interview with Rose Bell, called "961 Baby," about a teen mother who had nowhere to go. Rose runs a program for single teen mothers that is called 961-Baby.

David explains: "The story came out of Dora's own experiences and was published for the world to see as a kind of inspiration. I asked her why she had written the story and she said, 'I know a lot of people in this situation and I thought it might give them some hope.' Here's a person living in phenomenal poverty, that many people might find shocking, who is inspired to help *other* people.

"We had a publication party attended by school board members from Detroit and local media. The students got all dressed up and they read excerpts from their selections. I'm enough of an idealist to believe that publication will get them to commit to try to find a better life for themselves than their parents had. It may keep them in school. The dropout rate in inner city Detroit is anywhere from 60 to 70 percent. What are the chances that Dora or any other 6th-grader is going to make it through?"

RESEARCH BOOK ON RELUCTANT READERS

Jerry Phillips

Monticello, Arkansas

University of Arkansas

Elementary Education

GOING INTO THE FIELD

PRODUCING THE BOOK

"I'm just as happy as a lark to stand around and drink their coffee, eat their cookies, and watch them drill holes and sew."

"My students go out with their tape recorders and talk to reluctant readers from elementary school age up to 21-year-olds. I ask them to listen to their tapes three or more times, and then begin to write a narrative about their findings."

Jerry Phillips teaches elementary education at the University of Arkansas at Monticello. Jerry's students publish a research book every year on reluctant readers, the very kinds of students prospective teachers need to learn more about. He explains that the class continues to do research after the books are published. "We go through the cases to look for patterns and commonalities. When my students leave my classes they have a pretty good profile of a reluctant reader and a disabled reader, and they have done everything on their own. I just stand around and guide them.

"We go out into the public schools and find elementary, middle, and high school students who are in remedial classes or who have poor grades in English. We also talk to school dropouts." With tape recorders rolling, Jerry's students record the reluctant readers as they describe their problems with reading. They ask their subjects about their first experiences with reading and try to determine exactly when the problem with reading began. The students inquire about what kinds of reading material, if any, are interesting to them and try to determine the value attached to reading in their families and communities. And they ask what teachers can do to help reluctant readers.

"We devote quite a few hours of class time to crafting the interviews into narrative form. We have editing groups in which the students give and receive constructive criticism.

"Sometimes instead of putting together some pretty good-looking books at the campus Resource Center, we make our own bindings. We just bring in a lot of food on the last day of class. We use wallpaper and paste it on cardboard, get out our drills and sewing machines and stitch books together. The main reason we do it that way is so they'll go into their elementary classrooms and start producing books immediately with their kids. I leave it up to the students which way they want to bind the books. If they don't want to spend the four bucks at the Resource Center, I'm just as happy as a lark to stand around and drink their coffee, eat their cookies, and watch them drill holes and sew."

What is the purpose of this project? "Actually it has more than one purpose. The main purpose is to get these education majors familiar with the children disenfranchised in literacy. In addition, they are also learning a tremendous amount about interviewing techniques and writing.

They are learning the value of publishing, and that will come in handy in their teaching. And of course, they are learning about computer technology." To really understand why Jerry has these goals, you need to understand the demographics of the area.

"The college students I teach have low ACT scores. They come from low-income families and are mostly white. I would say that 40 percent are on some kind of government grant to attend this university. This is not the school that rich kids go to. We are located in a very poor neck of the woods, just on the edge of the Mississippi Delta. These are the kids who can't afford to go off to a state university or an expensive church school. I would say that in the neighborhood of 25 percent of them have gone to these types of schools and did not do well because of the social activities."

The book Jerry's students write helps them gain confidence in their own reading and writing abilities while they also learn the best strategies for teaching the next generation. "These kids have learned that they can write with the best of them, in part because they've published their writing. Three of them are going to make presentations at state and national conferences. We don't find too many undergraduates who are making presentations at national conferences."

Jerry's students have published monographs (single subject books) of information collected from parents of reluctant readers. They also have published poems collected from students all across campus.

The same sort of research and book production could be used for reluctant learners of math, science, or social studies, or at-risk children. Projects can be done by prospective high school or elementary teachers.

DEMOGRAPHICS OF MONTICELLO, ARKANSAS

ACHIEVEMENTS

OTHER PROJECTS

Anthologies by Correctional Facility Students

Grady Hillman

Austin, Texas

Artists in Education Program

Texas Commission on the Arts

"We take our kids to public libraries to do readings from their published works. There is always a bit of apprehension about kids from state schools and reform schools. The fear is that these kids might try to escape or that they're really terrible. When we do these readings, community people realize that these can be nice kids. They are really messed up, but given the backgrounds they come from, the fact that they are in these facilities is not unexpected."

It's rare to have the opportunity to read the work of adolescents in the criminal justice system. These are voices new to most of us. It's also unusual for these kids to get a chance to publish their work in their communities. Grady Hillman, a guest teacher and coordinator of artists in correctional facilities in Texas and other states, helps adolescents in prison write and publish their work in anthologies. Grady, a poet, was involved in the Artists in Education program of the Texas Commission on the Arts for many years. Now he does arts curriculum consulting all across the country and trains other artists to work in correctional settings.

Grady describes some of the young people he has worked with. "These are teenagers, ages 10–16, who have very low self-esteem. Many of them are victims of abuse or incest. Publishing, whether it's displaying work in the classroom or actually producing a small anthology, seems to be really helpful in building the kids' self-esteem. They are really excited about their work. In fact I just returned to the facility at Corsicana,

Cover from the Harris County Juvenile Probation Department 1990 Report

Art and poetry by youths on probation were used in the report.

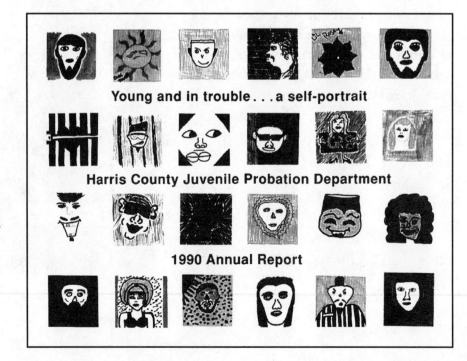

Texas, where we published an anthology six months ago. The students introduced themselves to me by saying, 'Remember me, I'm the one who wrote the poem about....' They really did identify with their work, and having it published just made it that much more concrete to them.

"I use an experience-based curriculum relating dreams, memories, and immediate sensory experiences to poetry, fiction, and drama writing. We write short stories as well as poetry and publish the work in anthologies. However, in the juvenile probation department of detention facilities, we have a relatively transient population. If you go in once a week, it's tough to do a lot of work with short stories or drama, because many of the kids won't be there the next time. So poetry is the most effective creative writing that you can do in this context."

It is increasingly difficult to obtain funding to bring artists and writers into the schools in these days of federal and state budget cuts. "Our budget for the juvenile probation department arts program in Harris County, Texas, is $225,000. At any given time we will have about 20 artists in residence. Right now there are about ten visual artists, five creative writers, two drama people, two dance people and a video person. There are no tax dollars funding this program — it is all foundation money."

"Many of these kids," Grady says "are very remote and not forthcoming about what is bothering them. Oftentimes in creative writing, things appear that the staff needs to know about. The kids can't confront the reality of murder and incest; it may come out in dreamlike episodes in their writing. The breakthrough often comes in creative writing. Later the staff uses the anthology as a diagnostic tool.

"Most kids in a correctional facility have fragile self-esteems; they give and take offense very easily. We try to build their self-images through writing and publishing the anthologies. Publishing gives us a chance to teach methods of criticism that encourage positive rather than negative thinking about one another's work. Also, being published seems to be recognized as being cool. So, previously produced anthologies are a good hook for getting new kids to do creative writing."

Publishing has also been a bridge from the reform institutions to the community at large. "The anthologies and the readings the kids give in public libraries counteract the public fear and hysteria about juvenile crime. People are frightened of these kids. Publication doesn't make the fear go away, but it puts a face on the kids. We're more afraid of what we don't see or don't hear. Publishing these anthologies allows us to know these kids a little bit."

I Am
by A.G.

I am the one I have to hold...
I am the one who watches me grow...
I am the one who loves me so dear...
I am the one who holds me so near...
I am the one who feels all my pain...
I am the one, only I change.

FUNDING

THE VALUE OF PUBLISHING

Drawing and poem above by A.G. appeared in the 1990 Annual Report at left.

ANNOTATED BIBLIOGRAPHY OF BLACK CULTURE

Sondra Nachbar

Bronx, New York

Bronx H. S. of Science

Librarian

Sondra Nachbar: "The students were from every ethnic group — they were Asian, they were white, they were black. I taught them how to annotate books, and they wrote annotations for all the books on black culture in the library."

Student editor-in chief: "This annotated bibliography was written by students at the Bronx High School of Science for all students everywhere. Twenty-four students representing diverse ethnic groups have become one group in the process of publishing this bibliography."

When a group of African-American students at the Bronx High School of Science wanted to set up a separate part of the library for books on black culture, librarian Sondra Nachbar suggested a different idea. She said that if the books on black culture were set apart, the same thing would have to be done for all the different ethnic groups, and then the library would become disorganized. Sondra presented the students with the possibility of putting together a bibliography of all books in the library on black culture. The African-American students who initiated the project liked Sondra's idea. They brought together a diverse group that eventually produced the annotated bibliography of books on black culture.

Sondra taught the students how to do annotations. They wrote all the annotations and organized the books in categories. For this cross-disciplinary project, students had to do a significant amount of reading and summarizing in a variety of subject areas.

Contributors to the bibliography felt that they had a mission. The student editor-in-chief said that it was his staff's desire to increase the awareness of the value of black culture for all people. Incredibly enough, the 24 students who produced this book worked on it during the sum-

Publication party, Black Culture, A Contribution to American Society, An Annotated Bibliography, *Spring 1985, Bronx High School of Science*

mer on their own time! Sondra also worked very hard correcting and entering the annotations on the computer — also on her own time. She recalls: "The students felt that we were producing a very meaningful resource, especially when we were able to publish over 300 copies of the 140-page bibliography. We sent a copy of the bibliography to every high school in the city of New York. We gave those away, but we did sell some.

"As a result of the bibliography on black culture, one of the social studies teachers came to me with an idea for a project. She asked, 'How would you like to do a bibliography on women in history?' I said, 'Sounds nice.'

"The first bibliography was subsidized by a former student. For the second project, we received a small grant from The New York Times Foundation. Again, we sent a free copy to every high school in New York City. There is really no reason why any student can't be involved in this kind of project. Yes, Bronx Science is a high school for gifted students, but I used to do this type of project in a regular junior high."

When embarking on a project like this, it is best to find the areas that students are most interested in. For her students, Sondra says, "The black bibliography was the better project of the two. Not as far as the results, but because it originated with the children, and because they were so enthusiastic about it. In the case of the bibliography on women, it took more effort on our part because we had to motivate the kids." Teachers can suggest to their classes book categories to annotate, then the class can add to the list.

Richard Smith,
cover art

Another way bibliographies can be integrated into the curriculum is in a newsletter format. Every few months, students in a given class or group of classes can read and annotate all the new books that come into the library. Then they can lay out a newsletter and send it to other classes and schools.

BIBLIOGRAPHIES IN NEWSLETTER FORM

NATIVE AMERICAN CALENDARS AND POETRY COLLECTIONS

Mick Fedullo

Pryor, Montana

Artist in the Schools

PROMOTING THE STUDENTS' WORK IN THE COMMUNITY

"I've had kids read at conferences, like the National Indian Child Conference in Phoenix."

"The calendars our kids made were distributed throughout the communities. Everyone needs a calendar. And when people buy one of ours, it hangs in their home. There they see the students' work; they see their writing."

For the last 13 years, Mick Fedullo, an artist in the schools, has helped students produce literary calendars and anthologies in Native American schools and communities in Arizona, Montana, North Dakota, and South Dakota. The centennial anniversary calendar for St. Charles School in Pryor, Montana, was one of the fancier projects. "That calendar," Mick said, "actually had photographs of the kids, as well as illustrations. It also had three or four of their poems for every month."

Mick's students' work ranges from relatively simple photocopied anthologies of poetry to fancy art calendars with poetry. With all these projects, Mick believes it is important to work with the community, and he promotes the students and their work in local newspapers, at public readings, and on local television.

"I've found it very useful to develop a professional relationship with someone on the local newspaper, someone who is in a position to use poems or stories as filler. It is good for the newspapers, the community and the kids.

"I often schedule poetry readings. Sometimes they're publication parties. The first time I did this was on an Apache reservation. A number of kids read their poems at an open reading. One of the best places to schedule readings is at universities. In Tucson, where I teach writing to Indian kids through a non-profit group, we do an anthology every year called *Dancing with the Wind*. We regularly have a recitation at one of the colleges around there. We promote the calendar or anthology at these events.

"I've had kids read at conferences, like the National Indian Child Conference in Phoenix. At that conference, there were several TV stations from Phoenix that wanted the kids to read into the cameras for their evening news broadcast. Afterwards, we were all watching the newscast at a friend's house, and one boy was so nervous about seeing himself on TV that he started hyperventilating. This brings out an important point. When kids get published and receive recognition in the community, they have to learn to deal with success. For many kids, especially kids with low self-esteem, dealing with failure is much easier. It's the pressures of success that we need to talk about with them."

Mick's goals as an educator and consultant are to help keep Native American cultural traditions alive, to give young Native American voices a chance to be heard in the wider society, and to promote education to these young people. He explains: "For over a hundred years, the Bureau of Indian Affairs was in charge of Indian education and its purpose was assimilation. Indian children were beaten if they spoke their own language. After generations of that, there were some pretty negative attitudes about education."

Mick turns kids' attitudes around by using and fostering cultural traditions. "On a reservation in Arizona, we did a quarterly newsletter that had a section in which we taught the Pima language. That was very popular. We also use art to bring people together. There was a Navajo school where we made calendars five years in a row. Navajos live so far apart from each other. They're all spread out in the desert. The school found that the calendars were an incredible vehicle to get people together and to recruit students.

"In addition to developing the arts, we help foster the oral tradition of Indian culture by always arranging readings at conferences, school board meetings, and parent advisory meetings. We also schedule TV and radio appearances.

"On a reservation in Arizona, we did a quarterly newsletter that had a section in which we taught Pima language. That was very popular."

1990-1991 Poetry Calendar entries from Ervin Begay, Terry Delgarito, and Eric Sandoval, Wingate Elementary School, Fort Wingate, New Mexico

Students' poetry and art fill the 1991 St. Charles School & Parish Calendar.

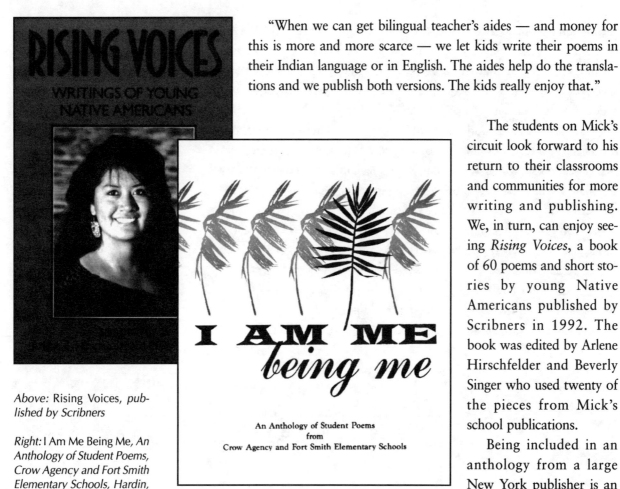

"When we can get bilingual teacher's aides — and money for this is more and more scarce — we let kids write their poems in their Indian language or in English. The aides help do the translations and we publish both versions. The kids really enjoy that."

The students on Mick's circuit look forward to his return to their classrooms and communities for more writing and publishing. We, in turn, can enjoy seeing *Rising Voices*, a book of 60 poems and short stories by young Native Americans published by Scribners in 1992. The book was edited by Arlene Hirschfelder and Beverly Singer who used twenty of the pieces from Mick's school publications.

Being included in an anthology from a large New York publisher is an achievement for any writer. Cameron Cuch, from Gay Head, Massachusetts, is one of the young Native Americans whose writing was selected for *Rising Voices*. His essay analyzes white settlement of Martha's Vineyard. Among other themes, Cameron's studies revealed that very early on Indians made the choice of being led by the settlers or resisting them. Forrest S. Cuch, Cameron's father, reflected on his son's essay and on the fact that it was published by Scribners: "The essay pulled no punches. It didn't help him get accepted at Dartmouth, but that's OK. Being published in *Rising Voices* gave him confidence and depth. He wants to pursue a career in government or politics."

Above: Rising Voices, *published by Scribners*

Right: I Am Me Being Me, *An Anthology of Student Poems, Crow Agency and Fort Smith Elementary Schools, Hardin, Montana*

ADDITIONAL IDEAS: HISTORICAL MATERIAL IN CALENDARS

A calendar with student poetry can also include social studies material. A class could study important dates in the community, in American history, black history, multicultural history, or the holidays of all cultures in the U.S. and briefly describe events on the appropriate calendar days.

"Most of the kids used what they knew of relatives' stories in their writing. It wasn't part of the assignment that they had to formally interview an elder. It was up to them to come up with their own setting, props, characters and plot."

FICTIONALIZED CULTURAL AUTOBIOGRAPHY

Bain Robinson

Kasigluk, Alaska

Akula Elitnaurvik

Language Arts

Bain Robinson, a language arts teacher in Kasigluk, Alaska, inherited a junior and senior class from Donna Murphy, and in addition, an interesting publishing project.

After reading *The Autobiography of Miss Jane Pittman*, the juniors and seniors invented a character, in much the same way Jane Pittman is an "invented" character. And just as the story of 100-year-old Miss Jane Pittman was a way of teaching about African-American history and culture, these students prepared to write fictionalized autobiographies to capture Yup'ik history and culture. Their six-chapter stories were compiled into the book, *Yuuciq: A Collection of Yup'ik Fictional Autobiographies*. The resulting stories are historical fiction. They are similar in genre to some of the work published by Ken Schmidt's students. As we will see, the process of writing these stories includes some of the same steps used in doing ethnographies.

DEMOGRAPHICS

Demography and geography have a lot to do with this project. Bain explains: "We're a village of 250 people on the Johnson River, which is a tributary of the Kuskokwim. This is about 30 miles straight west of Bethel on the Yukon delta. Like many rural villages in Alaska, there are two parts to the village, the old one and a new one. Our school, in the old section, is housed in an old Bureau of Indian Affairs building that has actually been condemned by the state for bad wiring. We're a subsistence village based on fishing and a little hunting. Most of the kids' parents speak Yup'ik. Many do not speak English fluently.

"There are some happy surprises in our village: The Yup'ik language is taught. In fact the man who teaches these classes has had writing process training. Also, we have more computers than you can believe. We are very well supplied for being so remote."

PROCESS: LEARNING FROM COMMUNITY MEMBERS

"As students read and discussed *The Autobiography of Miss Jane Pittman,* we analyzed the six parts of this novel and then they began their own six-chapter stories. During the process of writing, we invited elders and others from the village to come to class to hear what the students had written. The village people told the student writers whether what they had written could really have happened. The kids' work was really good — we had very few corrections. But the dialogue that was created as a result of these readings and the classroom discussions really helped them go on to the next chapter or the next incident they had planned.

"This was not an ethnography where the writer conducts interviews and remains literally faithful to them. However, most of the kids did try to use what they remembered of family stories and probably did go home and ask questions informally. Personally, I think fiction is way more interesting for students to write and is more interesting for the reader."

EVALUATION

In the foreword to the book, Donna Murphy, the originator of this project, describes the community involvement it generated: "The students' enthusiasm for this assignment exceeded my greatest expectations. Many students produced stories of much greater length than required. When the first drafts were shared, it quickly became apparent that parents and grandparents had become involved by offering details of the Yup'ik traditional lifestyle that were unavailable in our resource books. Enthusiasm spread to the 10th-grade, and, before long, fully half our school was involved in composing stories about fictional 100-year-old Yup'ik Eskimo men and women."

"...it quickly became apparent that parents and grandparents had become involved by offering details of the Yup'ik traditional lifestyle that were unavailable in our resource books."

"In our small town in the Central Valley of California we have probably one of the world's greatest experiments in multicultural living. We have a large Punjabi population, Indians from the Fiji Islands, Dutch, people of different Southeast Asian nationalities, Portuguese, and Italian-Swiss. Yet for many of these people, when they go to the library they see nothing of themselves."

Pat Egenberger teaches 7th and 8th-grade English as a Second Language in Modesto, California. Far from using the "drill, drill and more drill" approach to ESL, Pat bases her program on content or meaning based techniques that make sense when learning a first language. Pat's adult teacher's aide, Gloria Jenness, is essential to all her classroom activities. In her most challenging project, Pat has her ESL classes put together books of folktales from their countries of origin, in both their families' original language and in English.

There are two ways for students to do their bilingual folktales. They can write in the original language — optimally, they get stories from parents or an older person in the community. Or, they use folktales in their first language from one of the many books Pat is collecting in her room. Then, with the help of parents, students retell the stories in English. The other way of doing the bilingual tale is to start with parents' retelling of a tale in English. Then, students put the stories in their first languages. "I ask the kids to retell, not to translate, because I don't want them to feel that they have to sweat out each word. I emphasize how important it is that the stories be in their own words."

Why does Pat do such a challenging project?

"There are two main reasons," Pat explains. "First of all, so many of these children's languages are not looked at with respect; they go to the library and see nothing of themselves. Some languages have status like German or French. Japanese and Russian are in-between, while Spanish, Korean, and Vietnamese are often considered low status. I would like to help break down these destructive ideas. For these students to just get their original languages on the page is a way of making their parents' and their languages important. The second reason I do this project is that when students read and write bilingual books in their original languages and their new language, they make a big jump in literacy in the new language.

"It isn't easy for the kids to get started. They don't say, 'Oh goody, we get to do this multilingual folktale book.' They don't understand the purpose of it at first. It takes a while. And many of them are embarrassed about using their original languages in class, especially if there

MULTILINGUAL FOLKTALE BOOK

Pat Egenberger

Modesto, California

Somerset Middle School

ESL

79

PROJECT DESCRIPTION

"First of all, so many of these children's languages are not looked at with respect; they go to the library and see nothing of themselves."

ENGAGING THE PARENTS

are not a number of other speakers of their language."

Pat devises some ways of overcoming the shyness. "First I try to make the project very special. I send the kids home with pieces of very nice typing paper as well as paper that has lines drawn on it, that goes under the typing paper. I send home a nice black pen and whiteout. It all goes in a little envelope."

READING FOLKTALES AS PREPARATION

"It really helped this year to do much more extensive preparation. I had them read folktales from different countries. I introduced about eight different methods of storytelling. They did a presentation for the class, using one of these methods. They read more tales from their own countries, and this preparatory work validates the entire project for them."

Pat also did a storytelling project in which she taught everybody a folktale that is the Spanish equivalent of "The House That Jack Built." The class was divided in half, and half the class told the story in Spanish and the other half told it in English. "We shouted out lines, one after another, until the whole story was told in both languages."

PUTTING THE BOOK TOGETHER

"The entire process takes a couple of months. It takes a long time for the kids to get the stories from their parents. But, the parents help extensively. I see that the kids bring their work back and forth with corrections on it.

"It was a breakthrough when a kid who still had a lot of trouble finding a folktale came to me finally, and said, 'My dad does know a lot of stories. He told us stories last night in Laotian for hours.' Some of them wanted to learn their first languages better, and the kids who came here most recently became instant language experts. Children went over to the experts and asked for a few words in, say, Vietnamese. When it was all over, I was thrilled to see the excited faces of the kids when I passed out the completed books."

"The kids do their own typing or word processing of their tales. Since I don't have a typewriter for Chinese, Laotian, and some of the other languages, the way we were able to make the different kinds of writing look integrated in the book was by using borders. The kids help each other with word processing, and usually there are some who are real swift about computers. Once I learn PageMaker, and once the school finally gets the school edition of PageMaker, it will be fun to teach the kids how to do the layout.

"Since I don't have a typewriter for Chinese, Laotian, and some of the other languages, the way we were able to make the different kinds of writing look integrated in the book was by using borders."

Pat is planning to do more kinds of multilingual books with her ESL classes, including books of recipes and superstitions, and stories of how they and their families got here. She is also planning to bring multilingual storytellers into the classroom.

With some modifications, foreign language teachers might try to publish these sorts of books.

Tales by Lien Diep and Rick Gong, Wooyung Joo, and Alla Melnik from Stories From Many Lands

MULTILINGUAL BOOKS OF POETRY

Donna Clovis

Princeton, New Jersey

Princeton Regional Schools

ESL

"She uses publishing to heighten respect for all cultures."

"In the beginning stages of composing poetry, it's really fun because we do a lot of sharing. The kids are very interested in one another. The Russian students are showing their poems, which are in Russian, to a Chinese student. They can see why English is so difficult for some students. The Russian symbols and Chinese characters are so different from the Roman alphabet. They think that someone who speaks French has it easy when it comes to learning English."

Donna Clovis, like Pat Egenberger, teaches elementary and high school ESL. She teaches in Princeton, New Jersey, in a highly multicultural community. Like Pat, she uses publishing to heighten respect for all cultures.

"There are 37 languages in the district, and the socio-economic groups vary too. Some of my students come from Russia with just the clothes on their backs. We also have students from Haiti who are going to school regularly for the first time. We have children from Japan whose parents are at Princeton University. There are people from the poorest economic groups to the richest.

"Right now I'm editing a book of poems by ESL students from the whole district. Some will be in English, and some will be in the students' native languages and English. With my high school students, who are more literate in their native languages than the younger kids, we start with a poem they write in their original language. Then we translate it into English. We use bilingual dictionaries to make word for word translations at first, and then we try to make sense of the syntax later. To get the students comfortable with writing poetry, they read poetry in their own languages from books that I have in the classroom."

Six of Donna Clovis' Riverside students had their poems accepted for publication in The Acorn, *a children's magazine. The photo was published in Princeton, New Jersey newspaper,* Town Topics.

HOMESCHOOLERS PUBLISH

There are approximately 300,000 homeschoolers in the United States, students whose voices we rarely hear. But they, too, are beginning to write for publication. In fact, publishing is a crucial way for homeschoolers and their teachers to network with other homeschoolers and the public at large.

BOOKS

Homeschoolers around the country are publishing books. With computers, students can type, layout, and illustrate the pages of their books at home. Jesse and Jacob Richman, from Kittanning, Pennsylvania, are brothers who both have a great time writing books that they sell. Jennifer Goldman, from Roslyn Heights, New York, wrote a book about her travels with her uncle around the United States. Eleven-year-old Verity Bryant, a homeschooler in Santa Cruz, California, is planning to write a sequel to her first book, *The Adventures of Jumper*, and enrolled in a class for illustrating children's books. Verity did all the production herself using a computer, a laminating machine, and binding machine. She also calligraphed the titles and took the photographs for the cover. Verity says, "It took me nine months to finish this book and I was very proud when it was completed."

NEWSLETTERS

Susan Richman writes in her book, *Writing from Home: A Portfolio of Homeschooled Student Writing*, "A growing number of homeschooling families are finding that putting out their own family newspaper is motivating, fun for all involved, and even great PR with the relatives. The children come to feel that there really is an audience for their writing, a reason to write something about what they have been doing, or observing, and in the end there is a real product to hold in the hands after all their work."

Susan describes what it is like at their house when she announces that another issue of the *Oddfellow Gazette* has arrived: "Everyone comes racing in. 'Read it aloud at lunch! We want to hear it right away! Please!!!' So between bites of peanut butter and jelly, I read through this loved publication...It's another homeschooling family's own newspaper, published monthly. We've never met this family — they live 3,000 miles away — but we're getting to know them well through their writing and feel like whenever we do meet, it will be like meeting old friends."

HOMESCHOOLERS FOR PEACE "PEN PAL NETWORK"

The Gingold family from Midpines, California, like the Richmans, wanted to provide their homeschooled children with an outlet for sharing meaningful writing with other homeschoolers. They too have found that publishing a newsletter is an excellent way to counteract the potential isolation of children schooled at home. At first the Gingolds assembled whatever material was submitted by their children and a small group of other homeschoolers into a newsletter. Most of the students were very concerned about the condition of our world, and as they grew older, these interests were increasingly reflected in the newsletter. "When our daughter, Serena, insisted on using the name, *Homeschoolers for Peace*, we decided to take a bold step and make our newsletter a regular forum for kids to share their views on issues of peace and justice." The newsletter has grown in size and depth as the students have developed their comprehension of global issues.

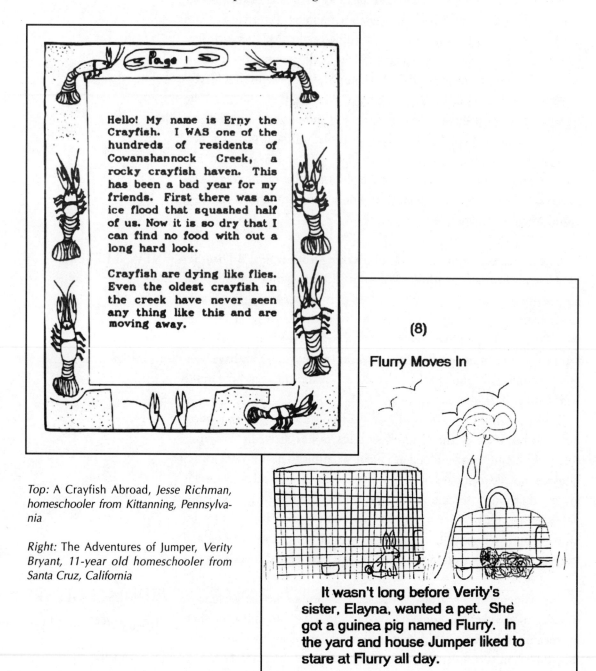

Top: A Crayfish Abroad, *Jesse Richman, homeschooler from Kittanning, Pennsylvania*

Right: The Adventures of Jumper, *Verity Bryant, 11-year old homeschooler from Santa Cruz, California*

Homeschooler Erica Dagle composes her ecology newsletter on a Sauvie Island beach, Portland, Oregon.

Photo by Marv Bondarowicz, The Oregonian

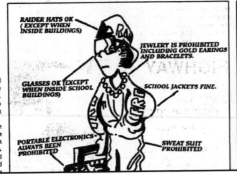

Chapter 4

EXPANDED AUDIENCES

When the audience for their writing is especially interesting to student authors, the hard work necessary to bring a project to successful publication is more rewarding. A variety of factors give audiences the power to inspire work.

For instance, the readers may need the published material. Young people, who often have a clear sense of what is right and fair, respond well to human needs. In one of the projects discussed in this section, students wrote books for their counterparts in war-ravaged parts of Nicaragua.

An audience can also inspire good writing if it is composed of influential people. Students, just like most of us, would like their words to be understood by influential people such as newspaper editors, city council members, state and national representatives, and business leaders. Some of the educators whose work is discussed in this section help students distribute their work to leaders in their communities.

Students can become more serious writers when they know their work will be distributed in a particularly exciting place or to an unusually large audience. Some projects reviewed in Chapter 4 target readers in places as far away as Japan. In another example, students write for *New Youth Connections,* which distributes 75,000 copies each month to high schools and libraries in New York City.

In addition, this chapter discusses journalism programs that teach students how to reach wide audiences with their writing. Some of these programs enlist the help of community members — like reporters — who have professional techniques to share.

New Mexico Students Make Books for Nicaragua

Nan Elsasser

Albuquerque, New Mexico

South Broadway

Cultural Center

Background

The Students and Their Books

"When I came back from Bluefields, Nicaragua, I went to Washington Middle School in Albuquerque, New Mexico, and I told the kids there what I had seen. I told them I had been appalled and saddened by the lack of materials in the schools in Bluefields. There were no pencils! There was no paper! Compared to Bluefields, Managua was like Sweden. During our discussion, someone asked, 'What can we do?' Then one of the students suggested that they write books for the children there."

Nan Elsasser and a colleague spent a semester at Washington Middle School as writers-in-residence. At the end of the semester, 1,200 books were delivered to Bluefields' Ministry of Education and a "storytellers" program was launched. After this first semester, Nan took the storytellers program to the South Broadway Cultural Center in Albuquerque, where students continue to publish books after school and on Saturdays. "The Working Classroom Storytellers program has sent 28 books to the presses in three years," said Nan, who is the project coordinator.

In 1986, after five years of teaching in the Caribbean, Nan traveled to Bluefields, a small town on the Atlantic coast of Nicaragua. Under a program organized by MIT, she helped develop a bilingual education program for the town's residents. Bluefields was once the capital of the British Mosquito Coast protectorate and was returned to Nicaragua in the mid-1800s. Spanish replaced English as the official language, but the people who live in this region are more fluent in a Caribbean form of English known as "English Creole." Nicaragua has long been an extremely poor country, ravaged by colonialism, greed, embargo, and war. In addition, the Atlantic coast was the least economically developed part of Nicaragua. After Nan told middle school students in Albuquerque about the history and conditions in Bluefields, they spontaneously offered to help the children there by writing and publishing books for them.

One key to understanding why the students in the program were so eager to help the children in Bluefields lies in the backgrounds of many of the young authors. Most of the students are recent immigrants from Mexico and Guatemala whose families currently live in Albuquerque's inner city neighborhoods. Their ages range from seven years through eighteen. Many of the young participants are in the process of learning English. The books, some written in Spanish, and some in English, are about eight pages long.

Because of their life experiences, the student authors often describe long journeys, like Miguel Pacheco's *El Viaje del Sapo*. The storytellers,

Nan says, put their troubles and hopes into their books. Loneliness and alienation are natural parts of a new immigrant's life, and these themes are often found in the books. There are also many happy endings and funny parts.

The appreciative thank-you letters from Nicaragua that the Storytellers received explained how the books were distributed to different schools and how the students loved them.

Because of their excitement about their audience, Nan's students were willing to put in long hours of tiring revision — on their own time. Students had to revise their works at least three times. Producing books for Nicaraguan children gave them a reason to write, many of them for the first time! Many students became more literate in their second language, English. Others became more literate in their first language, Spanish. Miguel, the teenage author of *A Hero From Mexico*, a story about his hero, Pancho Villa, has been in the United States for three years. So far his books have been in Spanish, but within a year he plans to write a book in English.

Robert Pedroncelli says that he writes as much as he can in one hour and then he takes an hour break before reading his work over to find things to revise. "I hate revising. It's boring and it takes a long time, but I want my stuff to look as good as it can, not like some little kid wrote it. I want it to look like a smart person did it. If I'm doing it for a lot of people, I'll put a lot of effort into it."

Like many other classroom publishing projects, this one has increased students' self-esteem. The father of 14-year old Robert Pedroncelli said, "Writing books has been a good experience for Robert. It has given him confidence. It has made him feel that his ideas are worthwhile, and that his dreams are good." The storytellers are acquiring not only new language skills, but are also learning to communicate in the larger culture. They have signings in bookstores in Albuquerque and Taos, where they read from their work, and they give interviews to the press about their successes.

Recognition of these students for their new skills also comes in the form of book sales. Bookstores in New York City are selling these books.

Educators and psychologists working with children who are recent immigrants from war-torn El Salvador are using the Bluefields project as a model. In this related project, Salvadoran children in the U.S. who are traumatized by and depressed about being separated from their villages and families in El Salvador will write books for children in their home villages.

KNOWING THE AUDIENCE INSPIRES NEW WRITERS

USING STUDENTS' LANGUAGE & CULTURE

"It's been a good experience for Robert. It has given him confidence. It has made him feel that his ideas are worthwhile, and that his dreams are good."

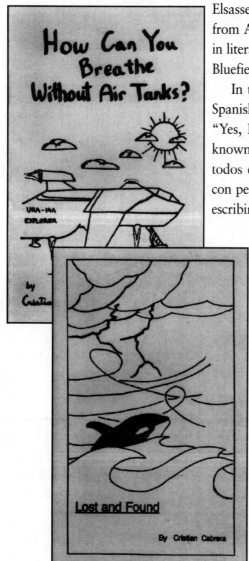

*Working Classroom books
by Cristian Cabrera*

In the play, *Suenos Sin Frontera* (Borderless Dreams), the Storytellers relate how the Bluefields project helped them gain literary skills and self-confidence. This play was written and produced by Working Classroom Storytellers with the help of playwright Monica V. Sanchez and Nan Elsasser. The action begins when Armando Cabrera, a young Chicano from Albuquerque, travels to Stockholm to receive the Nobel Laureate in literature. *Suenos Sin Frontera* incorporates within it stories from the Bluefields books.

In the play, the Nobel laureate, moving freely between English and Spanish, explains how his writing career began in Working Classroom: "Yes, I began to write when I was in Middle School, what today is known as Zapata Middle in Albuquerque. La classe era de espanol y todos eramos Mexicanos. Un dia, era un tarde, entro una senora alta con pelo enchinado, se llamaba Zena Faye. Nos pregunto si queriamos escribir libros para llevar a los ninos de Nicaragua. Yo era uno de los mas interesados… "(The class was in Spanish and all of us were Mexicans. One afternoon, Zena Faye, a tall woman with curly hair, entered the room. She asked us if we would want to write books to take to the children of Nicaragua. I was one of the most interested…)

As the play progresses, a reporter from the Excelsior newspaper asks the Nobel Laureate: "Senor Cabrera, sabiendo como es la vida del immigrante Mexicano en los Estados Unidos, como supero tanto Ud.? Como imagina que seria su vida si no hubiese pertenicido al proyecto que acaba mencionar?" (Senor Cabrera, knowing what life in the United States is like for the Mexican immigrant, how did you do so well? What do you imagine your life would be like had you not been involved in the project you have just described?)

Armando answers in a mixture of English and Spanish: "If I hadn't been a member of the project, yo a lo mejor ahorita estaria flipping burgers o limpiando officinas. Como otros companeros mios. This project gave me other choices which I pursued and here I am." (If I hadn't been a member of the project, it is as likely as not that at this very moment I would be flipping burgers or cleaning offices. Like others, my friends. This project gave me other choices which I pursued and here I am.)

Suenos Sin Frontera was performed at schools, universities, and libraries in New Mexico, Washington DC, and New York City. In addition, storytellers gave presentations about the Bluefields project in various cities.

WHAT'S NEXT?

Currently Nan's students are working with biologists from the University of Vera Cruz in Mexico to increase awareness about ecology, especially about the eagle that migrates between Mexico and New Mexico. The kids are writing stories about ecological issues and are sending them to Mexican students.

Looking ahead to new projects Nan says, "I plan to invite different non-profit groups to speak with the students. They will make their pitch, and the kids will decide which topic to study and write books about."

FUNDING FOR THE STORYTELLER'S PROJECTS

Although Nan finds it difficult and tiring to obtain funding for the projects, she does get the job done. The Storytellers are funded in part by the New Mexico Arts Division and the Albuquerque Community Foundation. National and local businesses also contribute.

Significant financial and moral support comes from *The Albuquerque Tribune,* which contributes $1,000 per year to cover printing and binding costs for the Storytellers program.

Tim Gallagher, editor of The Albuquerque Tribune, explained why his newspaper financially supports the Storyteller projects: "Newspapers tend to make a lot of money, and when they do, I think one of the things they ought to do with their profits is put them back into making us a nation of readers…Most of us in journalism agree with projects that are empowering to people."

ADDITIONAL IDEAS

Students can write books in English for English speaking children around the United States and the world who have little in the way of classroom supplies. Nan mentioned the possibility of writing books for children of black South African townships.

Children in ESL and foreign language classes can publish books and send them to Mexico, Guatemala, El Salvador, Vietnam, or Russia. Participation in this project would improve literacy for all students involved, as well as provide needed supplies.

Two Working Classroom books: Tiros Para La Libertad by Miguel Pacheco, El Valor de un Beso by Victor Manuel Facio Sanchez

A STATEWIDE ANTHOLOGY GOES INTERNATIONAL

"Treasures I, which included stories and art by Oregon students, was a success. Right before Treasures II — *also a compilation of Oregon stories — was about to be published, I asked myself what were we going to do next? It would be boring to keep doing the same thing. And there were already anthologies of stories by students from across the United States. Suddenly, I thought of Japan."*

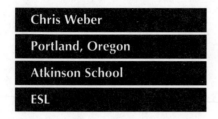

Chris Weber

Portland, Oregon

Atkinson School

ESL

Chris Weber, an ESL teacher in Portland, Oregon, has worked with students on a series of increasingly ambitious literary and art anthologies. As the scope of his projects grew, he sought more and more student involvement in many phases of the publishing process. Above all, he has attempted to expand the audience for the anthologies.

Treasures began with letters sent to all the public schools in the state announcing the first Starfire Art/Writing Contest. "We were looking for true stories — stories that gave you a good sense of who the writers were. That first year the contest was judged by a handful of writing teachers and myself. The funding came from an inheritance of mine, because we were waiting for non-profit status, and I had no grant writing skills."

In the introduction to *Treasures I*, Chris explains how the selections were chosen: "As all the stories were good, it was very difficult selecting which ones to include. Voice — the power of the words — and honesty — the extent to which writers or artists invested themselves in their work — determined the winning stories and pieces of art."

The selections are arranged by themes: "Me," "Places," "The Unexpected," "Life and Death," "Animals," "Refugee," "Sun and Rain," and "People." They do indeed give a very personal sense of the writers.

TREASURES III FIVE YEARS IN THE MAKING

"By the second year I had formulated some primitive grant writing skills. They certainly look primitive to me now! We received around $22,000 from various organizations and formed our foundation, the Oregon Students Writing and Art Foundation. The change between *Treasures I* and *II* was the use of high school students in the various aspects of publishing: public relations, sales, the whole operation from beginning to end. Students put the stories on the computer and helped with the copyediting. They were also involved with the layout a little bit, helping make decisions about the ordering of the stories and art. Basically the students who worked on *Treasures II* were Southeast Asian high school students from Portland, Oregon." These students not only learned about publishing and literature, they also had intensive training in English in a practical context.

After producing two Oregon statewide anthologies, Chris began looking for a new publishing project. He hit upon the idea of collaborating on a book with Japanese students. "I was always impressed with the quality of work the Japanese students did and the efficiency of their educational system. Also we Americans and the Japanese know so little about each other. If people could read firsthand what a Japanese child said and what an Oregon child said about what their lives were like, we would have a powerful cultural exchange."

Treasures III will have stories from Japanese and Oregon students. There will be two editions printed, one in English, the other in Japanese. Tentative publication date for the English version is March 1993.

Chris' projected budget is $250,000. So far, he has received grants from Avia, the Rose Tucker Foundation, and the Collins Foundation.

In order to make contacts with educators in Japan, Chris contacted Oregon Senator Mark Hatfield, sister cities organizations, and the Japanese Consulate. Through his research he found an education writers' group in Japan, a large grassroots whole language movement that is about 60 years old. Chris contacted groups of educators throughout Japan. "We sent the local groups guidelines and a copy of *Treasures II*, and asked them to send their most representative student work. We decided they should feel free to send us their selections in Japanese. We are receiving 30 to 40 stories, and are doing the final selection and translation in Oregon.

"We started this third anthology with three student editors who worked on *Treasures II*. Now we have 15 to 20 student editors who work on the project every week. A team of five students and five teachers selected the Oregon stories over a period of a year. We received 3,000 to 4,000 and selected 50. There is a group of students that reviews all the stories that come in. Another group of students does computer work, and there are students who take care of mailing, clerical work, correspondence, and invoicing. A group of students learning Japanese at South Eugene High School is putting the entire Japanese version into the computer."

A project with such breadth and such a large budget needs excellent marketing. Chris knows he needs to do homework in this area. He plans to mail books to national and regional distributors, like Baker and Taylor, Ingram, Bookpeople, and Pacific Pipeline. Chris' marketing plan also includes contacting local television and radio stations as well as writing lots of press releases.

Students and teachers talk about friendships and partnerships that were formed in the making of the *Treasures* books. Chris adds, "The

JAPANESE CONNECTIONS

"If people could read first-hand what a Japanese child said and what an Oregon child said about what their lives were like, we would have a powerful cultural exchange."

TO MARKET, TO MARKET

BENEFITS

previous students editors have talked about how giving became more important to them, after watching me run this foundation and do all this work for other people. Also it's an experience with other cultures that they will always carry with them. They have been impacted by the values of other cultures."

Speaking like a true publisher, Chris said, "I may be the spider, but there are lots of little strands that hold up the web. I just run around making sure everything's together." Because the targeted audience is so large, his role with *Treasures III* includes outreach, research, fundraising, and marketing. Chris acknowledges that *Treasures III* is a technically difficult intercultural publishing project. "But, if we succeed, then others can too. We can be a model for others."

Foreign language, ESL, social studies, and language arts classes can combine efforts to publish books, magazines, or newsletters with classes and schools in other countries on a variety of themes such as peace, the environment, science, school life, and more. For instance, students from the Pacific Northwest could collaborate with students from Central or South America to publish a newsletter on forest ecology. Foreign language classes could help with the translations. Such a project would be fruitful even if it were far more modest in scope than *Treasures*.

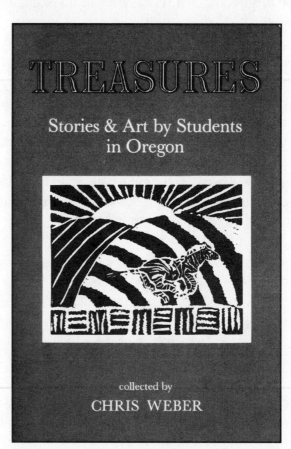

Treasures I, Stories & Art by Students in Oregon, *1985*

Mikell O'Mealy, age 11, cover art

"I had the seniors right after lunch, so on beautiful fall days, we just all took off. They loved it. They thought they were going to escape and have fun. Well, they knew they had work to do as well. We spent a few days downtown interviewing and doing the photography. They took it seriously."

Andrea Mayer, a professor at the State University of New York College at Oneonta, formerly taught high school English in a rural district in central New York state. The entire school population is under 500 students, K-12, and the senior class has roughly 25 students.

Producing a booklet on the Worcester community was the first of many publishing projects for Andrea's students. "Students went out into the community and interviewed business people about their jobs, what their days were like, and how well they liked what they were doing." The students found the interviewing to be a real treat, and it got them motivated to do the hard work of writing and revising. They wanted to do justice to members of the Worcester community, who would be their audience. "The local realtor asked for copies of the booklet to show prospective home buyers in Worcester a little bit about the community. It was a real document that had a purpose."

Dear Mr. Bobnick is a booklet of letters from Andrea's senior class to the superintendent, in which students wrote about what could be improved at the school and suggested possible solutions to those problems. "The students were upset because of a number of things. For instance, their driving privileges during lunch had been taken away. They were so upset, I thought I'm not going to get a thing out of those kids today. So I said, 'Let's get some of this down in writing.' I asked them to argue in a positive way. This was a good exercise in audience and tone. We sent Mr. Bobnick our book and invited him to visit. He came into the room, sat in a circle with the students, and gave his views on what they wrote."

This was an audience the students would not likely have had if they had not put together their letters in a book.

"Students chose a problem or an issue of national or international concern and wrote to President George Bush about it. They wrote on such topics as energy conservation, the greenhouse effect, the arms race, drugs in America, the homeless, toxic waste, segregation, the ozone layer, sex education, the need for cancer research, and abortion." They did not get a reply from the President.

"For four years I have had the junior class write a book about the graduating class. Juniors interview the senior class, and write short bi-

Andrea Mayer

Worcester, New York

Worcester Central School

Jr. & Sr. English

95

DEAR MR. BOBNICK

WE ARE CONCERNED, PRESIDENT BUSH

JUNIORS WRITE BOOK ABOUT SENIORS

ographies of the seniors. Students also take pictures and do the layout and paste-up. Our local vocational center prints the photos. My students do the collating and binding. It's a tradition now and I hope it continues after I am gone." Great care is taken in the production of these keepsake editions, and each successive senior class eagerly waits for its book.

Above: Reception for local merchants to receive copies of the booklet

Right: The Community and its Businesses published in 1987 by Worcester Central School's English 12 students with assistance from the Catskill Regional Teacher Center

THE COMMUNITY
AND ITS
BUSINESSES

The school newspaper, along with the literary arts magazine, has for many years formed the backbone of school publishing. In recent years, many school newspapers have been improving. Steve O'Donoghue, 1990 Journalism Teacher of the Year, told us, "A lot of the high school papers now are unbelievably good. Much more so than in the old days, because the kids do more. Very few schools had professional typesetting equipment, but now almost every school can get a Macintosh. Every school can be its own publisher."

Breakthroughs in technology as well as in the teaching of writing have increased the potential of the school newspaper. We'll look at three versions of innovative school journalism. Dennis Stovall advises an award-winning junior high school newspaper in Anchorage, Alaska. Steve O'Donoghue directs the Media Academy for at-risk high school students in Oakland, California. Carol Lange teaches and develops curriculum for classes in Intensive Journalism at a magnet high school in Alexandria, Virginia.

The Falcon Flash *May 12, 1992: "The American Scholastic Press Association in New York gave* The Falcon Flash *three coveted awards this year. First Place with Special Merit for* The Falcon Flash, *Outstanding Intermediate School Newspaper for 1992 (the #1 junior high paper in the USA), and Outstanding Story to two students: Shana Price and Lamond Venning for their coverage of sexual harassment during the Hill/Thomas controversy last November. They were the* only *junior high students to win this award."*

The Falcon Flash is a 70-page newspaper that the Journalism class at Clark Junior High School in Anchorage, Alaska, publishes about 12 times a year. The staff creates assignments and completes word processing, editing, and layout. In addition, all cartoons and photos in The Falcon Flash are produced by Clark students.

Dennis Stovall (See his previous segment in Chapter 1) motivates his journalism students to create a newspaper that is chock-full of lively, thought provoking articles in much the same way that he motivates his English students to produce books of provocative essays on a common theme. He challenges his students to tackle all kinds of topics, from those of schoolwide interest to issues of international concern, from human interest stories to very controversial topics. The students know they can go into depth on just about any topic. He gives them the confidence and freedom to investigate the world to find answers to their questions. Dennis communicates to his students that there is a wide audience of people beyond the school who want to read what they write.

INNOVATIONS IN SCHOOL JOURNALISM

Dennis Stovall

Anchorage, Alaska

Clark Junior H.S.

Journalism

Steve O'Donoghue

Oakland, California

John C. Fremont H.S.

Journalism

Carol Lange

Thomas Jefferson H.S.

for Science & Technology

Alexandria, Virginia

Intensive Journalism

A FLASH OF BRILLIANCE

What topics are covered in *The Falcon Flash*? "Sex, drugs, AIDS, sports, teen suicide, local politicians and politics, nuclear war, peace, movies, television, gossip, self-help articles, social services, charities, teen pregnancy, drugs, alcoholism, moral values, money, Christmas, homelessness, the rich, student government, classes, assemblies, garbage, computers, pizza, sexual harassment, the teacher's strike, biosphere, pornography, restaurant reviews, runaways, the economy, allowances, and religion. The only topic I have ever tried to avoid is abortion/choice," Dennis says.

THE REPORTERS INVESTIGATE

Good investigative reporting makes any newspaper interesting and this should apply to student papers too. In the October 1991 issue, student reporters interviewed many people. They spoke with Clark school administrators, secretaries, and students about a host of school and human interest issues and a Clark science teacher about his summer travels. For a story on an impending teacher's strike, a range of Clark teachers and district administrators were interviewed. Governor Hickel's office, the Anchorage superintendent of education, and a student were sources for a story on state budget cuts for computers in schools. Students even interviewed a diplomat from the Soviet Embassy in Washington, D.C.

DISTRIBUTION AND COMMUNITY SUPPORT

The newspaper is distributed to the school community and beyond. "Our newspaper," Dennis said, "has a mailing list of supporters that includes President Bush, our two U.S. senators, our congressman, governor, numerous state legislators, the mayor, city assembly representatives, our superintendent, the school board, area high schools, junior high schools, and elementary schools. In addition, we send papers to local businesses that have taken the time and expense to financially support our paper, and to local newspapers, TV stations, and the Associated Press. We put out over 400 copies of each edition, but we estimate the readership to be 3,000 people. The students know how much they are appreciated by their audience from the overwhelming financial support they receive from the police, local and state politicians, and local businesses. They gave us over $3,000 last year. Also, the students receive hundreds of letters of support for the writing they do." Creating a mailing list for distribution of the paper and contacts for stories is crucial for building an audience. This, in turn, is essential for fostering student motivation for writing.

The Falcon Flash, which Dennis Stovall and his students resurrected in 1985 when he joined the faculty at Clark, has been awarded first place by the American Scholastic Press Association from 1989 through 1992.

Section Editors for *Falcon Flash*, June 1992:

"Before the *Falcon Flash*, I was set in stone on being a scientist. Now my dream is to be a scientist and write a couple novels on the side."
— Shana Price

"I'm thinking about making a career out of journalism."
— Dusty Davis

"The journalism kids do a lot of topics that go way beyond the school. The topics in The Green & Gold *differ from what you find in many high school newspapers. They are a lot more nitty-gritty. The kids live in a neighborhood where the leading cause of death among teenagers is gunshot. They tend not to do too many stories about the 'club dance.'*

Steve O'Donoghue is the newspaper advisor and director of the Media Academy at John C. Fremont High School in Oakland, California. He helped design the curriculum for the academy, a three-year program built around journalism careers for at-risk students. These students major in newspaper publishing, magazine publishing, or broadcasting. "The academy," Steve explains, "has been in existence for six years and is basically a partnership between the state, which provides operating funds; the school district, which provides the teachers and the rooms; and industry, which provides speakers, mentors, job sites, and an advisory board."

In the Academy, the sophomores get a course in basic journalism: news writing, features, sports, and interviewing. In small teams, they produce a small newspaper and a magazine. They also get a short course in broadcasting. Then as juniors and seniors, they major in a particular area and they become the staff of the newspaper, magazine, or radio studio. Four of their six classes are in the Media Academy. Only one period a day is devoted to their major, but as Steve says, "they are here before school, after school, and at lunchtime, because nothing you do in publications or broadcasting can you complete during the regular school day."

Every three weeks, 1,800 copies of a new edition of *The Green & Gold* roll off the press. The articles, like those in *The Falcon Flash*, are controversial and persuasive. The topics, whether they are schoolwide or are national in scope, are close to Fremont students who deal with inner city issues daily.

THE GREEN & GOLD,
STUDENT NEWSPAPER

A sample of provocative articles on school and local issues from five editions of the paper covers a wide variety of topics. There are news and opinion pieces on dress codes and an opinion article on the lack of nutritious food in the cafeteria. Feature stories include an immigrant's first day at Fremont; Caucasians as a minority at Fremont; why ethnic groups don't mix on campus; and how street violence is turning Fremont students into stay-at-homes. An interview with a Fremont teacher recalls the days when Oakland had legalized segregation. News articles include a piece on public transportation service cutbacks and fare increases; and

COVERAGE WITH A
PUNCH

a story showing a majority of Fremont students regularly attend religious services.

POWERFUL NATIONAL ISSUES

As with school and local issues, articles with a national scope are written with clear voice and authority. A sample of national articles from five months of *The Green & Gold* reveals an array of topics. Opinion pieces range from an article criticizing affirmative action as being demeaning to blacks, to the case for not shunning doctors infected with the HIV virus, and an argument that parents should have a say in their child's decision about abortion. University of California tuition increases and a piece arguing that Black History Month should be celebrated all year are among the editorials printed. Feature articles include pieces on what would happen if David Duke were president, how teens are being raised by their grandparents, fashion and self-esteem, and how black entertainers give back to the community.

DIVISION OF LABOR

Steve says: "I give the sophomores training assignments, but the kids who are producing *The Green & Gold* come up with their own ideas. I may hear something and suggest, 'Hey, this is something you should look into,' but it's up to them. They have total autonomy. The kids have brainstorming sessions. Ideas come in the mail. Other teachers will suggest ideas. A teacher who is involved in something might come in and say, 'Did you know that next week a bunch of us are going down to picket city hall?'

"We're set up like a regular newspaper with an editor-in-chief, managing editor, and section editors. In the spring, the kids try out for the different editorial positions by producing a cub edition. The former editors and I make the decision, and the new editors remain in their positions for a year. There are 12 editors who do the layout of the different pages. Everyone, regardless of assignment, is supposed to do a story for each issue. The artist does a story, the copyeditors do stories, the photographers do stories. Everyone does research, interviewing, word processing, and editing."

THE NEWSPAPER IS A HOOK INTO LITERACY

The fact that the newspaper staff works collectively helps the students acquire language arts skills that are harder to come by in a regular English class. "On a newspaper staff, even if a kid's writing isn't world class, it is natural for another kid to sit down with him and help out," Steve explains. In addition, students rely on one another in their group, and this helps keep them in school — where they are developing their skills. "The great thing about publications," Steve says, "is that they allow you to bring kids along in their skills, because there are many nonacademic tasks that have to be done. Somebody has to distribute the paper. You don't have to be a genius, but it has to be done right. Kids doing these tasks are still contributing. Maybe their stories aren't so hot, but you can work them in. While you're working on improving their stories, they are still an integral part of the staff." The bottom line — Media Academy students have a better than average attendance record.

A second way publications attract at-risk students is by providing real motivation. Co-worker and audience feedback is far more potent than grades as motivation with these students.

Steve explains, "Because many of these kids have had so much failure, there is a good chance that if you say, 'If you don't do this, you're going to get an F, they'll say, 'Go to hell. Give me an F. I could care.' But this way, they get feedback from other people. If they mess up, someone is going to get in their face, saying, for instance, 'You misspelled my name, dummy.' Or, if they do well, teachers or kids come up to them and say, 'I really liked that story.'"

Because of the immediate feedback, the students learn a lot about accountability, which will help them with anything they want to learn. "Publication," says Steve, "is a very effective teaching tool, because it is one of those 'no excuses' things. Whatever the reason something is wrong, it doesn't matter to the reader. Your house could have burned down, but readers don't know that. They just say, 'This is messed up.' It's a very concrete thing, like sports for kids. You play well or you don't. The quality of the paper depends on the kids. They can't put it on someone else."

The bottom line — Media Academy students have a better than average attendance record.

SUMMARY

Reflecting on what he's learned at the Media Academy, Steve says, "I always thought that I had high expectations. When I compared papers from urban areas to those from suburban schools, I knew it must be possible to do better in the inner city. The kids proved me right on that, but they went way beyond my expectations. Our papers have earned 'All-American' from critique services in the past five years.

"The majority of these students won't end up in journalism careers," Steve adds, "but what we're concerned about is using journalism as a means to strengthen language arts skills, so that whatever they go into, they have a better chance."

INTENSIVE JOURNALISTIC WRITING

"One student, who wasn't at all confident about writing, was doing her investigative reporting project about shoplifting among teens. She came to me and said, 'Miss Lange, I was able to talk with the head of security at Sears. All I had to do was listen to him and he wrote my story.' I told her, 'That's it. Remember? That's what part of writing is about — observing and listening, and letting the story unfold.'"

Carol Lange guides her students at Thomas Jefferson High School for Science and Technology in Alexandria, Virginia, through a carefully constructed curriculum in Intensive Journalism.

She is one of the originators of this course in the U.S. and co-authored a curriculum guide called *Teacher's Guide To Intensive Journalistic Writing Courses* (see Resources). English teachers who don't have experience in this field can build their own course with the help of this book. It includes course outlines and lesson plans from six teachers. In addition, an annotated bibliography helps teachers find books that teach journalistic technique by lesson and example. Carol explains in the guide that her year-long course is designed to "teach journalistic writing techniques that employ critical thinking and reading." It is not a publication production class, although the skills students learn enable them to effectively reach the widest possible audience using journalistic techniques. They use these skills immediately because all students are encouraged to submit articles to national or local newspapers, as well as their school publications.

INVESTIGATIVE REPORTING LESSON IDEAS

Major assignments are based on earlier ones. "I want the kids to feel that I have thought this through and that I'm not going to ask something of them that they can't do. I want them to know that I've tried to prepare them." Units on the basic news story, press law and First Amendment rights, and interviewing techniques come early in the year. Each unit includes daily reading of excellent models of journalism and writing. Students are then assigned a beat and write a news story.

Other early writing assignments are the personality profile and the observation piece, both basic to feature writing. "For the personality profile, I have the kids close their eyes and select from a list of all the kids in school. They have one week to interview that person and write an article. In order to get an A, they must not only interview that student, but must also interview a parent, a sibling, and a teacher. Some of those profiles have been published in the yearbook. It helps give a little more depth to the yearbook.

"Also early in the year, I send the kids out to observe a scene around the school for 15 minutes and record what they have seen. I say, 'Don't talk, don't interact. Be an observer as much as possible.' Then I have them write up a human interest story from their notes that night. We read some pieces in which observation is central to the article — John McPhee is wonderful for the kids to read as a model — to show how setting is just as important to nonfiction as it is to fiction. For their end-of-the-year portfolio, they can go back to their first observation spots or they can choose another. Last year we had kids who sat outside a video rental store a half hour before it closed.

"I have the kids do a First Amendment research project. A number of the students took the option to do videos this year. Of course, they had to write scripts and still had to do their research and show that they had explored the First Amendment. The students also had to interview three authorities on their topics. For example, one group of three boys explored the KKK and the question of whether they had the right to assemble. Not only did they interview ACLU lawyers, they interviewed the Grand Dragon of the KKK in Maryland. They did their background reading, got his phone number, called him, went out to his home, and did the interview.

"By the time students get to their investigative reporting projects, they have a bag of tricks. They have practiced interviewing, they understand how to research the background of an issue, they have done personality profiles, and they've studied rhetorical modes. Plus they've also been reading models — Pulitzer Prize winners, or pieces from collections of well-written feature articles. They have an understanding of the writing process and of knowing one's audience. Early in the project I ask them to identify the newspaper or newspapers to which they will submit their pieces of investigative reporting. They have to read those publications and acquire a sense of their audience."

Good investigative reporting makes an impact on the audience. At its best, the project takes on a life of its own, as the author follows interesting leads. "One of the girls whose work was published worked in a yogurt shop and was going to explore the process of beginning a small business, using the yogurt shop as an example. In the early research, we read that several yogurt businesses failed to meet health standards. This student called a couple of folks, and the owners lied to her, saying that there had never been any violations. This girl is one of the quietest students — very studious, very reticent. I was just delighted to hear her say, as she called the shop owners from my room, 'But it says in this newspaper....' She gave the date of *The Washington Post*. When the owner continued to lie, she contacted the inspector and verified from him that the original news report was accurate. Her article was published in one of the local newspapers."

Not only did they interview ACLU lawyers, they interviewed the Grand Dragon of the KKK in Maryland.

THE REWARDS OF PERSISTENCE

> *"The next thing she knew, she was up in the room with the banks of cameras and TV screens. They actually saw someone shoplifting."*

ADDITIONAL IDEAS

The student who did an investigative feature on teen shoplifting was lucky to be in the right place at the right time. "Part one of her two-part in-depth feature was interviewing students who shoplifted in pairs and threesomes, almost like a game. As part of her background research, she interviewed the Fairfax County police to get statistics on teens who shoplift and statistics on economic loss to businesses. For the second part of her feature, she went to the local Sears store and talked to the clerks who introduced her to the head of security. The next thing she knew, she was up in the room with the banks of cameras and TV screens. They actually saw someone shoplifting. That was when she came to me and said that the head of security actually 'wrote her story,' that all she had to do was listen."

Teachers in a variety of situations and grade levels can use all or part of Carol's curriculum. Some may want to teach journalism as an advanced placement English class, as Carol does. Others may want to use her writing and thinking techniques in the production of a newspaper, magazine, ethnography, or other published work.

"Working with students is one of the best parts of my job as a reporter at The Seattle Times. *By explaining to them why I do what I do and how I do it, I get to look at my own career and remind myself why I'm in this business. Also, I like to pass knowledge on, because no one was there for me when I was in high school."*

Linda Parrish is one of a number of reporters at *The Seattle Times* who shares her journalistic expertise with area students. There are at least four programs at the *Times* dedicated to training young people and giving them a voice in the paper. The programs are fairly new and there are rough spots, but the commitment to youth shown by this newspaper should be a model for newspapers around the country.

It is in the interests of schools and newspapers to work in partnership to make students better readers and writers. From the schools' point of view, it is crucial to find ways to make students' work more meaningful in the real world. Working with local newspapers is a natural way to gain access to a large audience. In addition, newspaper staff can provide training to help students reach a wide audience in the future. Newspapers, for their part, need literate audiences, and we are becoming a less literate society. Newspapers must appeal to new readers and writers in order to be able to survive the era of the sound bite. Thus, it is beneficial for publishers to incorporate young voices in their newspapers. The programs for youth that are underway at *The Seattle Times* may give you ideas for using your local newspapers to enhance student literacy.

Jerry Large, education page editor at the *Times,* works with four education reporters, including Linda Parrish, to write the "In The Schools" page that runs each Tuesday. He explains the history and mechanics of this program: "Alex MacLeod, the managing editor of the *Times,* thought that we should bring student voices into the education page, in order to have a true picture of education. We have a group of ten high school students this year whom we treat as if they were reporters for the paper. We've engaged them in a variety of projects. We did a piece on books that kids read, a page about diversity in the schools, a page about applying to college, a page on political apathy among teenagers, and a page on why some teenagers choose not to have sex — among other topics. We had students involved in interviewing and writing pieces on these topics.

"In addition to features, sometimes the students are involved in writing news stories. On one occasion, a protest group at one school wanted to pass out condoms. We had one of the student stringers write part of the story that we ran on that. That was an actual breaking news story."

Linda Parrish
The Seattle Times
Education Reporter

Jerry Large
The Seattle Times
Education Page Editor

105

"IN THE SCHOOLS": THE WEEKLY EDUCATION PAGE

WHAT WE TEACH

High-school journalist Vanessa Arrington gets opinions about ethnic diversity from fellow students at Ballard High School. The article and photo were carried in The Seattle Times "In the Schools" section.

Photo by Peter Lidell

While Jerry oversees the general direction of the education page, it is the education page reporters who work closely with the student reporters. "The four reporters take turns figuring out the weekly education page," says Linda. "It's up to us to decide if there's a component where we can use a stringer. I've used students about half the time when it's my turn to do the page.

"What we teach is very basic — when to quote people and when not to. Staying focused is important. Lots of times they just start going into a story and have no idea of where they are going.

"It takes time to mesh schedules among ourselves on the staff and it is certainly difficult to do this with the high school students," Linda continues. "Although we are paid for our time with the students, for this program to work optimally, the paper has to commit to have us spend more time with them. The kids aren't going to get enough out of the program if they just turn their drafts in, and we clean them up whatever way we want and stick them in the paper without any feedback. That's definitely not our purpose."

Despite the problems, Linda considers the program to be positive. "The kids get very excited to see their work published. A lot of them get feedback when they go to school and their teachers and classmates say, 'I read what you wrote. That was neat.' Sometimes the whole class applauds them. They think twice about when they write now. It's not just, 'Well, this is okay.' They realize everybody is going to be reading this, so it has to be good."

"I found it touching how eager teachers were for our volunteer assistance. They welcomed help from other professionals who care as much as they do about reading, writing, and current events. They felt a kinship with us, because of the love of words. The photographer who spoke yesterday majored in journalism and talked about working with writers. 'Writing is so important to a photographer,' he said, 'If you can communicate in writing, it helps your communication visually.' The teacher said to him afterwards, 'I could just hug you for saying that.' The kids need to hear that no matter what you're doing, writing matters."

SEATTLE TIMES ADOPT A SCHOOL PROGRAM

Patricia Foote

The Seattle Times

Education Reporter

Patricia Foote, journalist for *The Seattle Times*, is one of the two dozen reporters at the Times working in the Adopt A School pilot project this year.

She explains the variety of ways people approach this program: "The participants have an arrangement with a particular school, and it is entirely up to the volunteer what the details of that arrangement might be. Some people have just enough time to be an on-call friend. They bring in speakers (for instance, music critics and political cartoonists), or set up a tour of the *Times*. Others are in the classroom every week, tutoring kids, advising the newspaper staff, helping the classrooms put out newsletters. And then there is a bunch that fall in between. They might go out and spend six weeks on a unit on newspapers during the year and that might be their only link with a school. So it's a very individual program, but the people who are into it are pretty excited about it."

KID TALK

Pat describes Kid Talk, a feature in the Saturday edition of the *Times*, written by elementary age kids. "It's in our Weekend section, which gives ideas for fun things to do on the weekend. Different classes in the Adopt A School program work on this page.

"When I did the Kid Talk page, the first thing I stressed to students is that everybody will not get published, and that is just the way it is for writers in the rest of the newspaper.

"We also talked about the focus of the Weekend section and how what they wrote had to fit that focus. I also wanted them to understand the importance of showing readers what makes something fun, not just saying that it is fun. We discussed the need to write about a variety of things to do. We had to include some activities that cost money and some that don't, some that are outside, and some that are inside. We talked about accuracy, about getting names and numbers right. If you're sending someone to an address, it had better be right. Finally, we looked at the role of illustrations and how to fit them on the page. Overall, they learned that a newspaper has to appeal to a lot of interests and it has to be accurate and lively."

TEACHING HOW TO INTERVIEW

Pat invited a toy store owner to come to class (a combined 3rd and 4th-grade) to help students learn how to interview. "They learned by interviewing this person with me. Another reporter in the Adopt A School program, who has adopted the Indian Heritage School, teaches interviewing technique by doing her interviews for the *Times* in front of the class. She chooses people who might be interesting to the students, for example, authors and dancers of Native American heritage. She leaves time at the end of the session for the kids to ask interview questions. In fact, she receives letters from the people interviewed saying how that classroom experience was the high point of their promotional tour. They like being among the kids."

WHERE TO GO FROM HERE?

The Adopt A School program is still in its formative stage. "We will sit down at the end of the year and decide if this program is something we want to continue, and if we do, how we should make it better. There is talk of trying to extend the program past the newsroom and see if other people in the company would want to participate. I think people are feeling a lot of satisfaction, but for many it is a real time commitment. Many of the reporters in the program talk about 'my kids' or 'my class.' You can hear in their voices the pleasure they get from watching their kids develop an interest in writing, reading, or newspapers."

"We turn the students into little attack journalists by the time the workshop is over. When they get to their last interview, they're whipping it. They've interviewed the mayor, the chief of police, community activists, and city council people."

Don Williamson

Seattle Times

Director, Urban Journalism

Don Williamson organized Urban Journalism summer workshops for high school students of color at three different newspapers across the country. Currently, he is a reporter at the *Times* and the director of the Urban Journalism workshop. Urban Journalism programs have been in existence for 25 years, and there are 50 such summer workshops in the United States.

IT'S A BOOT CAMP FOR JOURNALISM!

The Seattle Times program provides an intense, organized approach to journalism for 20 high school juniors and seniors each summer. The *Times* staff, under Don, has to work fast; it has only the two-week summer program and four follow-up meetings during the year.

Don explains, "We call this a journalism boot camp. We run the students from 8 in the morning until 10 at night. They have to meet deadlines, and we're very demanding. We beat them into shape for two weeks, but they get a real sense of everything that might happen to them in this business in that short amount of time. They are just dead, and they always complain that they're tired, that they didn't get enough sleep. They say they should have fun. We just tell them that they can have fun when this is over, that for two weeks they are really going to have to work. And it's just amazing to me what these young people accomplish in two weeks — when I look at their raw copy when they start and their finished work when it's over."

THE PURPOSE

"The program has multiple goals," Don says. "There are not enough people of color in this business or who are attracted to this business, and that is one of the reasons we have this program. In these two short weeks we let these students see if they like to write. If they do, then we want to give them an idea of what the publishing industry is like. Sometimes people of color drop out, not because they can't do it, but because they didn't have proper expectations. I think it's important for the students to see other people of color who are in this business.

DIVISION OF LABOR

"Each summer the group of 20 students produces its own workshop newspaper. The students are involved in everything. They do the writing, they take and develop the pictures, they do the editing, layout and design. They do everything except print the paper. During the first week, we divide the students into groups and present evening sessions in which some students learn how to be editors, some learn photography, and some specialize in layout and design. During the day, we have hour-long sessions covering all aspects of newspapers, so that all of the students get to hear about how the entire process fits together. In the second week production starts. At that point, each student has to write a story for the paper, but students also have their additional responsibilities within the division of labor. During the entire two weeks, students have to read the *Times* before arriving at the workshop, and they get tested on the paper every day."

THEMES EMPHASIZE DIVERSITY

"We develop a theme, and all of the stories center around that theme. We try to choose a theme that speaks to the diversity of our students and the city. For example, last year we wrote about historic Yesler Way, which was Seattle's original Skid Row. Now, if you go from one end to the other, you'll touch quite a variety of districts. First you'll come to the Port of Seattle, where trade is so important, especially trade with Japan. Then you'll come to the area of the homeless, where many people of color live. Bordering this impoverished area, you find areas of gentrification. Then you'll go up the hill into the international district where the Asian-American community is. You'll then cut through public housing, where there are a lot of people of color. Next is the Central District, which is probably as much of a black area as we have in Seattle. And, finally, you'll arrive in areas where people have fairly substantial incomes. By choosing that street, we were able to have students write about so many topics. They wrote good news stories that also spoke to the issues of diversity."

INTERVIEWING

"Because we only have two weeks, my staff and I decide on a theme and have the interviews already set up by the time the students come on board. We try to allow a little flexibility, in case they have something special they want to do, but the basic meat of the program is set up when we start.

"Learning how to interview is one of the main parts of the program, and it is always difficult for the students. They have to learn to ask far more than a couple of questions to get the job done. When their notes turn into two paragraphs, but they need to write fourteen more, they realize they didn't ask enough. Or sometimes they get caught up in the interview, and they start having a conversation and forget to take notes. That is why we have sessions on note taking. Or they go to the mayor or someone they are intimidated by, and they are afraid to ask questions, or they think it's impolite to take notes when the person is talking. So you have to work through all these things. But, when they get to their last interview, they're whipping it!

Photos from Prism, *Urban Journalism Workshop '91, printed in* Urban Explorer

Left: Janey Lee, a 1990 Urban Journalism Workshop participant, now works for The Seattle Times' *circulation department. Photo by Anita Lee.*

Bottom: UJW participants grapple with a practical exercise in a classroom at the University of Washington. Photo by Anita Lee.

111

"The first year I did the workshop in Philadelphia, a young woman in the program and I did not get along. She was smart, but she always seemed to have a serious attitude whenever I talked to her about doing something. I was real surprised to see her standing at my desk one day with scholarship books in her arms wanting to know if I would help her apply to college. I said, 'Sure,' but we still didn't get along very well. When we did the first follow-up session, she was not there, but her mother was. I found out that she had been pregnant during the workshop and that was probably the reason that she had an attitude, in general, and maybe had one with men, in particular. She still wanted to attend college, and with the help of her mother's extra work, she continued school after the baby was born. *The Philadelphia Inquirer* felt that she deserved two internships. She did this all in spite of an experience that stops some girls dead in their tracks."

Don Williamson, the University of Washington, and *The Seattle Times* are committed to the Urban Journalism workshop. This is the first year that the Dow Jones Newspaper Fund, which helps finance many of these workshops around the country, has given a grant to the *Times*. The University of Washington helps to pay for room and board for the students. It also provide classrooms and computers. The paper finances everything else, including giving Don and his core staff two weeks off to run the program.

"There are not enough people of color in this business, or who are attracted to this business, and that is one of the reasons we have this program."

Opposite page photos by Hariharan Sreenivasan
Upper left — Graphics staff cut, paste and measure away to come up with just the right layout.
Lower left — Intense instructions, one on one: Anita Lee gets help from Don Williamson, while Linda Parrish poses serious questions to Gerald Choung.

L.A. Times Incorporates Student Work

Carol Hallenbeck

Fullerton, California

Sunny Hills High School

English

"When the editor of the Orange County Edition of the L.A.Times, saw the quality of the material submitted to the paper from the high schools, she decided to add a high school page to the new Life section she was developing for the Orange County edition. That edition has approximately 150,000 subscribers and reaches a circulation of about 350,000 to 400,000 readers."

Carol Hallenbeck teaches English and journalism in Fullerton, California. Her Advanced Journalism class produces *Accolade*, the school newspaper. A number of Carol's students also reach the vast audience of Orange County when they are published on the "High Life" page.

Carol explains, "The story begins with Narda Zacchino, the editor of the Orange County edition of the *Times*. She had worked for her high school paper and wanted to do something to honor high school journalists. So she started a contest with nice financial prizes for best newspaper, best editorial, best feature, best sports story, best photo, and best art. In fact, *Accolade* won prizes for best paper and best stories. When Narda saw the quality of the material students sent in, she decided to add a high school page to the Orange County edition."

Students Reporters Get Paid

There are a variety of ways that students get published in the *Times*. "High schools in Orange County send Bob Rohwer, the new editor of the High Life page, copies of their papers. If he likes a story, he calls our staff and asks for permission to use the story. The reporter is paid $75 and usually makes arrangements for photos to be taken. Sometimes our reporters call Bob Rohwer and suggest stories they would like to cover for him — either from our campus or anywhere in Orange county. If he is interested, they cover the story and sometimes go to the *Times* office to write their stories. They really feel like professionals. At other times, they call the *Times* and read their story to computer operators who send them electronically to the Orange County edition offices. Sometimes Bob has a story that he wants covered. Then he will call a reporter who has given him good material in the past and ask if that student is willing to cover this new assignment. He hires two students to work for him each summer, so there is competition to get on his 'call' list."

What's Covered

The *Times* has selected stories about interesting personalities, school activities, teenage problems, humor, larger cultural problems and teen response to them, teenage achievements, and leisure time activities.

Students respond to the experience of being published:

Benson Chang: "Your parents expect you to get grades, so they don't pay much attention to what you do at school as long as you don't screw up. But when your story appears in the *Times*, then they notice you."

Shara Cohen: "It's always nice to know that someone is reading your stuff. I know that a lot of students here at school don't read what we write because it just doesn't interest them, so having a story published in the *Times* is a way to reach a wider audience. Besides, it is an honor to have Bob Rohwer call you up and say, 'I want your story for the *Times*.' It makes you feel like a big-time player when professional people are looking for you to go out and do things for them."

Neha Gupta: "When my story is published in the school paper, none of my friends say anything. But when the story is reprinted in the *Times*, my friends say, Wow, you made the *Times*.'"

Jason Tu: "And don't forget the money. That's nice too."

Carol discusses how she evaluates students in her classroom publishing program. "Students are asked to assign themselves two goals each issue — a personal goal (i.e. meeting deadlines or getting along better with the editor-in-chief) and a professional goal (handling leads or headlines better). They rate themselves on reaching their goals, attach what they have produced to their evaluation sheet, and tell who helped them and who they helped. Then the adviser rates them for a grade. The evaluation sheet is to help them realize that in the long run, their own evaluation of their work is the best motivating guide."

"When my story is published in the school paper, none of my friends say anything. But when the story is reprinted in the Times, *my friends say, 'Wow, you made the* Times.'"

EVALUATING AND GRADING

New York City Magazine by and for Youth

Keith Hefner

New York City

Director

Youth Communication

Origins of *New Youth Connections*

"Our circulation averages 75,000 copies a month. Our magazines go to all the public schools and public libraries in New York City. So we have a huge readership. Probably as many as a quarter million kids read it. The tone of the magazine says unmistakably that it is by teens, for teens."

Keith Hefner is executive director of Youth Communication, a program that trains 150 teenagers a year in writing, research, graphic arts, photography, typing, and computers in the process of publishing the monthly magazine, *New Youth Connections*. The students are 50 percent African-American, 30 percent Latino, and the rest are divided between European-American, Asian-American and other groups. They range from poor to middle-class.

Keith describes what unites these students: "First, they are all teenagers struggling to grow up in New York City. Second, they refuse to be victims. No matter how bleak they have been told their future is going to be, the youngsters who arrive on our doorstep want to gain control of their lives and make them better. Third, they soon learn that while working here they have the opportunity to help their peers, as well as to improve their own skills."

We asked Keith about the origins of *New Youth Connections*. "In the early 1970s, the Robert F. Kennedy Memorial Foundation had a contest for the best writing from high school students on issues like poverty and injustice. Judges found that the entries were so bad that the foundation established a Commission of Inquiry into High School Journalism. The commission found that the two biggest problems in school journalism were censorship and racism. It decided that the solution was to start independent, citywide papers in major urban areas. There are about a dozen cities with newspapers or magazines by and for youth. We started Youth Communication in New York City in 1980 so young people would have a voice and be able to make their views known to each other and to people in power."

Today, there are many examples of student publications — including books, magazines, and newspapers — produced within the school system that contain the thoughtful, powerful, and honest voices of a diversity of teenagers. It is very likely that in the last decade, the quality of school publications has jumped dramatically because of the spread of writing programs and the increased use of computer technology. If the Kennedy Memorial Foundation were to have a new contest today, the results would be quite different.

However, independent citywide newspapers and magazines are also a proven vehicle for helping young people acquire skills and find their voice. The fact that *New Youth Connections* pulls together a staff of socially concerned student writers from all over New York City puts it on the cutting edge of youth publications.

In December 1987, before it was more common in the press, *NYC* had for its lead story, "Thinking about AIDS." The cover also showed an opinion contest on Howard Beach, as well as a related story, "I was Homeless at 14." Several times a year, the staff devotes a large part of the monthly 28-page edition to a single topic supplement. In recent years, these supplements have focused on: "The Best of the High Schools," "Science and Technology," "Prenatal Care: What It Is & How To Get It," "Museums and Historic Sites," "Race Relations," "Changing Roles For Young Women," "Responsible Sexuality," "Good Health Is No Accident," and "The Urban Environment."

The November 1991 *NYC* focuses on multiculturalism. Keith describes the contents of this issue: "Some girls wrote about why they feel insecure when they read *Teen* magazine; a Panamanian girl expressed her anger about people saying that she is not Hispanic; and a Korean girl wrote about her boyfriend who complains that she is too Americanized. There is an article about the problems of speaking English with parents who speak only Chinese. Another piece is about a girl whose grandfather was Chinese and whose grandmother was Dominican. She described all the stereotypes she faces about being Chinese-Dominican American. We have an article about coming to America from the Dominican Republic and going up to Massachusetts and freezing, and not finding the promised land. A student wrote an article about spending the summer in the Israeli Army. One student wrote about what it was like attending an all black Afro-centric school. A Saudi Arabian and Lebanese student debated in print about how Americanized they should become. We have an article by a student whose parents enrolled her in a school for the deaf for a year so she would understand what it was like to be a minority."

"For many of the kids, working on the magazine is therapeutic. They write strong personal stories about abortion, alcoholic parents, rape, and other life traumas. For many students, this is the first time they have confronted their feelings about these things. They feel supported here by their co-workers, and they know that their articles will help other young people confront their own experiences and move on with their lives."

"Typically, new writers will call up and say, 'I'd like to write for your newspaper.' Another way we get people is by putting notices in the magazine. We're also listed in a lot of catalogs, so students might be sitting in a counselor's office trying to figure out whether they want to work in an office to get credit for work experience when they see our listing in the catalog. Most of them do get credit for their work experience with us."

TRAINING

Using the same phrase as Don Williamson, Keith describes *NYC* as "a boot camp" for young writers. He continues, "Most come to us with very uneven skills, and we drill them in basic grammar, usage, and the principles of clear readable writing. Students also learn research and interviewing techniques, as well as word processing and database management. Most articles go through four or five drafts, and sometimes students must rewrite a story ten or more times before all relevant facts are included, the style is clear, and all errors are corrected. This can be a daunting experience, but we have found that when young people are taken seriously and are offered the opportunity to help themselves and others, they can overcome bad neighborhoods, poor skills, prejudice, and other obstacles, and offer hope for themselves and their peers."

DIVISION OF LABOR

Students do the writing, illustrating and photography. "We don't have any teen editors," says Keith. "We found that work progresses most smoothly when students do not supervise other students. However, decisions on content are made in a collaborative process. Every Thursday all the important matters about the magazine are discussed for two hours in an editorial board meeting. Some of the kids who have trouble writing are often very good speakers who help crystallize issues for the kids who are going to be writing some of the stories. For instance, we had weeks of discussion about articles on AIDS back in 1987, debating about what would be effective language for this sensitive topic. All points of view were put out, but we always came around to what is going to communicate the information to the reader the best. The arguments aren't often between adults and students; they are more often between students and students."

CAREER DIRECTIONS AND PERSONAL GROWTH

Although the largest number of students on the magazine are interested in communications industry jobs, a large number of students are interested in law, social work, politics, business, science and technology. Many of the students, according to Keith, go into social services. "They are the ones who realize at the end of the program, or several years later, that what they really liked was not the journalism, but the support of working with concerned and caring people."

Whatever career students choose, they believe that working on *NYC* has helped them. Sixty-five percent of the students felt that the program helped them get into college. Sixty percent said they learned to work with different kinds of people. Eighty percent said that their work at the magazine improved their public speaking skills. The same percentage of students said that their library/research skills improved. And the same percentage said that the program helped them feel like more capable and effective people.

Teen reporters, New Youth Connections
Photos by Tony Savino

119

Publishing: who, what, when, where, why, & how

How to Use Section 2

Publishing is the selection, preparation, and distribution of printed matter. But the term is used loosely for everything from the private production of single documents to mass market distribution of the latest popular novel.

The complexity, sophistication, and purpose of publications have an even broader range. And the possible divisions of labor, of specialization, increase quickly from one person doing everything to many people handling only individual elements of the whole process. A surprisingly small amount of the work involves special talent in either writing or editing, though those activities are fundamental to modern literacy and publishing.

Classroom publishing covers a similar range of possibilities, from handwritten, one-of-a-kind documents to the complexity and sophistication of commercial books, magazines, and newspapers. There are important similarities in the way all publishing is done, a certain natural progression. But there are significant differences requiring a host of skills — many points of view and various ways of working. By exploring publishing's process, ways to adapt it appropriately to the classroom — or adapt the classroom to it — should become apparent.

While we hope every student appreciates the whole of publishing, it would be wishful thinking to imagine all our

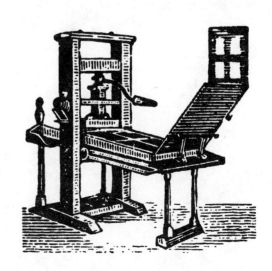

students as professional writers — even those who love to write. Yet, most people — writers or not — never consider publishing careers. While instilling a love of the world of words and ideas, classroom publishing can open avenues of access to employment in that world.

Through a rich publishing program, students can try the many roles and pursue those they like best. This section, besides giving an overview of the history and process of publishing, discusses career opportunities, including the impact that technology is having on them.

Three related subjects are presented in Section 2.
• Publishing: history and process
• Floss to Gloss: how-to information
• Career options in writing and publishing

The first two are laid out in adjacent columns on each page — history and process on the left, how-to on the right, each in a different typeface, we've done on this page.

Chapter divisions are based on the progression of a manuscript from author to reader. At the end of each chapter is a discussion of related current and prospective career opportunities. Individual job descriptions are not deeply probed, since the text on process and how-to has covered the essential work and the usual division of labor.

Much of the material in the *Floss to Gloss* column is drawn from case studies presented in the first section of this book. Additional techniques, sources of materials and support, useful tips, and innovative alternatives are included and explored. But reading the case studies in Section 1 will doubtless stimulate or reveal other ideas. Teachers, librarians, and their projects referred to in *Floss to Gloss* can be found through the index.

This graphic goes with the text on history and process. Throughout this section, historical and theoretical discussion is in the left column.

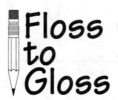

This graphic indicates practical information on how to help students publish, based on the experiences of teachers, librarians, and publishing professionals. This material appears in the right column, and the graphic serves as an occasional reminder.

The title, **Floss to Gloss**, comes from the range of methods used to create publications, from simple booklets, hand sewn with dental floss (Diane Goddard's projects), to polished, glossy commercial productions.

☞ This graphic appears at the beginning of each item or discussion in **Floss to Gloss**.

This graphic introduces the career guidance information at the end of each chapter in the section.

Chapter 5

PUBLISHING: A BRIEF HISTORY

The development of modern publishing revolves around interrelated cycles of technological advance and social upheaval. The four most important technological leaps have been writing, paper, printing, and the computer. The important social changes have been those that increased literacy or arose from its increase. They have had a tendency to broaden democracy, i.e., the rise of the commercial cities, the revolutions against feudalism, and the industrial revolution.

Moveable type

The two principal publishing categories are periodical and non-periodical. The former includes magazines and newspaper, while the latter usually refers to books. In either case, the process is similar and the role of the publisher is only different in focus, not responsibilities.

If we think of the beginnings of publishing at all, we likely imagine Johannes Gutenberg, a German printer, inventing moveable type around 1450 and using it to set his famous Bibles. Printing with moveable type was revolutionary. Abruptly the meticulous copying of texts by scribes disappeared. The tedious carving of complete pages in a single block for printing was made obsolete. Suddenly, it was "easy" to create as many exact copies of a document as one wanted. With Gutenberg, a technology that had appeared earlier in China and been abandoned for nearly a century was reinvented — and this time, for good.

In fact, long before moveable type, there had been something similar to modern publishing much earlier, in ancient Greece, Rome, and China, where literature was copied

Floss to Gloss

Oh, those ubiquitous words! They're everywhere. They're so much a part of our everyday lives — our consciousness of who we are — that we often take them for granted. We forget their awesome power — to inform, inflame, educate, entertain, sooth, smooth, transport, report, and otherwise give our lives the context of collective experience and ideas.

WHEN STUDENTS PUBLISH, they join those millions of others before them in one of humanity's truly exhilarating activities.

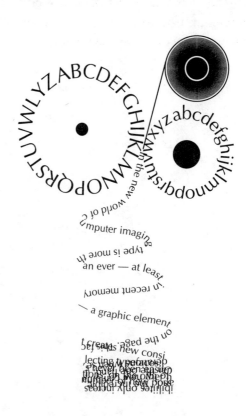

and distributed to a fairly wide group of readers. Among those cultures, China was the major contributor. Paper was invented there (AD 105) and block printing emerged about 500 years later. The Chinese even worked with moveable type, but it was inappropriate to their picture-based language and, so, it disappeared. It was Arab traders who brought paper to Europe from China. But from Gutenberg on, the new methods spread like spilled ink over most of Europe.

Before mechanical printing, writing was mainly a way to set down laws of religion or politics and a way of keeping track of ownership and wealth so they would be remembered exactly. With the development of commerce and the rise of the cities, the need increased to keep books of accounts and lists of goods. Better communications, in general, were required.

Literacy, both writing and reading, spread rapidly. In turn, this made those who were literate more powerful in their societies. When their growing influence led to conflicts with their rulers, the changes that followed set the stage for our modern world. Literacy is now highly prized as a right of citizenship in most countries.

Universal literacy is still a dream — only half the world's population can read or write, including many of our fellow citizens — but the invention of movable type really changed forever the nature of literacy. It also gave publishing the definition we use today: to make words or other images public.

☞ **TEACHING PUBLISHING HISTORY**
can be exciting and interactive. Consider having students publish replicas of early scrolls, tablets, and books.

☞ **TOPICS FOR INVESTIGATION.**
There are a number of important individuals and dates in printing and publishing history that could be subject matter. For instance:

- What were clay tablets mostly used to record?
- When was paper invented? By whom?
- How is paper made?
- Who published the first known newspaper? What was the first newspaper in North America?
- What has ink been made of?
- Why did the Chinese abandon moveable type?
- Why was movable type such an important invention? Who is credited with it? Who else invented it?
- What is digital type? What other forms have been used for type.
- What are the parts of a character of type (letterform)?
- How have printing presses evolved? Why are they called presses?
- Where were the first known libraries?
- Why was freedom of the press an issue in the European and American revolutions of the 18th and 19th centuries?
- When did publishing become a form of entertainment?
- Has there always been censorship?
- Who were Garamond and Caxton?
- Who was Gutenberg?
- What is the relationship between printing and literacy? Between literacy and democracy?

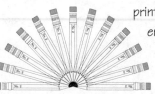

Printers and publishers

It's easy, then, to think of publishing and printing as one and the same, since they're so intimately related. But they're different beasts. Printing is the mechanical or electronic transfer of images to paper or some other medium.

For several centuries, and until quite recently, printing was a handicraft. Each letter, space, ornament, or element of punctuation was carefully arranged by hand. Ink was applied and paper was pressed against the type to leave the desired impression. And impression it was. If you find an old book done with formed type, you can actually feel the depressions created by the letters being pressed into the paper and you can also see the irregularities that are missing from today's precise electronic type. This old technology had lots of mechanical variations and enhancements through the years. It is still in use by many small press publishers specializing in limited editions of poetry chapbooks, broadsides, and "fine letterpress" printing.

The next major advance in printing came with its mechanization in the 19th century. This automation continues today, with computers creating high quality type and art and monitoring printers and presses capable of printing hundreds of thousands of pages each hour.

The age of computers has only begun, so the real impact of this new technology on publishing has yet to be seen. We have some hints of how it will make vast amounts of information nearly instantly accessible — both documents already published in traditional forms, then converted, and new publications that couldn't have existed before.

Let's look at how our printed media have evolved.

BOOKS

Books have a long history — over 4,000 years. They are the

☞ You can **USE OUTSIDE EXPERTS AND RESOURCES** to explain specific aspects of publishing. They can come to the class, or vice versa. Many, especially those in business, will donate their time. Who can you ask?

- Newspaper editors or staff
- Archivists (for instance, employees of state, university, or local historical collections)
- Antiquarian book dealers or collectors
- Book arts guild members (these could be papermakers, endpaper designers, specialty binders, or letterpress printers)
- Book restorers

Depending on grade level and your proximity to appropriate sites, students can **VISIT PAPER MILLS, PRINTERS, BINDERIES, LIBRARIES, BOOK AND PERIODICAL DISTRIBUTORS, OR BOOKSTORES.**

☞ Classroom publishing projects can **USE THE TOOLS AND TECHNIQUES OF LETTERPRESS PRINTING.** The Spruce Street School, a private elementary school in Seattle, Washington, has its own letterpress with complete fonts of old type. Students aged 5 to 9 make books, cards, and broadsides entirely by hand. The antique presses, 350 cases of type, and typographical ornaments were acquired from print shops that no longer used them.

Only original work is published. Students working with an experienced adult printer who assists in

125

oldest form of publication. At first, they were written on scrolls made of papyrus, or they were inscriptions on tablets of clay, leather, parchment, vellum, bark, or leaves.

We get our word *paper* from papyrus. And we also maintain a connection with the earliest books through other terms. For instance, the Greeks got their supplies of paper at the port of Byblos, so they called paper by that name, and we inherit the word *bible*. To the Romans, the scrolls of papyrus were *volumen* or *charta*, from which we get *volumes* and *charts*.

What separates books from other publications is their singularity. Their primary role is to give permanence to our thoughts, whether fact or fiction, and to record our histories. Every year in North America there are over 50,000 new books published. To appreciate their great variety, all one has to do is visit a large library or bookstore.

126

PERIODICALS

Magazines and newspapers are the most common periodicals. They differ from books by usually being less permanent and appearing as part of a series at regular intervals. Not only the style, but the pace of the work is distinct.

Defining the content difference between magazines and newspapers is difficult because they frequently publish the same things. Size often determines which is which, but it's not always definitive. Newspapers generally have a larger format, are published more often, and are less permanent. Magazines are likely to have a different, heavier, or coated paper for a cover. They are usually bound in a manner

designing, typesetting, and printing — often in more than one color. Projects take from a few hours to over a year, with young students able to sustain interest.

Each author receives a number of copies of his or her work, with the rest of each edition kept by the school. Student work is also sold at public events (arts festivals, museums, etc.), with commissions going to the students whose work sells. Prices range from one to twenty dollars per book.

☞ FORM AND CONTENT: Is the medium the message? Have students COMPARE AND CONTRAST VARIOUS NEWSPAPERS AND MAGAZINES. Have students bring samples from home. Discuss how form and content are related — or not. How do audience and purpose affect choices of size, quality, design, etc.? This discussion is most fruitful when it's part of defining an actual project.

"One of the things we did very early," says Linda Clifton of Seattle, "is collect literary magazines from a variety of places, but mostly ones published in high schools. …we spread this stuff out on a table and start looking at it, saying 'What do you like? What do you not like?' And from that we would work up our own design."

But literary journals are only one form of content. Mick Fedullo of Pryor, MT has created a poetry calendar project that similar to books and booklets, while newspapers are only folded and inserted.

Historically, magazines grew out of a desire for entertainment, though their role has grown to include the regular publication of news and analysis of ideas and events.

Another difference between the forms is that periodicals, even those that are quite serious, are much more likely to include advertising than are books.

The number and range of periodicals is staggering. They truly run the gamut of possible sizes, bindings, purposes, frequencies, sophistication, and quality. Those that readers are likely to save are published in durable formats, while others look like the throw-aways they are. To a significant degree, all commercial periodicals depend on advertising for their definitions. Few survive on subscription revenues. And this means that we read most newspapers and magazines almost like we watch TV — around the commercials.

Periodicals comprise one of the primary marketing tools for business. Audiences are clearly defined and dependably reached. In fact, readers are generally so well defined that the sale of mailing lists may be the most important source of revenues. Repetition, so necessary to effective advertising, is easy when you have real names.

Most less commercial and non-profit periodicals — church bulletins, PTA newsletters, organizational magazines, literary journals, school newspapers, and the rest — have a different relationship to their readers. We all depend on them for a level of communication and information that's not available elsewhere.

The rapid spread of literacy in the past century has relied heavily on periodicals of all sorts, just as those publications have depended on a broadly literate audience for their growth. And, of course, it couldn't have happened at all without the dedication of teachers and librarians.

keeps the work of his Native American students in front of their audience for an entire year.

Cheryl Shackleton of the Bronx leads high school students in the creation of books that are themselves art — words are incidental. And Carolyn Tragesser's Moscow, ID, junior high students emphasized striking covers as a way to make URSA MAJOR, a literary magazine, attractive to other students.

☞ **DEFINE THE FORM OF PUBLICATION** early in the project to provide focus. When students discuss what they hope to accomplish — and who they expect to reach — they will select the appropriate form of publication.

The familiar publication types have evolved around clear functions. But this does not mean that a particular form cannot be adapted to other purposes, new or old. Many student publications straddle traditional definitions. Magazines resemble newspapers or books. Newspapers look like magazines. And books are anything between covers.

However, form does dictate a cascade of subsequent decisions, including budget, materials, and distribution. There may be little choice in the matter when methods or materials are dictated by economic or institutional circumstances. This may mean that the original question is changed. Instead of "What form best suits our message?" it is "How do we use the given form to best convey our message?" In either case, the discussion must **CONSIDER THE NATURE OF THE AUDIENCE** — its desires and expectations from reading material and from life, in general. **WHO ARE THESE READERS, ANYWAY?**

127

Publishing In North America

Publishing arrived in the Americas shortly after the first European colonists. The highly prized independence in religion and politics which brought many people to this continent rested heavily on the printed word.

And it was the newspapers of the day — actually broadsheets, or single pages — that played a critical role in the movement toward independence from Britain. Printers were generally publishers, the two roles had not yet separated. They were politically powerful individuals in their communities. But when life was more intimate — without modern electronic media and still on the scale of villages, printers' roles were more clearly defined. We all learn their importance when we study Ben Franklin, Thomas Paine, and other early leaders who used the power of the press to foment rebellion and to organize the former colonies into a nation.

As westward expansion accelerated, printers quickly set up shop in each new town. Newspapers thus played a role not only in the geographic development of a nation, but helped spread literacy at the same time.

Books developed later and more slowly than newspapers. They were more expensive to produce, more difficult to distribute, and the segment of literate citizens who appreciated them was still small. This changed as population centers developed, so that book publishing first gained a foothold in such places as New York and Boston — still important centers today.

Even when growing literate populations in the West created a market, it was the newly established east coast publishers who satisfied it. Gradually, books became a popular form of entertainment, following on the heels of cheap magazines. But it was not until recently that the publishing centers of the East started giving way to a growing book industry in the Midwest and West. This trend toward decentralization in book publishing has speeded up lately because of major changes in the industry — some having to do with economics and some with technology.

☞ **DISCUSS FREEDOM OF THE PRESS**, the power of the press (cultural & political), and the responsibility of the press — with cases of the press doing both good and bad. While such a discussion may seem too advanced for very young publishers, it can be introduced with concrete examples, such as how another student's feelings would be hurt if something untrue were written about him or her and a lot of people, not knowing it was false, read it.

The other side of freedom and power is shown to be responsibility and discipline. Alaskan Dennis Stovall's students have learned how seriously the press is taken, especially by public officials and businesspeople — how it can be used as a tool for affecting public policy and opinion. These 8th graders publish compilations of essays as books intended for adults: One about Vietnam veterans had an audience of people who went through the Vietnam experience; another, titled, *TRUTH AND LIES THROUGH 14-YEAR-OLD EYES*, was distributed to local lawmakers, school administrators, and workers in the criminal justice system.

Another classroom exercise in responsible journalism comes from Carol Lange's students in Alexandria, VA, who are required to show both sides of any issue they choose to write on. The exercise is difficult — often painful. But it's an eye-opener.

☞ The powerful political role of publishing allows **CLASSROOM DISCUSSIONS OF HISTORY, LAW, AND RIGHTS**. Our society places high value on freedom of the press and freedom of expression. Discuss how ownership and control of the media affect

CONGLOMERATION

Perhaps the biggest change in publishing is who owns and controls the major houses. The largest and most important book and newspaper publishers were for years independent of each other, competitors in a market of ideas. In the past thirty years this has changed. Larger and larger corporations have bought up the major publishers. Where there were once dozens of companies, there are now a few. Newspaper chains dominate their markets. Giant media conglomerates control most of the production of books and magazines.

OPENINGS FOR SMALL PRESSES

These changes paved the way for a newly invigorated small press movement to grow in the shadow of the giants. Like the small publishers who grew large in the last century, these new presses frequently develop around the immediate concerns or interests of one or two people. In the past decade, there has been explosive growth in this area. The number of publishers increased by the tens of thousands all across the country.

This rapid growth has been facilitated by opportunities overlooked or thought unprofitable by big publishers. Advances in computer publishing technologies spurred it on by making the preparation of publications faster and less expensive. These advantages, in turn, were enhanced by better access to national markets and more competitive prices for printing short runs.

The difference between the large and small presses is tra-

> "...slant and bias are always encouraged so that students will recognize the same in [other] publications. In History Media [class], we use current journalism styles to create newspapers as if they existed in the American Revolution, West or Civil War. ...content is always multidisciplinary."
>
> — Michael Bergen
> 10–12 English,
> Appleton, WI

these. We also put high value on property. Where does intellectual property fit into things?

☞ In any modern democracy **LITERACY IS FUNDAMENTAL TO FULL CITIZENSHIP** and to the protection of basic rights. **LITERACY CAN BE DISCUSSED FROM MANY PERSPECTIVES,** but good discussions might focus on what we mean by "literacy." Is it only the ability to read road signs and fill out job applications? Is it a reasonable level of cultural understanding and critical thinking? Or is reading only one side of the literacy equation, with writing and publishing being the other?

☞ Publishing wields power in other areas of our lives: preservation, education, and entertainment. Students are familiar with these types of publishing, but may not understand how they relate to the issues of the power of the press and freedom of expression. **CONSIDER POINT OF VIEW AS IT AFFECTS ALL WRITING AND PUBLISHING.** Students might discuss whether or not it's possible to have unbiased writing or reporting — or if we'd even want it.

Learning about bias and slant in the media is a major theme in the History-Media class taught by Michael Bergen of Appleton East High in Appleton, WI.

☞ **RESEARCH THE PUBLISHERS AND PUBLICATIONS NEAR YOUR SCHOOL.** Invite some of the publishers to visit the class. Or take the class to them. Find out
- how they define publishing,
- how they felt about publishing when they began,

ditionally much greater than size. The large tend to concentrate on work that will most likely sell in great quantities, which means they're less willing to take risks on unknown authors or subjects that may have narrow audiences. Small publishers have taken up the slack in this regard, as they always have. But most of the new small presses have concentrated on nonfiction, because it's easier to sell. The more speculative literature — new novels and poetry — are difficult and risky for them, though they seem to be taking those risks more and more often.

The mainstays of new fiction and poetry are the small literary magazines and book publishers who view their work as a mission, not as a commercial venture expected to make lots of money. Many of these publishers are non-profit organizations, or are associated with non-profit groups, such as universities. They rely heavily on grants to subsidize their publishing programs, rather than expecting sales alone to underwrite them. They are, in many respects, most like classroom publishers.

While predicting the future is always rash, it seems safe to say that from the large pool of new publishers there will develop some bigger ones — more commercial and more general in their selections of writing to publish. These will not be in New York or Boston or Chicago or Los Angeles. They will be distributed throughout the country, since modern communications have nearly removed the disadvantages of being geographically remote from markets.

PROSPECTS FOR CHANGE

The important changes in the publishing industry noted above are only the beginning. The pace accelerates with each new advance in technology, but what we've discussed so far is only print publishing. Computers and other electronic media open the door to whole new ways to publish both words, pictures, and sounds. Talking books are modest cross-overs. Multi-media publications are the next wave.

These developments were unimaginable a few years ago — or imaginable only as science fiction, and few of us would have believed we'd live to witness them. But they're here, and the technological changes that drive them are occurring so fast that the next level will be reached even more quickly.

- how they feel about publishing now,
- why they started publishing,
- what their points of view are, and
- about their backgrounds.

To track down local publishers, use LITERARY MARKET PLACE (LMP), THE INTERNATIONAL DIRECTORY OF LITTLE MAGAZINES & SMALL PRESSES, WRITER'S MARKET, a regional guide like WRITER'S NORTHWEST HANDBOOK or CALIFORNIA PUBLISHING MARKETPLACE, and the telephone directory. Supplement these by asking printers, bookstore owners, and local and state librarians who the most active publishers are. There may also be associations of different types of publishers that can help.

☞ **REGIONAL PUBLISHERS' ORGANIZATIONS** serve as resource centers and incubators for their members. Most would welcome student members, and the contact with other publishers would be invaluable to students and teachers, alike.

☞ **CLASSROOM PROJECTS CAN ENJOY A REAL PLACE IN THE GENERAL PUBLISHING WORLD.** Student publishers are in the tradition of small press publishing everywhere. Most school publications remain modest in distribution, but access to bookstores, book fairs, art fairs, county and state fairs, and other markets means that audience can be more broadly defined.

Teacher Chris Weber formed the Oregon Students Writing & Art Foundation to publish anthologies of student writing and art. Students are fully involved in all phases of the process. And the foundation has been able to fund its projects, at least partially, through grants from such corporations as Avia. Titled TREASURES, the first two books brought together work from throughout the state of Oregon. The third book is a collabo-

On-line data bases provide today's most basic computer networks and information sharing systems. They depend on high speed transmission over phone lines, and they link computers and their operators worldwide. Such networks give us access to vast amounts of information. We can select articles from thousands of magazines and newspapers, getting only those that match our momentary interests or needs. We can scan complete libraries for the references we want, and do so nearly instantly.

But it's not only previously published material that computers provide. Original publishing is being done in electronic form. Many computer bulletin boards encourage users to publish on-line.

Interactive electronic books are appearing on the market. They suggest more of the computer's potential for literary experimentation. Fiction in this form remains crude, though it's exciting to see the effects on a story's outcome of one's decisions as the reader. Currently more powerful and refined are the nonfiction offerings, especially references that offer virtually infinite routes of access to their information. Research has never been easier or more enjoyable. Not only words, but associated illustrations and sounds are available. The better realized teaching programs also use a combination of text, graphics, and user input to design the progress of lessons.

But, frankly, what seems so magical today will soon seem crudely primitive. Publishers of the next generation will have ever more impressive tools and will apply them in new ways.

This does not mean the end of books or reading, but only the introduction of new techniques to communicate, educate, and entertain. It will, however, call for writers and publishers to acquire new skills as classrooms, libraries, and bookstores respond to technological change. Best of all, perhaps, the new technologies are reintroducing democracy in publishing, since they are affordable for and accessible to many more people than ever before. This development ought to enhance literacy, rather than threaten it. And it's a good part of what classroom publishing is all about.

ration between students in Oregon and Japan. Because this project is not limited to one school or community, the books are marketed just like titles from commercial publishers. Additionally, Weber and his student staff can frequently be seen selling their wares at regional teachers' conferences.

Chapter 6

PUBLISHING: HOW IT'S DONE AND WHO DOES IT

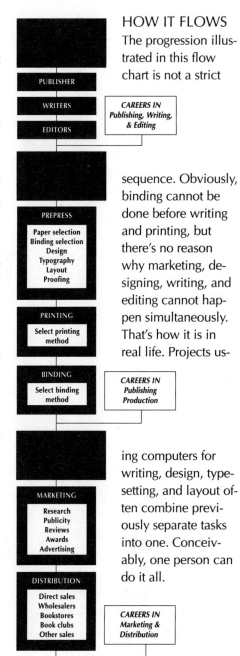

As we've already mentioned, selection, preparation, and distribution are at the heart of publishing. But these pieces of the puzzle have no clear, simple relationship to each other. While we can say, "Okay, here's step one, now let's do step two," in reality all the elements must be considered together from the beginning. For instance, because publishing means distributing or marketing the finished documents, it is always a relationship between the writer, the publisher, and the audience. So, a publisher must consider this relationship carefully before beginning any project. The essential questions are: What is the purpose of this publication? Who will read it? And who will write it? The physical details of producing it and distributing it then fall into place. *In the column to the right is a simple flow chart of the process. It's also the way in which the chapters of this section are organized.*

No matter the final form of a publication, each goes through a series of predictable steps. Someone must first decide what sort of material to publish. The next step is to target the writers and materials that fit that need, and then to select those few pieces that are best and most appropriate. Once the material has been found, it must be refined — rewritten and polished. Finally, the finished manuscript enters the production process, from which it emerges in a magazine, book, or other medium.

But creating the final product is not the end of the process. Then, the real work of the publisher begins — getting the finished work into the hands of readers.

Each step in the life of a publication, from conception to the turning of the last page by a reader, involves different skills. This is just as much true when the publication is created in the classroom as when it's done by a major publisher in New York, Paris, or London.

HOW IT FLOWS

The progression illustrated in this flow chart is not a strict

133

sequence. Obviously, binding cannot be done before writing and printing, but there's no reason why marketing, designing, writing, and editing cannot happen simultaneously. That's how it is in real life. Projects us-

ing computers for writing, design, typesetting, and layout often combine previously separate tasks into one. Conceivably, one person can do it all.

PUBLISHER

WRITERS

EDITORS

CAREERS IN
Publishing, Writing, & Editing

PREPRESS
Paper selection
Binding selection
Design
Typography
Layout
Proofing

PRINTING
Select printing method

BINDING
Select binding method

CAREERS IN
Publishing Production

MARKETING
Research
Publicity
Reviews
Awards
Advertising

DISTRIBUTION
Direct sales
Wholesalers
Bookstores
Book clubs
Other sales

CAREERS IN
Marketing & Distribution

Manuscript Selection & Preparation

PUBLISHERS

Selecting what to publish and the form in which to publish it usually begins before any manuscripts are evaluated. Publishers have goals and interests that dictate what's acceptable. Sometimes these arise from a sense of mission, i.e., promoting a particular philosophy or hobby or writing genre. Other times they result solely from a business decision, i.e., books on cats are selling well for other publishers, so let's do something about cats.

Successful publishers can be found doing just about any imaginable subject. The key is finding the audience. Naturally, if the publisher plans to stay in business, it's also important that the audience likes what it gets.

Given that a publisher has a focus, it's first and foremost the writers or artists who do the basic creation. It may be helpful to think of publishing as being like producing a concert, where the musicians are the writers, and the concert promoters are the publishers. Without the musicians, it wouldn't matter how large the hall was or how good the speakers or how much publicity there was — no music, no concert.

WRITERS

At the beginning are the writers. Because they have as many interests as publishers, perhaps even more, it's a matter of matching the right material with the right publisher. The possibilities are almost limitless, not only can anything be a subject, but writing can be practiced as either art or craft. Again, learning how to find the right publisher is the trick.

There's a method to this, whether it's convincing the editor of the school newspaper to use an article or getting a book publisher to take your novel. Savvy authors study pub-

The first impetus can only be traced to a man who, all alone, is groping to give form to his ideas in a manuscript. It is the writer upon whom the whole inverted pyramid rests. It is upon him that the publishers depend. On him the presses wait.

— Paul Standard, calligrapher & historian

☞ **PUBLISHING'S DIVISION OF LABOR CAN BE USED TO THE ADVANTAGE OF TEACHING.** Depending on teaching philosophy, project goals, student needs, and the type of publication, the process can be adapted. Teachers following the Foxfire model generally use the small press approach of each person learning and doing some of everything. Others emulate larger publishers, fitting roles to individual students or classes, either to teach them new skills or to take advantage of special talents.

☞ **PROJECT SELECTION** means considering

- curriculum goals,
- budget,
- time constraints, and
- intended audience.

With these things in mind, decisions can be made on

- type of publication,
- number of copies,
- design,
- quality of production,
- subject matter,
- division of labor, and
- distribution or marketing.

The process is essentially the same in commercial publishing, and students can be brought into the discussion at any level.

lishers to learn who needs what. They target their work to the markets most likely to accept it.

A majority of manuscripts are rejected immediately, and it's worth looking at the most common reasons.

Foremost is that the writer did not first check to see what the publisher wanted — a sure route to rejection, and an easy problem to avoid by doing a little research.

A close second is sending the publisher an unpolished presentation, which may keep even a great idea from being recognized. This is also easy to avoid. Again, a little research about the publishers will indicate how they want to receive queries and manuscripts.

A similar mistake made by many writers is sending unsolicited materials without an SASE (self-addressed, stamped envelope) for their return. Publishers swamped with queries and submissions cannot afford to return manuscripts or even respond to queries unless the author makes it possible. Some publishers find this little breach of etiquette so annoying that they won't even read the proposal. They simply dump it in the trash and get on to the next one.

Most editors are too busy to read long letters from authors. At least, they won't read them unless they're hooked by the first sentence. So, another way to a quick rejection is to waste an editor's time at the beginning of a query or cover letter. This is done by not quickly getting to the point of the proposal, or by wasting time telling how great the story is or how good the writer is or how rich this will make everyone. All the editor wants to know is what the writer is selling; the editor or publisher can make up his or her own mind about the merits of the idea, the promise of the manuscript.

On the publisher's side, guidelines are sent to writers or listed in directories. But keep in mind that much more writing is turned away than accepted, and of the manuscripts that make it into print, many fail to find their audience — or satisfy it, if they reach it. When all of this works well, happy writers get into print with happy publishers.

EDITORS

In the division of labor within publishing houses, it's one or another kind of editor who will evaluate new submissions — or even solicit them. In a big publishing house, this person

☞ **MANY PUBLICATIONS ACCEPT STUDENT WRITING.** Some pay in cash, some in copies, some in experience — all are valuable.

For example, when Steve Charak, an ex-teacher founded YOUNG VOICES in Olympia, WA, he made two decisions: to pay student writers and to pay them on acceptance.

Some of Mick Fedullo's Native American students were anthologized by New York publisher Charles Scribner's Sons and were paid cash and copies. (See Resources for established markets.)

A national magazine for kids, *Essential News for Kids*, out of Tempe, AZ, uses cub reporters. Editor Bob Henschen holds workshops and trains some students to give cub reports on local radio and television.

Native Monthly Reader, a newspaper for young adults in Crestone, CO actively seeks student writers and reporters, and issues an official press card.

Check the resources section for market directories and other publishing opportunities outside school.

☞ **SUBJECT AND FORMAT SELECTION** in the projects we surveyed was amazingly broad. The age of the student publishers did not much limit general choices, though it restricted topics. Remember, all projects used as examples here are discussed in the first section, along with many others.

There were middle school publishers researching and producing sophisticated **histories** and **biographies** (Bill Coate, Madera, CA). Many projects involved students from elementary through university in publishing **books written for younger students** (both entertainments and texts). Annotated **bibliographies** of books on black and women's history (Sondra is called an acquisitions editor. In a smaller publishing operation, one person will wear this title as one of many. Besides such editors, many publishers rely on literary agents to act as filters, sending through only appropriate submissions. Final decisions on what to publish are often made by committees, and they may involve readers from outside the publishing house who have special expertise in some area or whose opinions are highly valued.

After a manuscript has been accepted, a contract is written to set out the rights and obligations of both the author and the publisher. A literary agent often acts on behalf of an author in the sale of a book, while writers negotiate for themselves on other kinds of writing.

Now, another type of editorial work begins. Depending on how well written and complete the manuscript is, an editor may be assigned to work with the writer to make major changes to the work. This is called substantive or content editing. There are people who specialize in this, generally concentrating on only a certain genre, like juvenile fiction or technical manuals. Sometime these editors are referred to as "book doctors."

Nachbar, Bronx High School of Science) were among references and resources published by students in high school.

Newspapers, literary journals, and **yearbooks** remain the most common forms of classroom publishing, though generally treated as electives or extra-curricular activities, rather than regular course work.

Anthologies of every type abound, with **poetry** predominating. Most unusual among them were **multilingual** poetry anthologies (Pat Egenberger, Modesto, CA). Anthologies lent themselves to **collaborations among schools** in a district, a city (Gabriele Stauf, Victoria, TX), a region, a nation, or the world (Chris Weber's project between Oregon and Japan).

Individual **books** or **booklets** of a single student's work were common on the elementary level, as well as among homeschoolers (Susan Richman, Kittanning, PA), who also created **magazines** and **newsletters** linking them with other students around the country.

School and community/business directories were popular because of practicality, renewability, and community support (Andrea Mayer, Worcester, NY).

Besides publishing in the classroom, many students were encouraged or required to **submit for publication outside of school.** Some teachers had students submit to a variety of freelance markets (Dennis Stovall, Anchorage, AK), while others concentrated on particular ones, such as the annual contest of Landmark Books (Janis Cramer, Bethany, OK). To guide students through the submission process, proper techniques are taught as part of some classes (Donna Clovis, Princeton, NJ).

Sample Query Letter
(done only after reading the guidelines of each publisher)

Date

Editor's name & address

Dear (editor/publisher):

Attract the editor's attention immediately with your best writing. Perhaps, lead with the actual lead ¶ of your work. In your style.

Detail your proposed work. Be brief!

Tell why this proposal is appropriate and why you're the one to do it. Who? What? When? Where? Why?

"...I try to give my students writing with a genuine purpose that goes outside of the classroom walls, to show them that writing is a tool for communicating and accomplishing a goal, whether it be to entertain, reflect, inform, or persuade. ...(m)any of the projects are also multi-disciplinary, which strengthens learning by reinforcement and makes education more meaningful to the students, since they're seeing how science and social studies can be related to English, instead of being taught separately. Education is not just academics: it's also relating to others, both within the class and outside, ...with peers as well as adults."

— Andrea E. Mayer
10–12 English
Worchester, NY

☞ **EVALUATING PURPOSE AND AUDIENCE.** Will the project be for

- only the teacher, the student and her or his family;
- fellow students and teachers;
- the community around the school;
- general public; or
- a highly targeted, narrow group.

The project must have a clearly understood purpose in relationship to the audience. Why is this project being done? What will it accomplish? Will it

- educate,
- record,
- persuade,
- entertain, or
- provoke?

The most successful projects are those with greater student participation in deciding purpose.

However, publications done from year-to-year, with an established role, can hold their own when each new class determines how the purpose is fulfilled. This provides teachers with an exceptional opportunity to **DISCUSS SUCH ISSUES AS COMMUNITY STANDARDS, DEMO-GRAPHICS, AND TASTE.**

☞ **EDITORIAL SELECTION CRITERIA** depend on teaching philosophy, student sophistication, age, and project type. The two approaches most used when a publication will have more than one author are to:

- include everything submitted so that no student feels left out; and
- select only the best work for publica-

137

An edited and revised manuscript is turned over to a *copy editor*, who corrects spelling, grammar, punctuation, and usage. This process cleans up the inconsistencies and minor problems that are always left after the author is done. When the manuscript is clean, it is passed on to the production phase.

NOTES/IDEAS _____

USE THIS ISLAND OF WHITE FOR YOUR ADDI-
TIONS, AND LET US KNOW ABOUT 'EM TOO.

138

tion, rejecting what the editors consider poorly done or unsuitable.

Where selection and rejection are practiced, it is handled in several ways:

- the teacher decides;
- all teachers and students involved
  decide collectively; or
- a student editor or editorial committee decides.

The means by which a method is chosen is
handled the same way, except that it is ultimately the teacher who establishes the
level of democracy in any project.

☞ Projects may be ad hoc, or permanent publishing companies may result. Even
if a publishing program is not on-going, it
can get the same **REGISTRATIONS** for itself and its publications as other publishers. These include

- the **International Standard Book
  Number (ISBN)**, which ensures that
  books are listed in *Books In Print* and
  can be found by buyers anywhere;
- the **International Standard Serial
  Number (ISSN)**, which designates
  periodicals for cataloging and distribution purposes;
- the **Library of Congress Catalog
  Number (LCCN)**; and
- the **Library of Congress Cataloging
  In Publication Data (CIP)**, which allows libraries to easily catalog new
  books in a standard way.

Addresses for these are listed in the Resources section of this book.

☞ **ORGANIZING AND DIVIDING THE
LABOR.** There are only a few basic models:

- producing one or a few copies of complete personal books by individual students; or
- producing a publication (multiple cop-

ON DIVISION OF LABOR
AND
PROJECT ORGANIZATION

"It [division of labor] depends on what the agenda is. If the agenda is the acquisition of skills in writing, then…to allow kids to evade the issue just perpetuates the problem. I don't think that can be defended. If the kid has no writing skills, and if the point…is to teach writing skills and the kid instead takes a bunch of pictures, that's a dead end."

— *Eliot Wigginton, Foxfire founder, Raybun Gap, GA*

"I wanted them to do everything, to the extent that it was humanly possible. Essentially I was just there to consult, to monitor, and to cheer them on."

— *Anne Sullivan, Robert E. Lee H.S., Baytown, TX*

"I have a big layout committee and they spend hours out of school…putting pieces of artwork next to writing, seeing what works with this, what works with that, what two pieces of writing would work well together. Then they start to notice the evolution of things coming together. You know, we have these feelings, or these topics; we want to go from here to there. It takes a long time, because there's no plan."

— *Nancy Gorrell, Morristown H.S., Morristown, NJ*

"I run it this way. …in the fall…a volunteer staff that comes in before school, after school, at lunch. [They] help do the advertising, solicit the materials, and…determine what's going to be in the magazine that year. Then I teach — usually in the spring — Advanced Creative Writing, and those kids…sift through the selected materials to determine what theme arises out of this work. They determine the layout. …so it is pretty much 100 % student produced and edited."

— *Cheryl Sackmann, Flagstaff H.S., Flagstaff, AZ*

ies) as a class — or as a team that involves or integrates classes, schools, states, or nations.

In the first case (common in elementary schools), there is either no division of labor in the project — each student does it all — or part is done by the student and part, i.e., copying or binding, by an adult.

In the second case, the range is from relatively equal participation by everyone in all phases and tasks to a strict division of labor and responsibility. Actual divisions of labor may be decided by the

- teacher,
- teacher and students together, or
- students alone.

Some projects work across the curriculum. The different courses create a natural division, i.e., English organizes editorial, art illustrates and designs, social science formulates issues, business handles marketing, shop builds displays, etc.

From our surveys, the only clear conclusion is that there are unlimited ways to handle organization — and students will suggest innovative solutions to organizational problems, if they're asked.

139

Career options: writing, editing, agenting, publishing

WRITING

For writers, the publishing game is quite a gamble. But when the bets are well placed, it's a gamble that pays off in the tremendous satisfaction of having one's words in print. It may even pay off as a lucrative career. As we've noted, there are innumerable possibilities for writers to specialize. Training is available at most colleges and universities, though some programs are better than others for certain kinds of writing. Finding the right school is a matter of studying the current curricula of many.

Specialized writing areas are often entered from the specialties, rather than from writing schools. For instance, the best science writing is usually done by scientists who love to write. They may have taken classes to improve their writing, but it's the love of the subject that makes them so effective at conveying it.

But careers in writing, except for journalism, rarely demand a degree — or even special academic study. Looking at great writers, both past and present, suggests that it's much more important to have a love of words, of reading, of writing. And that, finally, the best writing comes from those whose lives are as rich and varied as the work they hope to produce.

The one thing to remember about writing is that, unless the writer is on a payroll, it requires self-discipline, the ability to work alone without much feedback for long periods, and the temperament to handle frequent rejection without giving up. It can also call for lots of cash management skills, since freelancing generally means an unpredictable income.

EDITING

Several types of editing have been mentioned. There are actually many more, each a specialized role. Editing is virtually synonymous with publishing. In fact, the Latin root of the word means "to publish." Editors do everything from selecting and managing a publication's content and directing its staff to ensuring that all the i's are dotted and t's crossed in each manuscript. They may concentrate on a certain type of writing, oversee broad project areas, or they may be general editors.

One thing that holds true for most editing jobs is that working with others is at the core. Obviously, strong language skills are essential, but people skills are equally important. All publishing involves editing. Staff editors are employed by larger publishers, often with editorial assistants working under them. For example, Geraldine Albert, an associate managing editor for Van Nostrand Reinhold (VNR) in New York, is responsible for non-technical books in the categories of architecture, computer science, travel, and culinary. She oversees the work of three production editors, each of whom has an assistant production editor. They produce over 100 books per year. Albert evaluates manuscripts for copyediting and art needs; she gives guidelines to production editors on scheduling and editing; and she serves as a production editor on some titles

Careers are now available in...
Writing
Publishing
Editing
Graphic arts
Photography
Printing
Binding
Bookselling
Marketing
and more...

herself. She feels that the future holds fewer staff editing positions as large publishers continue to merge and downsize. Already, most copyediting and proofing is done by freelancers. Other editing may follow the same path.

This sentiment is echoed by another VNR editor, Bob Argentieri, whose responsibilities are acquiring new manuscripts, negotiating with authors or agents, and acting "as shepherd through the whole process, a go-between with the author." He travels extensively, looking for new books, and he "keeps in touch with hundreds of authors." He sees technology entering the picture slowly, but holding potential for dramatic changes in the types of work acquired and the media of their publication. Like Albert, he sees staff jobs shrinking at major publishers, as more of the process is subcontracted to freelancers.

Often, editors learn their craft on the job, either as apprentices to more experienced editors or as writers who have decided to broaden their freelance employment possibilities. From what was said by editors interviewed, the in-house apprenticeship method of learning editorial skills may not be as available as it has been.

Editing is taught in journalism schools and in some writing programs. Geraldine Albert of VNR took a degree in English, intending to teach, but fell instead into publishing. Editors of all sorts have recommended working on student publications as a way to learn. Computers have aided editors without threatening to make their jobs obsolete. Anyone considering an editing career should know the new tools.

Both small and large publishers hire freelance editors if they have more work than they can manage with their staffs. Or when, as the editors we've interviewed note, publishers decide to employ fewer people full time in favor of hiring freelancers

141

COMMON PROOFREADER'S MARKS

SIGN	MEANING	USED IN A LINE	MARGINAL NOTES
∧	Insert	A big dg	⌒/
#	Space	found out	#/
ℓ	Delete	about of	ℓ/
⌒	Close up	the contest	⌒/
	Delete & close up	for canines	ℰ/
n	Transpose	liked who	n/
∧	Semicolon	to jump	∧/
∧	Comma	he'd, unfortunately	∧/
⊙	Period	missed it before	⊙/
⊙	Colon	They asked for ID	⊙/
∨	Apostrophe	his sires middle name	∨/
∨ ∨	Quotation marks (open & close)	and his bark	∨ ∨/
cap	Capital (≡ under)	this was	cap/
lc	Lower-case (/ through)	not What	lc/
/=/	Hyphen	he expect	/=/
1/m	Dash	ed the procedure	1/m
⊗	Defective letter (circle)	seemed odd.	⊗
wf	Wrong font (circle)	So he	wf
/	(Use to separate corrections)	trotted Home	t/lc/
ital	Italic type (underline)	without once	ital/
rom	Roman type (circle)	wagging his tail.	rom/
sc	Small caps (= under)	From an old story	sc/

on a project by project basis. So, as with writing, career opportunities in editing range from the security and predictability of full-time employment to the uncertainties and freedom of freelancing.

AGENTING

Literary agents serve as intermediaries between writers and publishers or editors. They negotiate contracts, try to sell work, and generally earn their keep by knowing the business side of writing. This is another people-oriented career; one that demands strong negotiating skills as well as an understanding of how best to market an author's work. Some agents serve as front-line editors, helping their author clients prepare their manuscripts for sale. From the point of view of publishers, good agents serve as first readers, passing along for consideration only the best and most appropriate work.

Agents usually specialize in types of writing or in specific markets, i.e., films, foreign rights, and audio.

Most agents are in the major publishing centers, but a growing number choose to live elsewhere. With telephones, postal and other delivery services, fax machines, and computer modems, they can maintain close contact with the markets. If they need to meet editors face-to-face, they can travel.

Agents make their livings by taking a percentage of each sale they make. So, this is another speculative career, like freelance

writing or editing. Most people learn to agent by working in an established literary agency, since it takes considerable time and effort to develop both strong, deep contacts within the publishing industry and a group of writers to represent.

PUBLISHING

Being a publisher means managing an entire publishing business or only a section of one and seeing its projects through to publication — to reaching their readers. In small houses, the publisher is probably the owner, typist, receptionist, editor, and mailroom clerk. But, large or small, the responsibilities are basically the same. Publishers must have the broadest possible view of the process, including the financial and legal issues. Publishing can be risky, so anyone pursuing it must learn the basics of running a business in addition to understanding the selection and preparation of material.

The path to becoming a publisher can begin with the decision to start a publishing company, or it can begin with an editorial position in an established house. There are a number of excellent publishing programs in universities, and there are special intensive publishing institutes that pack everything into a few weeks. Through regional publishers' associations there are often seminars and classes on aspects of the business. And, of course, classroom publishing projects provide an exceptional introduction.

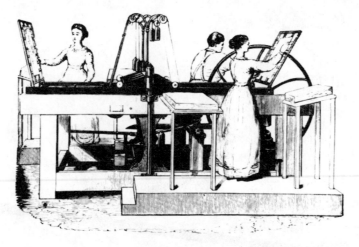

Production

Production is the invisible part of the process. Few of us, unless we know printers or typesetters, have an accurate sense of how a manuscript winds up as a printed and bound publication.

There are several steps in production, and they are quite similar across the range of publications. All begin with the decision to publish a particular piece of writing, which we discussed in the previous section. At that point, editors and publishers start paying attention to questions of length, style, illustrations, format, and production schedule. From one publisher to the next, who is in charge of scheduling all the elements of production varies. It may be a publisher, an editor, a production manager, or someone else.

Production has three major stages if the publication is bound; two stages if it is not. Prepress work includes everything that goes into preparing material for the printer. This stage potentially involves the greatest variety of skills. Printing is the next step; and binding is the finishing touch.

PREPRESS

PAPER SELECTION

Paper is often taken for granted, but it's another element that reveals its complexity at second glance. Papers are manufactured to an amazing number of specifications — from cheap to pricey, from handmade to mass produced, from environmentally benign to toxic in its production, from hard to toothy, from natural hues to brilliant white to any color, from transparent to opaque, from smooth to embossed, from acidic and temporary to alkaline and archival. Choices are made according to use, budget, size, aesthetics, etc. Publishers rely on papermakers for accurate, consistent specifications. The paper industry employs specialists who understand the differing needs of publishers.

Despite that, knowledge of papers is part of any publisher's or graphic artist's stock in trade. Knowing which

Floss to Gloss

☞ What was said at the end of the last chapter about division of labor and organization in projects holds for production as well as editorial.

We noticed from our surveys, interviews and workshops, that **STUDENT PUBLISHING CENTERS** are becoming more common. They come in all forms, and with the changing roles of media specialists/librarians, many are part of the library.

But too often, despite the overwhelming evidence of its value, school systems give publishing little support. In fact, those we interviewed commonly support their programs out of their own pockets — or with their own time. Dennis Stovall (Anchorage), for instance, couldn't get needed computers from the school, but through much personal effort, got them donated by a manufacturer. Other teachers report paying for supplies, printing, and travel.

☞ **MATERIAL AND EQUIPMENT NEEDS** depend on the production techniques used in individual projects — from floss to gloss. Wonderful projects can be accomplished with nothing more than paper, glue, writing/drawing/typing tools, and imagination. Dedicated space, computers, camera equipment, darkrooms, photocopiers, laser printers, and simple binders open the way to a host of more complex possibilities.

However, there is strong evidence that computer technology is a very powerful lure, getting students involved who might otherwise never dream of working on a publication. For some exciting examples, check out

143

papers work best with photos, certain colors, various inks, and types of presses becomes important quickly. Most publishers delegate paper selection to book designers, graphic artists, or production managers. Many small publishers rely on their printers to help them choose. And it's not always as straightforward as it might seem.

No matter who makes it, paper is fundamental and must be selected by someone before printing proceeds.

BINDING DECISIONS

To bind or not to bind? It's a real question. Newspapers and some magazines opt for nothing more than pages folded and inserted. Tradition, expense, and type of publication generally dictate the choice of whether or not to bind. But once it's been decided to bind, new options appear, each with its merits. The physical differences are discussed later.

For now, we'll consider this as one of the design decisions usually made by a publisher or designer and having a lot to do with the intended use of the publication, i.e., how durable it must be, what size is it, what quality paper is used inside, how many are to be printed, who will read it and where, how will it be marketed, etc. The person making this decision may rely on printers or binders for recommendations or may have studied the various bindings carefully.

INTERIOR DESIGN

Book or publication designers evaluate what is to be published and choose layouts, formats, and typefaces that befit the budget, the message, and the audience. Book design is both art and science. Successful book design combines an understanding of how books are built with an aesthetic appreciation of the ways ink, especially as type, can be laid on paper. Good design also considers how readers respond to dif-

TRIM SIZE refers to the measurements of a page after binding and trimming. A publication can be almost any size, but because of manufacturing standards, certain sizes are most common and economical. With width first, they are

Pages bound long side vertical are in portrait format.

Pages bound with the short side vertical are in landscape format.

11" x 17"
8 ½" x 11"
6" x 9"
5 ½" x 8 ½"
7" x 10"

144

the projects of Steve O'Donoghue (John C. Fremont School, Oakland, CA) and David Schaafsma (Detroit, MI).

☞ Paper is anything but uncontroversial because of its environmental costs in production, its contribution to solid waste management problems when discarded, and the impact different papers have on the longevity of publications. Simply consider that because of cheaper high-acid papers, there are acres of books in the Library of Congress which can only be handled by archivists — they're that brittle, that fragile. So, **PAPER SELECTION** for a classroom project can lead to interesting and useful discussions. It may also provide a way to involve classes in the sciences: chemistry, biology, ecology, etc.

☞ Except for crude forms, paper is not generally made as part of classroom publishing projects, though it could be. Handmade papers are appropriate for printing with an old letterpress or for making limited editions, publishing poetry or broadsides, and similar publications. In fact, **PAPERMAKING MAY BE AN OPPORTUNITY FOR COLLABORATION BETWEEN A SCHOOL'S ART AND LANGUAGE DEPARTMENTS.**

☞ **PAPER HAS GRAIN** as the result of fibers aligning themselves in the direc-

BOOK

BOOK

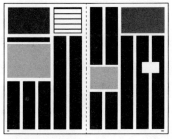
MAGAZINE

There are standards and expectations in design for different types of publications. Besides looking at available newspapers, magazines, and books for inspiration, you can mock-up interior designs by creating empty, white two-page spreads — full-size or proportionally smaller. Cut out blocks from a darker paper to represent various elements: columns, text blocks, photos, graphics, folios (page numbers). Move these around on the page until the effect is agreeable.

One thing to avoid is the temptation to cram as much as possible on each page. White space is an important design element that enhances readability when used well.

Note too, that the type of binding affects how far the gutter margin opens, thus how wide it should be.

Placement of text and graphics has a rhythm on the page that helps the reader move smoothly through it. Our culture reads from right to left and top to bottom, and this establishes a natural path for the eye that should be considered in all design — even when the intent is to jar the reader from usual habits.

NEWSPAPER

Below are the basic elements of a printed page (left facing).

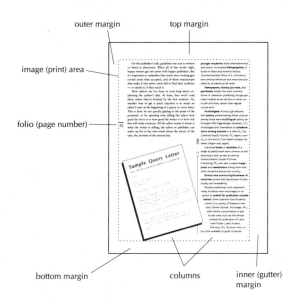

outer margin   top margin

image (print) area

folio (page number)

bottom margin   columns   inner (gutter) margin

tion of pulp flow when it's made. Generally, grain should run parallel to the bind. This is because it changes size with moisture content more across the grain than with it. Books bound "cross-grain" show waves and puckers along the outer edge. **AN ENTERTAINING TEST** of a paper's grain direction can be done by having students tear a small square of paper, then moisten only one side; the paper will curl around the grain direction.

☞ On the theory that imitation is high praise, classroom publishing projects can do what publishers everywhere have always done: look at a wide range of publications similar to what's wanted and **EMULATE DESIGNS THAT ARE MOST PLEASING AND EFFECTIVE.** Simply looking at how information is consciously presented gives students insight into the complexity of communications.

☞ **BUDGET DICTATES PROJECT CHOICES.** It's no different for commercial publishers, except that binding type and cover are critical to marketing.

That may seem too crassly commercial for classroom projects, yet we all know that an attractively produced publication is more likely to be read. Binding and cover are important parts of design. Students who have control over budgets for their projects can investigate the relative merits and prices of various bindings and decide on the style that best suits the project — and their ability to finance it.

Attractive covers do not require large budgets — better bindings are simply more costly to produce. **STUNNING COVERS** — on any binding — depend on the artistry and design that goes into them. Some of the most beautiful covers are the

145

ferent typefaces and designs, so that the form of a publication enhances its effectiveness. On detailed projects, the publication designer may have a lot say about the organization, order, and placement of editorial material, working closely with editors. Successful design goes virtually unnoticed. Bad design is obvious and disconcerting to the reader.

COVER ART & DESIGN

With the exception of some very small publishing houses, the design of the inside and the cover are done by different people. Quite a few folks can be involved at this stage, including the publisher, a graphic artist, the cover artist, the designer, and possibly someone from marketing. All too rarely are authors consulted.

When a cover requires the incorporation of artwork or photographs in its design, other people become involved. While some fine artists, illustrators, and photographers specialize in cover art, designers ordinarily purchase art they want from whomever has produced it.

We've all heard the saying: "You can't tell a book by its cover." In the publishing industry they add: "Maybe not, but you sell a book by its cover." Competition is keen on bookstore shelves and magazine racks. Each cover tries to outdo the next for our attention. That's how seriously cover design is taken — it often costs more to produce the cover than to print all the insides.

TYPOGRAPHY

Typography is changing at a remarkable rate because of computers. While a book designer creates the specifications, including such things as the typefaces, sizes used for headlines and other elements, line lengths, lines per page, etc., it has always been skilled typesetters who made those choices real. Until fairly recently, type was set physically, one character at a time. That changed to creating bars of set type in one process from molten metal. The next step was setting type photographically by exposing film or pho-

simple drawings and paintings done by small children.

Additional doses of labor can overcome lack of cash. Hard covers can be made and applied by hand to printed pages that have been folded, gathered, and sewn (with anything from silk thread or fishing line to dental floss or yarn). Perfect bindings, as softcover bindings are called — can be created from a wide range of material and applied by hand to loose book pages with padding glue, which is readily available at printing supply stores. There are excellent books on the craft of hand binding — and book building, in general.

This wonderfully minimalist cover (on the back is a wink), was designed for the 1984 Matrix, the annual magazine of Fairfax H.S., Fairfax, VA, (Carol Lange, advisor) by Anne Birdsall.

tographic paper to images of letters by shining a light through a template. Now, most type is set digitally, using patterns of tiny laser-made dots on film or paper to create letters and other images.

Since the end of handset type in commercial printing, text has been entered from a keyboard, along with instructions for size, style, and format. Skilled operators knew the relationships between various elements and visualized the final type as they fed complex codes to machines that looked like typewriters on steroids. That's how it was until quite recently, when "desktop publishing" came on the scene with its acronym WISIWYG (what you see is what you get). It gave the ability to set type to thousands of new people — both skilled and unskilled.

This was heralded as the death of fine typography, when, in fact, it simply allowed more interested people to learn about it. Certainly, the democratization of the process that this engendered resulted in more examples of ugly documents, but it enriched publishing with just as many fine and elegant experiments. Unfortunately for typesetters with traditional skills — long a priesthood of sorts when it came to composing type — the change has meant "either change with the times and accept the technology or get out of typesetting." Which is not to say there isn't a need for skilled typesetters who also understand the creative flexibility that computers offer in the overall design and composition of pages. Fine type is still worth the effort, no matter the tools.

Put your best face forward…

Choose type conservatively — no more than three faces per document. Avoid pages that look like ransom notes, with too many type styles, sizes, etc. scattered about.

For major text areas, stick with one serif face (that's type like this one [Sabon], with ending strokes or short cross lines terminating main strokes).

Use the same face for titles — larger and perhaps in bold or caps — or apply a san serif face (*san serif* means "without serifs" like the titles used in this book [Optima] or the **Stone San Serif** in the sample on the next page or that old familiar **Helvetica** or Swiss that almost everyone with a computer has).

Avoid script faces except for wedding announcements and invitations. Resist the urge to use every ornament available; select them purposefully.

Remember that type is a graphic element on the page.

Later, break the "rules" for effect.

☞ **THE RIGHT TYPE** depends on its use — that means understanding the purpose of the publication and who will read it. As research, students can bring type samples for discussion. And if computer publishing systems are available, they can print a range of samples, and they can imitate some of the example they found.

Typeface are indicated with a shorthand form. A number like 10/12 means 10 point type with 2 added points of lead (space between lines). Remember that there are 72 points per inch, 12 points per pica, and 6 picas per inch.

☞ Many lessons taught in typing classes run counter to **TYPOGRAPHICAL PRACTICES**. It's crucial that student typesetters know the differences — the special characters, spacing attributes, and type variations. The display of Stone Informal (next page) shows all the familiar characters and even more that are new to most students. Here are a few **COMMON PROBLEM CHARACTERS**.

- Em dash. When we want a long dash — like these — on a typewriter, we use two hyphens (--). Depending on the computer, there should be a way to enter —. The — is supposedly the length of the M in a given typeface.
- En dash. Equal to half of an em dash, it is used to show a range, as in 10–

147

aA bB cC dD eE fF/Caslon
aA bB cC dD eE fF/Caxton
aA bB cC dD eE fF/Palatino
aA bB cC dD eE fF/Times

Sabon 11/15. To appreciate how important type is to the success of the message, one need only compare the readability, mood, and color of different typefaces set at different sizes and leads.

Stone Sans 8/8. To appreciate how important type is to the success of the message, one need only compare the readability, mood, and color of different typefaces set at different sizes and leads.

Zapf Chancery 12/18. To appreciate how important type is to the success of the message, one need only compare the readability, mood, and color of different typefaces set at different sizes and leads.

American Typewriter 10/11. To appreciate how important type is to the success of the message, one need only compare the readability, mood, and color of different typefaces set at different sizes and leads.

LITHOS LIGHT 10/12. TO APPRECIATE HOW IMPORTANT TYPE IS TO THE SUCCESS OF THE MESSAGE, ONE NEED ONLY COMPARE THE READABILITY, MOOD, AND COLOR OF DIFFERENT TYPEFACES SET AT DIFFERENT SIZES AND LEADS.

Bauhaus Demi-bold 10/12. To appreciate how important type is to the success of the message one need only compare the readability, mood, and color of different typefaces set at different sizes and leads.

Palatino 10/12. To appreciate how important type is to the success of the message, one need only compare the readability, mood, and color of different typefaces set at different sizes and leads.

Stone Informal 8/10

abcdefghijklmnopqrstuvwxyz
ABCDEFGHIJKLMNOPQRSTUVWXYZ
1234567890`-=[]\;',./#$%^&*()~!@_+{}|:"<>?
`¡™£¢∞§¶•ªº–≠œΣ´®†¥¨^øπ"'«åß∂ƒ©˙∆˚¬…æΩ≈ç√∫~µ≤≥÷
Ÿ/¤◊fifl‡°·‚—±Œ„‰ÂÊÁËÈØ∏""'»ÅÍÎÏÌÓÔ ÒÚÆÛÙÇ◊ıˆˉ˘˙˚¸
regular/*italic*/**semibold**/***semibold italic***/**bold**/***bold italic***

12 or 1951–68. It's longer than a hyphen. Hyphens show word breaks and word links.

- This (") is an inch mark and this (') is a foot mark. Open and close quotes should look like these (" ") and single quotes and apostrophes should look like (' '). These characters are either automatic or need special keystrokes.

- Putting two spaces at the end of a sentence is bad typography. Not only is one space conventional, but type-setting programs use the space as a flexible element, which causes unpredictable results on two or more spaces.

- On a typewriter, each space is the same size, so if you space over five on one line, it's always going to match if you do it on another line. Not so with typesetting, where letter spaces are in proportion to each letter, and spaces are flexible. You cannot reliably line up columns using spaces — even if it looks right on the screen, it may print wrong. Use tabs to set absolute stops.

In the resources section of this book is a **BIBLIOGRAPHY** including titles on the art and craft of typography and the use of computerized page composition software. We recommend that a few of these be available for study. Not only the composition of type, but the design of new typefaces is an important artistic and technical skill. Given reasonably equipped computers, it is possible for a classroom publishing project to include the creation of its own typeface, if for nothing else than a cover or special titles.

CAMERA-READY ART: LAYOUT, PASTE-UP, & STRIPPING

When publishers, graphic artists, and printers refer to camera-ready art or copy they mean that all of the type, photos, illustrations, lines (rules), etc. that are wanted on the printed page are assembled and mounted on some sort of stiff layout paper or artboard, ready for a camera to take a photo. From this photographic film, a printing plate is made.

This was not a step that existed before photography and modern printing. Today, the preparation of camera-ready art is more and more often done on computer screens, and there is no longer a step between doing that and generating a film image from which to make the printing plate. Though not yet as common, going directly from computer screen to printing plate is a simple step. But most projects require a mix of new and old techniques, which will probably be the case for some time.

Type may be completely composed and output as one piece of camera-ready art, but photos, illustrations, and other art may have to be added mechanically (by hand). Computer scanners are getting better, which means some elements can be scanned and then manipulated (cropped, resized, otherwise edited, and positioned) electronically, but the mechanical skills of stripping and paste-up still need to be part of the graphic artist's repertoire.

When the various pieces that will go into the design of a finished page are ready, they are pasted-up (mounted) in their proper positions. Spaces are left for elements that have to be created separately, such as film for screened photographs, color overlays, or 4-color images.

PHOTO PREPARATION & COLOR SEPARATIONS

Even when they are pasted-up as part of camera-ready art, photos call for separate preparation. They must be screened if a full range of colors or grays are to be reproduced on the press. Screens create a mesh of tiny black dots or lines in the new photos taken through them of the originals. The smaller the dots (the finer the screen), the higher the resolution of the resulting print. However, different types of printing presses have their own limits on resolution, which means that the person in charge of preparing photos for the

☞ **LAYOUT WORK IS DONE ON A LIGHT TABLE,** which is a special box topped with translucent glass with an even light shining through. This allows pieces of copy to be aligned by using a grid which can be seen through the layout. The pieces are held in place with adhesives. Commonly, hot wax is applied to the backs of the elements with a special roller. This allows them to be repositioned easily, but holds them firmly. Besides wax, anything that doesn't harm the layout can be used.

Light tables are expensive to buy, but relatively cheap to make. This just might be a way to involve the carpentry class — the mind boggles at the possibilities.

You can also print your own gridded layout paper when you have a stable design — just be sure to use a pure blue ink that is not photographable. There are also pens and pencils this color so you can write notes and instructions directly on layouts without having them appear on the printed page.

☞ Black and white photos are most common in classroom publishing. The cost of **4-COLOR REPRODUCTION** of color photos, except for limited use, quickly goes beyond the means of most small publishers. The exception may be the cover of a book or magazine. However, between 1 and 4 are 2 and 3 — colors that is, which can be affordable, simple to prepare, and printable on the most basic equipment. And acceptable 4-color is getting cheaper and more available from color copying machines, those especially handy graphic arts tools.

The use of inks of a second or third color is generally referred to as **SPOT COLOR.** Rather than creating a complex color from the four basic ones using overlaying, separated screens of each, inks are press must know how to screen correctly for the best results on a particular press.

Likewise, a camera operator has to be able to use the camera to enlarge, reduce, crop, or otherwise manipulate images in ways that help them fit prescribed spaces and reproduce well. Instructions on how to handle photos is passed on by the graphic artist to the cameraperson.

When color photos are used, their preparation requires that the constituent colors be separated, since each must be printed separately. Colors are reproduced using four inks — cyan, magenta, yellow, and black (CMYK). Color separation (seps) are still best done by professional services that specialize in them, though high quality scanners and computer software are gradually taking over this area, too.

Once photos have been prepared, they are made part of the art in one of two ways. If they are screen prints (PMTs, Veloxes, etc.) they are pasted in place with the type and other elements from which a negative will be made, then a printing plate. If photos are screened negatives, the film must be positioned on the negative that includes all the other type and art ready for shooting to a printing place. This process is called stripping in, and those who do it are strippers.

PROOFREADING

When printing was done with cold type in the old manner of letterpresses, a piece of paper was laid on the inked type and a first impression taken after all type was placed. This was a proof copy, and making it was called "pulling a proof." This was essential when one considers that hand-set type had to be positioned one character at a time in trays where it was a mirror image of the way it would print. So, reading proof provided the last check on composition, spelling, and other typographic elements.

We still call it proofreading, but it's not quite the same

mixed to the final color and can be applied as solids or screened for tints or other effects. Without the costs and technical requirements of 4-color process printing, spot color provides a surprising range of design possibilities. Amazing colors can be created — beyond the possibilities of 4-color. Popular color matching systems, such as PMS (Pantone Matching System), Trumatch, and Focoltone market swatch books of thousands of available or mixable ink colors.

If a school has **PHOTOGRAPHY CLASSES**, it's possible to handle much **BLACK AND WHITE** work completely inside the publishing project. Photo supply stores are a source of screens for creating halftones. A little carpentry results in a frame for shooting artwork, or catalog suppliers generally carry ready-made paraphernalia for almost any need.

Finally, **COMPUTER SCANNERS** and special editing software can supply art — black & white or color — ready for the electronic page and easily manipulated.

☞ Bain Robinson of Kasigluk, AK, relates **AN APOCRYPHAL PROOFREADING TALE:** It seems that after the books his 9 and 10th grade students published were off press, one student discovered a serious mistake and swore that she hadn't typed it that way. Bain asked her to check, and said that if she had not made the mistake, they would reprint. She stomped off, got

using modern equipment. Today, when the film is ready to make plates, an image is created on special photographic paper that shows all printing areas in blue. These proofs are referred to as bluelines, and they are provided by the printer so that the publisher can make one final check of the work. It's the last chance to change copy, though it's more expensive than correcting mistakes before the film is made.

When the printing begins, the press operator will still "pull a proof" and use it to adjust the press so that the image is properly positioned and the inking is correct. Generally, the publisher is not involved, though some try to be there for a "press check" before giving the printer an "OK" to run the job. Press checks are more important if the job is high quality 4-color work, where tolerances are critical.

Computerized page composition (desktop publishing) has shifted the proofing process toward the publisher's end of things, since it allows virtually finished pages to be proofread long before camera-ready copy or film goes to the printer. Still, it's important to check bluelines to ensure that no mechanically placed art has been lost or that no pages have been misplaced, inverted, or damaged.

her disk, and returned chagrined. The mistake had been typed and proofed by her. She couldn't believe it. "That was the most lucid moment in that whole process for me," Bain says. "It indicates a kind of learning having taken place there. What you strive for, really, is to be able to be impassioned while you work, but when you're looking back over your work — to see what your passion has created — to have the coolness to say, 'Well, okay I can see this with a different eye.' I felt like we achieved that as a result of having done this book."

NOTES/IDEAS _____

USE THESE ISLANDS OF WHITE FOR YOUR ADDITIONS, AND LET US KNOW ABOUT 'EM TOO.

Career options: prepress

Careers are now available in...

Writing
Publishing
Editing
Graphic arts
Photography

Printing
Binding
Bookselling
Marketing
and more...

Prepress careers are among the fastest changing due to new technologies. The traditional division of labor is being compressed into fewer and fewer jobs. Old methods will still be used by choice or necessity for a long time, so anyone seeking such employment needs to know both old and new methods.

careers are concerned, this in an area in which both old and new methods will always co-exist.

DESIGNER

Qualified, skilled publication designers usually emerge from apprenticeships within the industry, though there are a few schools that teach this art. Once a designer's work has been recognized, it's possible to either work for one publisher or freelance to many. Most designers study graphic arts and production, with a new emphasis on using computers for part or all of the process. This means that keyboard skills are more important than ever.

Cover designers specialize in an area where talented graphic artists can always find work, either as full-time employees or as freelancers to a variety of publishers. We've noted how crucial it is to have good covers, and publishers are willing to pay for the talent to create them.

ARTIST/ILLUSTRATOR

Cover artists and illustrators are important in many kinds of publishing. They are usually not involved in the production process, the creation of mechanicals or camera-ready art. They simply do the art, using the medium they choose or the one requested by the publisher. Until recently, art has been supplied in traditional formats, but computers are changing fine art as well. More publishers are now seeking fine artists who do original work on computers, since this allows the final art to be manipulated and pasted up electronically. But as far as

TYPOGRAPHER/ ELECTRONIC PAGE COMPOSER

Career options in typography and electronic page composition area are rich, though the future remains as unpredictable as the next revolution in technology. As with any craft, anyone can claim to be skilled, but those who are most talented will come to the fore and find employment. The industry has shifted rapidly and almost completely to the composition of complete pages, including type, on computers. This has opened employment opportunities for a whole new generation of people trained from the beginning in desktop publishing technologies. But the shift also means that many of the separate jobs required by the old methods are being rolled into one on the computer. Not only should anyone planning to enter this field know how to use the equipment — both hardware and software — but skills in typing and an understanding of typography are essential; graphic arts training would certainly enhance employment potential.

LAYOUT ARTIST/ STRIPPER/GRAPHIC ARTIST

Like typography, the mechanical production of camera-ready copy is being replaced by computer composition. This means that those who have prepared camera-ready art for a living — layout and paste-up artists and other graphic artists — must learn to use computers for at least part of their work, while retaining some of the mechanical skills that are needed for special jobs. As the old functions are done more and more on computers, this part of the prepress process will involve fewer people, and it will likely become the job of a graphic artist, working on a screen, who also acts as a publications designer, typographer, and photo refinisher.

PRODUCTION MANAGER

Overseeing the prepress process is a job in itself, but only with larger publishers is it treated that way. A production manager plans production schedules, selects outside vendors (typesetters, imagesetters, color separators, typists, artists, etc.), arranges for the timely delivery of outside work, gets competitive bids from printers and others, arranges shipments of finished publications, and generally ensures that the process works smoothly.

In a small publishing operation, the publisher usually does this. Larger publishers may have several production managers, each responsible for a type of prepress production, i.e., covers and insides. In any case, production managers understand all the aspects of publishing, though they may not be experts in any of the areas. Most often, though, a production manager is someone who is promoted from work in one of the prepress disciplines.

153

These two lovely perfect bound books are part of a major project sponsored by the Montana Arts Council and coordinated by Julie Smith, Director of Artists Services for the Artists in Schools/Communities Program. Funding came from the Arts Council, the Montana State Legislature, and the National Endowment for the Arts. While the material is all by Montana students, the editing, design, typography, and printing were contracted out by the Council.

Printing & binding

It may seem like a long haul to press time, but that's when the publication finally becomes real — once it's printed and, if necessary, bound and ready for its readers.

PRINTING

LETTERPRESS

Printing can be done one page at a time on a *letterpress*, a technology that has been in place since before Gutenberg created moveable type. Production like this straddles the line between fine and industrial arts. It's advantage is complete, hands-on control of publishing. It's disadvantage is slowness and lack of flexibility. Considerable skill is involved.

OFFSET

Offset printing is the method of choice, offering a wide range of cost, quality, speed, and flexibility. It is easily integrated with prepress technologies. For most printing, but especially 4-color, it is the only economical choice. In offset printing, a printing plate is exposed photographically through a film negative of the complete type and art. After it is developed, it retains an image of the areas to be inked, and once on the press (wrapped around a drum), only treated areas will pick up ink and transfer it, as an image, to another drum which has a thick rubber blanket. Paper is fed through and the inked blanket transfers the final image to it.

Offset presses fall into two categories — sheetfed and web. Sheetfed presses use cut sheets of paper, taken one at a time through the press, while web presses run continuous rolls (webs) of paper through the press and cut the sheets at the other end. Web presses are much faster, but less precise. A press of either type that can print both sides of the paper at once is called a "perfector."

Presses used for 4-color work generally act like four presses in a row, with separate plates applying each color (CMYK) in sequence. Four-color printing can also be done

Floss to Gloss

☞ Because few commercial printers still use **LETTERPRESSES**, it may be possible for a school to acquire a workable press with complete fonts of type at little or no cost.

☞ Projects must have a way to print or reproduce their publications. This can be done with whatever equipment is available, from an old spirit duplicator to a district offset press. Or this can be handled outside the school at a photocopying service or a commercial printer. Services may be donated or purchased. The teachers we interviewed handled printing and production in all of these ways. You can associate methods with projects by referring to them in the index and finding them in the first part of the book. Here's **HOW THEY DID IT**.

- Andrea Mayer of Worcester, NY, used the local student vocational center.
- Nan Elassaser of Albuquerque, NM, has arranged for the *ALBUQUERQUE TRIBUNE* to print her students' books.
- Anne Sullivan of Monticello, FL, had the students reproduce their publication on a high quality photocopier in the district print shop.
- Jerry Phillips at the University of Arkansas/Monticello uses the campus resource center.
- Donna Clovis of Easthampton, NJ, has a publishing room equipped with Macintosh computers and printers; parents of her elementary kids form a committee, get training, and then handle the printing and production.
- Bill Coate of Madera, CA, says, "We

on 1- and 2-color presses by first printing one or two colors and then feeding the paper through again until all colors are applied. Some commercial presses have six inking stations, allowing special inks or finishes to be applied in one pass.

ALTERNATIVE PRINTING METHODS

Alternatives to presses are laser printing, photocopying, spirit duplication, and mimeography. These are fine for less demanding applications or for tight budgets. None is yet adequate for high resolution reproduction or large quantities.

CHANGING PRINTING METHODS

Modern printing technology is rapidly adapting itself to the latest electronic prepress techniques. But because of the high cost of new equipment, it will only be the largest printers who stay on the cutting edge, and even they will continue to handle much work in more traditional ways. The near future holds the promise of going directly from computer files to the printing press.

Alternatively, high-speed photocopiers are moving toward higher resolutions and better color reproduction. They can work directly from computer files, since they are basically sophisticated laser printers. They can print both sides of pages, collate them, and then do simple bindings, such as saddle- or side-stitching. There will soon be equipment capable of the more commercial bindings necessary for most publications, especially books. This should lower the cost of very short runs of publications, to the advantage of all small publishers. Even more exciting, is the ability to publish on demand, which will mean that publishers, especially of books, can avoid investing their money in large inventories.

BINDING

Methods of binding have changed little considering the technological advances that are affecting prepress and even printing. More automation has speeded up bindery work. Better glues have given certain kinds of bindings broader application. And a few new methods — actually just variation on old ones — have given publishers options they didn't have before. But, overall, bindery work remains much like it's

take our final copy to a job printer. They print the pages for us. And they design the dust jacket. We used to use the school district, but we had to conform to their time schedule, and it just didn't work out."

- Carolyn Tragesser of Moscow, ID, had her students compose on the computer in the classroom and take the disc to a laser printer place where they photocopy the print-out.
- David Schaafsma of Detroit, MI, had access for students to Macintosh computers with a laser printer that was borrowed from Educational Improvement Through Collaboration program at the University of Michigan.
- Sondra Nachbar of the Bronx, NY, found an alumni who subsidized the printing of the book through two editions.
- Steve O'Donoghue of Oakland, CA , says his students "do all the writing, they do all the editing, they put it on computer, they knock it out camera ready. They do the photography. Everything. We send it to a local commercial printer. The magazine is bound outside."
- One teacher told us her school is next to a photocopier plant and that she easily got the company to donate high quality, high speed reproduction of her class' publications.

☞ As with printing, all manner of solutions come into play with **BINDING**. There are, by the way, excellent craft books on custom binding, so there are many possibilities to explore. Handcrafted, limited edition covers exemplify many of the elementary school projects. When press runs are small, mechanical bindings see considerable been for over a century.

The whole point to binding is to keep finished pages together. The method depends on the use of the publication, its budget, the desired look, and publisher preference. The broad categories are mechanical and non-mechanical.

MECHANICAL BINDINGS

STITCHED BINDINGS

Stitched bindings are actually stapled, like most magazines. But any stapling approach can be used. One staple in the top left corner is familiar to us all. Another common stitch is through the left margin of the gathered pages, generally using two or more staples. The most refined method is saddle stitching, with the pages stapled down the center of the spine at the fold line. Stitching is inexpensive, but it has a low limit on the number of sheets that can be bound before it becomes unwieldy.

COMB, SPIRAL, AND SIMILAR BINDINGS

These types of bindings, and there are many variations on the theme, are used when the bound material must open flat. Common applications include manuals, calendars, notebooks, and reports.

All of these bindings require some sort of machine for drilling or punching precise holes in stacks of paper and finally inserting the mechanical apparatus.

METAL POST AND RING BINDINGS

Three-ring binders are the best known of these. Metal posts are two-part pins with a flat, washer-like piece on either end that are screwed together through holes in the paper stack. Posts can also be clips that are inserted through the holes and then bent. Neither approach is either very elegant or cheap for publishing, but both are great when pages will often be added or subtracted for any reason.

NON-MECHANICAL BINDINGS

With the exception of saddle stitching, where each sheet has two pages on each side, the mechanical bindings fasten together individual sheets with one page on each side. Non-mechanical bindings generally hold together pages that have

use. And longer runs, especially of books, graduate to commercial perfect binding. The list that follows indicates how some of those interviewed solved the binding question. To learn more about their individual projects, use the index to refer to their mentions in the first section.

- Bill Coate of Madera, CA, says, "We buy dissertation covers from General Binding Corporation and we have a strip binding machine. It's very simple, and yet, once [the book is] inside that hard cover with the flyleaves and the adhesive and once that jacket comes around it, you can't tell it from a [sewn] book. It will hold together better than a glue bound book."

- Andrea Mayer of Worcester, NY, was able to purchase a spiral binding machine.

- Linda Clifton of Seattle, WA, says, "Any way you bind them is time consuming. Comb binding has the advantage of laying flat when you open it. I don't think it looks as good. It allows you more pages. I remember doing hand stitching, like you do with chapbooks, with thirty sheets folded in half. That one looked nice. I remember us going to a mother's house one time in Ephrata, and she stitched them all on her heavy duty machine. Those were wonderful. They looked great. Another time it didn't get bound at all, it all got stuck in a paper bag."

- Jerry Phillips of the University of Arkansas/Monticello, relates, "We have wallpaper, we paste it on some kind of box, board, whatever; and we use our drills, we use our sewing machines, we stitch it together like that. Mainly the reason I do it that way is so been printed in larger signatures (groups of pages printed in an arrangement of both sides of a large sheet so that, when folded to single-page size and trimmed, they create pages. Signatures run 2, 4, 8, 16, 32, or 64 pages per sheet.

When signatures have been folded, one edge is the spine. Since most books or magazines have multiple signatures, when they are gathered and stacked in proper order, they are called "F & Gs" (folded and gathered). The spine edges are lined up, and binding can begin.

PERFECT BINDINGS

Perfect binding produces the books that we call softcover or paperback. It's the most familiar and economical binding method for publications of more than 60 pages printed in large quantities. As one would expect, there are several perfect binding methods, but all have in common the application of a stiff paper cover using glue applied at the spine. Both books and magazines make use of the method.

The most expensive and durable form of perfect binding is very much like the best hardcover binding, except that the cover is paper. This type is sewn with thread through the spine of each signature (much as staples are used in saddle stitching). These sewn signatures then have hot glue applied at the spines and a cover wrapped on.

Most perfect binding entails notching or grinding the spine folds of all the gathered signatures (so that the glue holds better), applying the hot glue, and wrapping the cover.

Once covers are glued to the spines, the books or magazines are trimmed on the other three sides to remove the folds there and to make the edges even.

SIGNATURE SAMPLES

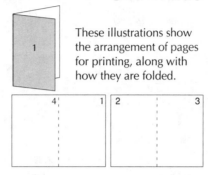

These illustrations show the arrangement of pages for printing, along with how they are folded.

You can often get scrap samples of printed signatures, either folded or unfolded, from local printers. These make great show and tell. Also, any blank piece of paper

can be numbered and folded as shown. The final step is to trim the folds from all edges except the spine.

they'll go into these elementary classes and start producing books immediately with their kids.

- Janis Cramer of Bethany, OK, has her student publishers construct simple hardbound books using the "cardboard that comes from the backs of art tablets." They cover this improvised binder's board with construction paper; then holes are punched with a push pin and the books are sewn together with a carpet needle and thread.

- Pat Muggleston of Madison, CT, teaches her elementary school publishers a "Japanese method or blanket stitch...to sew the books together. Covers are cut from 1/8 inch binder's board and covered with fabric. Cloth binding tape is added to the spine of the books. A title block is attractively mounted on the front cover. A library card and pocket are placed on the inside of the back cover."

- Bob Hughes of Orange Glen HS in Escondido, CA, has his marketing students publish their *NATIONAL FUND RAISING DIRECTORY* with a

157

CASE BINDINGS

Case binding gives us hardcover books. Production follows the same pattern as perfect binding, with most of the same variations from sewn signatures to cased perfect bound.

The stack of signatures (or book block) is put inside a case which may be manufactured of special paperboard, plastic, or leather. When cased with paperboard, the outside is usually finished with some other material, such as cloth, plastic, or leather.

The highest quality case binding uses sewn signatures. Case binding may also be used to give a fancier finish to a book bound by another method, such as side stitching or ordinary perfect binding.

Other finishing techniques are used to add a touch of artistry and quality. These include special endpapers glued to the inside of the case and braided bands of cloth at the top and bottom of the spine that are known as head or foot bands. There are variations on the casing theme that impart a special look, such as round or square backs and fancy dust jackets.

158

OTHER BINDINGS

Binding methods have remained fairly constant, but there are recent innovations that create useful compromises between mechanical and perfect bindings. One of these creates a book that opens flat like a mechanically bound volume but with a cost closer to that of a perfect bound one and construction similar to a case bound book.

saddle-stitched binding. Ten thousand copies printed and bound in school print shop.

- Diane Goddard of Yarmouth, MN, is a parent volunteer: "In the publishing center we have the paper that they use to type on and cardboard …[for]…bookcovers, which are made by volunteers and covered with wallpaper or contact paper. Sometimes the children like plain white covers so they can decorate their own. We have **dental floss** to sew the books with,…stencils to do any kind of correcting,…construction paper that …[backs]…the paper that is typewritten and folded. So you have typewritten pages and a page of construction paper sewn together, then rubber cemented to the cardboard cover. It's really hand sewn."

- Through the Center for Book Arts in New York City, Cheryl Shackleton taught a workshop in bookmaking for high school students. Three book structures were taught (accordion, single section pamphlet, and concertina).
  - Home school teacher Susan Richman of Kittanning, PA, published WRITING FROM HOME a 384 page anthology of writings by home school students across the US. The book was commercially printed in both hardcover and perfect bound editions.
  - Janis Cramer of Bethany, OK, says, "When they are through …we have a knot-tying ceremony. They get…a standing ovation from everyone in the room."

Writing from Home

A Portfolio of Homeschooled Student Writing

Susan Richman

Careers options: printing & binding

Printers learn their craft either through apprenticeships or by training in schools. The possibilities range from the fairly simple operation of small printing presses, such as those used in quick-print shops, to the highly skilled operation of technically sophisticated 4-color presses, such as those used in the production of museum catalogs.

Since more documents, not less, are being published each year, it's likely that employment in printing will remain stable or increase. The countervailing weight to increases in printing jobs is the need for fewer printers to produce the same quantity of work from more automated presses. It's also the case that more advanced technologies are changing press operators into computer operators.

Because bindery equipment is so specialized, only large printers have their own. Most bindery work is done by businesses that do only that. Classroom publishers will gain an appreciation for the work that goes into finishing a book by touring a local bindery. And students interested in working in binderies should know that, except for artistic bindings, the trade is learned on the job. On the level of craft, binding techniques can be learned in art schools and institutes.

Printing and binding use complex machinery and electronic equipment. Mechanics, electricians, and computer technicians are all employed to keep everything running smoothly. And, as one would expect, the industry always needs people to sell services, supervise the production processes, and do other types of production labor.

Careers are now available in...
Writing
Publishing
Editing
Graphic arts
Photography
Printing
Binding
Bookselling
Marketing
and more...

159

There have been many arguments over the relative merits of justifying both margins of text blocks. Some hold that ragged right makes it easier for the reader to mark his or her place, generally. Others maintain that there's no real difference, except with unusually long lines of text. But all would agree that trying to fully justify lines that are short in relationship to the type size leads to awkward word and letter spacing. Careful use of hyphens

There have been many arguments over the relative merits of justifying both margins of text blocks. Some hold that ragged right makes it easier for the reader to mark his or her place, generally. Others maintain that there's no real difference, except with unusually long lines of text. But all would agree that trying to fully justify lines that are short in relationship to the type size leads to awkward word and letter spacing. Careful use of hyphens can help.

There have been many arguments over the relative merits of justifying both margins of text blocks. Some hold that ragged right makes it easier for the reader to mark his or her place, generally. Others maintain that there's no real difference, except with unusually long lines of text. But all would agree that trying to fully justify lines that are short in relationship to the type size leads to awkward word and letter spacing. Careful use of hyphens can help.

There have been many arguments over the relative merits of justifying both margins of text blocks. Some hold that ragged right makes it easier for the reader to mark his or her place, generally. Others maintain that there's no real difference, except with unusually long lines of text. But all would agree that trying to fully justify lines that are short in relationship to the type size leads to awkward word and letter spacing. Careful use of hyphens can help.

There have been many arguments over the relative merits of justifying both margins of text blocks. Some hold that ragged right makes it easier for the reader to mark his or her place, generally. Others maintain that there's no real difference, except with unusually long lines of text. But all would agree that trying to fully justify lines that are short in relationship to the type size leads to awkward word and letter spacing. Careful use of hyphens can help.

Marketing & distribution

After everything that goes into production, it may not seem like building a publication is the easy part. But for anyone deeply involved in publishing, distribution and marketing are the crux of the matter — and the more difficult part, simply because these areas are less predictable and mechanical. Publishing, after all, means to make public.

That's easy if the intended public is small and local or easily defined. Nonfiction generally has such an advantage, since it is directed to an audience that can be identified — perhaps even by name. It becomes complex when that public is scattered and large. Imagine the marketing problems that face a publisher with a new novel by a previously unknown author. Who will want it? If the subject or genre is narrow, that will help. Mystery readers or lovers of romances can be expected to go to certain bookstores or read particular magazines. But those potential readers are still scattered all over the country and the world, and they have thousands of other similar books to choose from — many by better known authors. So, you can see the challenge.

MARKETING

Marketing and sales go together, but are not quite the same. Marketers identify the potential audience and learn as much about it as possible. They then work with sales people to create marketing programs that will get as many of the potential buyers as possible to know about the publication and to think about it when they want something to read. Sales people take advantage of what marketing has done to get bookstores, wholesalers, magazine distributors, newsstands, and others to stock the book or periodical so that readers will have it as a choice.

Marketers might emphasize getting the publication directly into the hands of readers by mail promotions or through specialty catalogs. Someone with a different, but related, product could be convinced to use the publication in a promotion, i.e., a book of dog stories can be ordered at a special price by clipping a coupon from a box of dog food.

Floss to Gloss

☛ **MARKETING SUGGESTIONS.** If your classroom publishing project is **a directory** to student services near the school, it has a natural, easily identified market. If your project is an anthology of **oral histories** of the elderly in the neighborhood around the school, the potential public is different, but it's still pretty easy to target, though a publication like this might generate interest elsewhere among people interested in history. But if your project is to publish **short stories and poetry** by students from your area and from a sister city in another country, the potential audience suddenly becomes much larger, less easily described, and more difficult to reach.

☛ **MARKET RESEARCH.** A classroom publishing project could have certain students research and describe the prospective audience. They would present this material to the editorial staff and the designers so that the tone of the publication and its presentation fits the market. These same students might then be the sales force that creates a promotional campaign directed to the audience — or to others who might distribute or sell the publication.

For instance, if a student publication lists local resources, the sales and marketing staff might arrange with local real estate agents to buy copies that they can give to new families moving into the area.

☛ **PUBLICITY** can be frustrating. It may seem that no one is listening — or even cares. As with advertising, publicity

Even the most rarefied literary magazines engage in marketing and sales. They may not be driven editorially by their markets, as are many commercial publications, but their editors and publishers will know who their readers are and what they like. Most publishers want audiences (and sales) at least large enough to justify the effort and expense of producing the books or magazines.

PUBLICITY

Publicity takes many forms, but its essence is letting potential readers know of a publication's existence and availability. If this is done properly, it dovetails with advertising and reviews. Publishers who can afford it hire publicists — professionals who specialize in promoting publications.

Publicity is not effective if the market is misunderstood. Just as a publication ought to be directed to an identifiable audience, so should publicity.

Publicity can be generated by creating an event associated with the publication or by associating the publication with an event.

The best publicity is often the least expensive. Sometimes

A PUBLICITY EXAMPLE

You have just published a student cookbook.

- *Mail press releases to the editors of newspaper living sections or education editors, rather than to the book reviewers.*
- *Send information to periodicals interested in student publications.*
- *Send information to periodicals interested in anything on cooking, health, or diet.*
- *If the recipes derived from student interviews with their grandparents, publicity would also go to periodicals targeted to the elderly.*
- *If the cookbook is for holidays, then every holiday is a new opportunity for publicity.*

---

calls for persistence and repetition, in the same way that some of us need two alarms in the morning. The trick is to look for the best angle for each of your publicity targets. Then don't let up. Sell the newsworthiness. The timeliness. The topicality.

Sometimes, the publication itself is a newsworthy event — the press loves stories of students doing unusual or exciting projects.

- Donna Clovis of Princeton, NJ, got attention for her student publishers. "Three students and myself are appearing on cable TV...each Thursday in May to discuss poetry and the publication process. We are very excited!" She was also photographed for the local newspaper with six of her ESL students whose poetry was accepted for publication in THE ACORN, a children's magazine.

- Mick Fedullo of Pryor, MT, notes, "We did the centennial calendar...photographs of kids...three or four poems for every month. First we got some publicity through a Billings newspaper, THE GAZETTE. An article was done on the book. ...they started getting flooded with requests. In Phoenix, three Pima kids recited their poems for an evening TV news broadcast."

- Michelle Takenishi of Honolulu, HI, invited local TV news and newspaper reporters to their authors' tea to celebrate publication of her middle school students' books.

- Ken Schmidt of Death Valley, CA, announces new publications with press releases and gets interviews on TV and radio news.

161

Your Letterhead

NEWS RELEASE
Date

For Immediate Release
Contact: Your name
             Your phone

Strong lead sentences make news releases more effective. Let
the first sentence position your publication as a solution to a
problem or as an answer to a need. Newsworthiness.
Mention the names of the book, author, and publisher.

A news release should answer the who, what, where, when,
and why news questions. Who will be interested and why?
What is it about? When was it published? Why was it done?
The information must "sell" the editor on the importance
and timeliness of your publication.The credentials of the
author(s) will help develope human interest.

Ideally, this release should require only one page. It should
be typed, double spaced, and on letterhead, if possible.
When practical, it should be personalized to the editor.

The final information should contain the price and
availability details. Be sure to include your address.

Publication's title
Author(s)
Size, cover style, and binding
ISBN or ISSN
Publication date
Price

# # #
(signifies the end)

162

it's word-of-mouth, or maybe a mention in print or on television or radio that comes directly from a press release.
Whatever it is that does the trick, it will vary from one publication to the next, from one locale to the next.

And one more thing: be sure the publications are available before the publicity hits.

REVIEWS

Reviews are a great source of publicity, but they're not so
easy to get because there are many new books and magazines, but few reviewers. If the general rules for getting publicity are followed, though, there's a good chance of getting
some. And once you've gotten one, it can be included in the
next publicity packet to help get others.

Since it can be costly to send a lot of books or magazines
blindly out in search of reviews, careful selection of poten-

☞ Book reviewers may not be **THE
MOST LIKELY REVIEWERS**. It is often an
editor or publisher or writer who happens
to be interested in your subject, so try to
find such people or publications.

Reviews are absolutely worth the effort,
whether to sell the publication or to reward
students with notice and feedback. Some
media solicit reviews by students, while
others don't care who writes them, or they
assign publications to their own people.
Here are some likely ones.

- *SCHOOL LIBRARY JOURNAL*
- *PUBLISHERS WEEKLY*
- *LIBRARY JOURNAL*
- *ALA BOOKLIST*
- *SMALL PRESS*
- *HORN BOOK*
- Regional or state publications of
  Councils of Teachers of English (and
  other disciplines)
- *WILSON LIBRARY BULLETIN*
- *THE BOOK REPORT*
- *MIDWEST BOOK REVIEW*
- *BLOOMSBURY REVIEW*
- *HUNGRY MIND REVIEW*
- *WRITER'S NW*
- Review groups and lists for state and
  regional school librarians
- State library review committees
- *VOYA*
- *THE SCOOP, A CHILDREN'S BOOK REVIEW
  NEWSLETTER FOR BOOKSTORES & THEIR CUS-
  TOMERS*

☞ **ADVERTISING** was seldom part of
the projects we surveyed, since most depended on easily accessible audiences:
other students, school and public libraries,
relatives, or a few local bookstores and
businesses. Limited ads appeared in school
newspapers.

Advertising makes sense when the po-

BEFORE PLACING ADS

- *Establish a budget for advertising.*
- *Consider alternatives to paid advertising i.e., trades.*
- *Study those that others have placed in the same publications and ask which of them appeal to you or your class.*
- *Ask which have stayed in over many issues; this is usually a sign of effectiveness.*
- *Request a media kit (rate and circulation information) so you can assess the actual cost of reaching readers.*
- *Determine the size ad you can afford to repeat in at least three consecutive issues.*

tial review media makes sense. Many publishers send information and an invitation to request a review copy. Even when a publication takes a copy, that's no guarantee the book will be reviewed.

As with any publicity, it's only useful if the interested readers can find the publication. If it may not be in most bookstores, reviewers should be told how it can be ordered.

ADVERTISING

Advertising is both art and science. It can also be quite expensive and should almost never be used alone for publicity. But when integrated into a complete marketing plan, it can make a big difference in sales.

As expected, ads need to be carefully targeted. And there has to be a budget so that priorities can be set. One of advertising's rules: repetition is essential; it's better to place a series of small ads than to buy one or two large ones.

Ads must be well-designed, since they have incredibly little time to get and hold the attention of readers. When budgets allow, advertising is designed, written, and placed by professionals. Low-budget publications must rely on their own resources. In such cases, it helps if successful ad campaigns done by others are imitated.

tential audience is beyond personal reach or the project is a commercial, as well as a literary, exercise. It must be approached judiciously, but it can be an excellent training ground for students.

Based on its previous popularity, Ken Schmidt of Death Valley, CA, plans to "advertise his students' book in the newspaper." Bob Hughes of Escondido, CA, teaches marketing, so it's logical that his students advertise their NATIONAL FUND RAISING DIRECTORY, though they do so through mailers, rather than display ads.

☞ **AWARDS** not only provide great publicity opportunities, they enhance the self-esteem of the students involved.

Local printers and booksellers will know of trade and industry honors. And there are lists of competitions and awards in directories like LITERARY MARKET PLACE (LMP) and publications like LIBRARY JOURNAL and PUBLISHERS WEEKLY.

Announce awards to all the media targeted for previous publicity, as well as to any new ones that seem appropriate. Include a photo of the book and the presentation of the award (if one is available).

There are several ways to track down possible awards. First, any professional organization with a relationship to the project or to the subject of the project should be approached. These might be councils of teachers of English, social science, art, history, etc. And they may be anything from local to national. Directories like LITERARY MARKET PLACE have lists of awards.

☞ When you can identify potential readers, marketing by mail becomes one of the most effective means. Good sources for donated **MAILING LISTS** exist in most

PROMOTIONAL MAILERS

One sure fire source for a mailer is the cover of the publication. At print time, pay the printer to run as many extra covers as you'll need and can afford, but with nothing printed on the back. Then go to a local printer, or use the press in your school, to print targeted copy on the back (leave space for an address label and postage).

For a book of normal trade dimensions (around 6" x 9"), this results in an appealing postcard. Larger publications may require a separate printing of the cover reduced to post-card size, or the cover will have to be sent in an envelope, raising the expense. However, the oversized sheets may make excellent insertions in someone else's publication or mailing.

This method is effective because the recipient sees the attractive cover immediately and is less likely to treat it like junk mail.

Awards

An award is a wonderful occasion for publicity, and publicity can do nothing but help.

For almost every type of publication there is at least one award category. Usually there are many. They range from recognition of the value of the project to awards for quality of production. A publication can be recognized as the "Best of Category by Classroom Publishers," "Finest Example Since July of a Local History in Our State," "Best Cover Design," "Best Use of Type in a Trade Format Publication," "Regional Booksellers Selection of the Year," and on and on.

After receiving awards, publishers often have a stick-on seal made that shows the award. These are put on the covers of the books.

communities. These may be the membership lists of organizations or the client lists of businesses. If your project is seen as a worthy cause, it's not hard to get the use of such lists. Alternatively, many groups, especially those devoted to community service, will gladly include your mailing piece with their own. Even a local newspaper may be willing to do the same. And we've all opened utility bills to have an assortment of ads fall out, so don't overlook that possibility — they might print it, too.

Since different audiences need different approaches, design one or more mailing pieces. Besides using the publication's cover as a mailer, attractive leaflets and brochures can be part of the project. During the project development, have everyone collect such promotional pieces from other sources — no matter what they promote. These can be studied for ideas.

☞ **ANY OPPORTUNITY TO PROMOTE.** While television is tougher to break into, it's worth the effort. Morning talk shows should be approached, and it doesn't hurt to contact the news director. One good interview or news story will be worth its weight in gold — just remember to tell the viewers how to order.

☞ Another way to use **STICK-ON LABELS** is to apply one that says "Local Authors" or "A Special Project of Your School."

☞ One author we know successfully promoted her new book to reviewers by sending with review materials a tin of fresh, homemade cookies. The book had nothing to do with food, but reviewers paid attention to this **UNUSUAL DEVICE** and reviewed the book. Imagine how effective this would be for a student-published cookbook.

SPECIAL MAILINGS

Using the mail to promote a book makes great sense if the audience is easily identified. The important thing is to select mailing lists carefully. Naturally, the best list is one comprised of previous buyers, and most publishers maintain such in-house data bases. Lists can also be purchased from a wide variety of sources, including brokers who resell and compile special lists, and there are consultants who design and manage direct mail campaigns. Recently, direct mail has replaced space advertising for many publishers of books. Magazines have long used this technique successfully.

OTHER PR OPPORTUNITIES

A surprisingly accessible medium for promotion is radio. Local stations, especially talk-radio, are constantly looking for people to interview. Anything with a unique slant will be newsworthy. Television is less accessible than radio, but many local talk shows regularly feature authors and books — generally around topical issues. Local public broadcasting affiliates are a good bet, sometimes sending an interesting story national.

☞ Other **GIVEAWAYS** can be effective, too. Bookmarks, small postcards, buttons, and other imprintable items can inexpensively keep your publication's sales alive.

☞ Be creative. **BRAINSTORM** with the project participants to come up with as many ways to associate the publication with other people's lives as you can. You'll be amazed at the innovative ways a book or magazine can be marketed.

165

DISTRIBUTION

How do you get publications to market, even after the marketing campaign is history? There's no easy answer. But an understanding of how this part of the industry works will provide insight.

First, there are levels of distribution from narrowly local to international. Second, there are almost as many specialists in distribution as their are specialty publications. Effective distribution, whatever it might be, makes your publication available to the right audience.

Every savvy publisher looks at a new title and asks, "Where should this be sold?" Most of us will immediately think of bookstores, but a surprising number of books will not be distributed there. They may be so specialized that no bookstore wants them, or the publisher may decide that the hassle and expense of selling through bookstores isn't worth it, so other ways to distribute are found.

Signatures from Big Sky is a Montana student literary/art magazine (8 ½" x 11", saddle-stitched) published by the Montana Assn for Gifted & Talented Education, Montana Assn of Teachers of English & Language Arts, and the Montana Art Education Assn.

☞ Step back from your own project to evaluate its needs. You may not need or want to use **TRADITIONAL DISTRIBUTION**, and you may have neither need nor desire to distribute outside your locale.

A classroom publishing project should have immediate appeal near the school. Interest diminishes with distance — all kinds. So, bookstores and other retailers nearby can probably be approached individually. Friends, families, and neighbors can likewise be contacted in person. But if you want distribution beyond the geographic area easily reached by foot or car, other means will be necessary.

☞ Here's how some of the teachers we interviewed handle distribution.

- Mel Jones teaches 7th-8th grade composition and computers (*comp & comp?*) in suburban Philadelphia, where he's undertaking a new project with his students. They will produce magazines to be placed in offices throughout the community: doctors, barbers, beauty salons, etc.
- In Worcester, NY, Andrea Mayer's student publishers extended distribution beyond the immediate school/parent audience by selling THE COMMUNITY & ITS BUSINESSES through the Worcester Historical Society. It is also used by a local realtor to acquaint new residents with the town.
- Homeschooler Sarah-Kate Giddings of Rochester, MA, markets her monthly magazine, *Rainbow*, to other homeschoolers by subscription sales — $6/yr.
- Sondra Nachbar, Bronx HS of Science, has distributed the annotated bibliographies published by her students free to all NYC high schools.

WHOLESALERS

Wholesalers buy books and magazines from publishers and sell them to bookstores, newsstands, and other retailers. Rarely do they market books; instead, they take orders and fulfill them. They are convenient for booksellers because they stock titles by a lot of publishers, so only one order needs to be written.

While there are some national wholesalers, there are many that are regionally based. Larger companies may carry thousands of titles, but most specialize in some way.

Most wholesalers who accept publications from small publishers will only do so on consignment, which means they pay only after a sale is made. Since they sell to retailers, they want a large discount — from 50–60 percent of the retail price.

DISTRIBUTORS

BOOK DISTRIBUTORS

Distributors differ from wholesalers in that they usually represent fewer publishers, and they actively try to sell those they handle. They do this by hiring sales representatives who visit the booksellers in their territories several times each year. With few exceptions, distributors don't represent publishers with only one or two titles.

They also take even larger discounts than wholesalers, but that's because they bear all the costs of selling (including to the wholesalers), warehousing, shipping, etc.

Some distributors are highly specialized and may take a single title because it fits so well with the rest.

PERIODICAL DISTRIBUTORS

This category includes specialized operations as well as the large businesses that service the magazine and paperback racks in chain stores, usually in one area. They're also known as IDs, which stands for Independent Distributors. Like wholesalers, they take a hefty discount.

SALES REPS

Most sales reps are employees of distributors, though they may also work directly for one or more publishers. They travel their territories introducing new titles to their custom-

• According to Project Coordinator Shirley Olson, SIGNATURES FROM BIG SKY, a statewide lit/art mag by Montana students, is "sent to all school libraries in Montana (750) with the aid of private grants." They plan on pushing for a solid subscription base.

☞ Ask bookstore owners and librarians for the names of **WHOLESALERS AND DISTRIBUTORS**. There are also lists published in LITERARY MARKET PLACE, PUBLISHERS WEEKLY, and elsewhere. Contact those who seem best as early as possible in the project. That way you can plan for things they could demand — like bar codes, ISBNs, competitive pricing, steep discounts, and slow payments. A school project may be able to negotiate better than usual terms. Give it a try.

☞ In a particular locale, an independent distributor (ID), a general trade distributor, or a rep may want to help with a classroom publishing project's **DISTRIBUTION**. They are more likely to increase your audience than wholesalers, since the latter are really only order takers. IDs and distributor's reps actually go into the stores. IDs often determine which books or magazines will go on the racks, while reps make presentations of the titles they represent to the stores' buyers.

NOTES/IDEAS _____

USE THESE ISLANDS OF WHITE FOR YOUR ADDITIONS, AND LET US KNOW ABOUT 'EM TOO.

167

ers, checking shelves to be sure nothing they sell is out of stock, and taking orders. Sales representatives know both their lines of books and the types of customers served by the stores. This knowledge allows them to make intelligent suggestions to the stores and give feedback to the publishers.

BOOKSTORES

We all think of bookstores when we think of books, but there's no way a bookstore can stock all the books in print. So, bookstores specialize to one degree or another, and selling to them means knowing what each one wants. That's easy if it's part of the title (Murder By the Book), but tougher if it's not. Publishers use catalogs, reviews, direct mail, trade shows, advertisements in trade publications, and distribution networks to alert appropriate bookstores to their titles.

The discount that bookstores expect is around 40 percent. And they reserve the right to return unsold copies for a credit or refund.

☞ Local **BOOKSTORES** should be willing to sell your publication. Beyond your community, you'll need to approach those most likely to be interested.

In every region of the country there is a **BOOKSELLERS ASSOCIATION** that keeps a list of all the stores, who owns them, manages them, and their specialties. They often have special projects and awards that you should know about, and they will likely have a newsletter where they'd be happy to announce your project.

Bookstores may only take your publications on consignment, but even if they pay up front, they usually reserve the right to return unsold copies later for a refund.

Several of the surveyed projects found local booksellers receptive and supportive.

- Carolyn Tragesser of Moscow, ID, after discovering two willing stores, pursued placement of her junior high publishers' literary magazine in others: "I took some of the writing club kids on a field trip downtown, because there was a bookfair where an illustrator and an author spoke. Two bookstores were there and offered to carry URSA MAJOR. So then we went around to all the bookstores in town."

- CORRIDORS, published by David Schaafsma's Detroit, MI, students was sold by a small, regional bookstore chain, Borders.

- Not part of our survey, but worth mentioning, is BOOKS WE LOVE BEST: A UNIQUE GUIDE TO CHILDREN'S BOOKS (Foghorn Press, San Francisco). It's nationally distributed by the small press that published it. This compilation of book reviews by students was part of an accredited publishing program done with the San Francisco Unified School District.

ISSUE # 8 HALLOWE'EN 1991

RED ALDER TRUNK
The Magazine for Young Writers

"Nuts, say you?" cried young Angus; "then there you are like us of the North. For sure Hallow E'en is Nutcrack Night with us ..."

source: "The Little Donna Juana" - A.D. 1340
An October story of the Moors of Spain and Lord James of Douglas.

Red Alder Trunk is edited and published by home schooling educators/ publishers Thea and Dan Chapman and their daughter Liane of Vancouver, British Columbia. The format is 8 ½" x 11", saddle-stitched.

Book Clubs

Clubs are a terrific way to distribute a lot of books quickly. They do highly targeted marketing, mostly by mail, and they generally buy books outright for a huge discount — up to 80 percent. But they do all the work, and it often pays a publisher to get the extra publicity the club generates, despite the low profits. Some publishers create their own clubs based on a catalog of books around a subject, often including complementary titles from other publishers.

Direct Sales

Small publishers — and many large ones — swear by direct sales. Payment is immediate, there are few or no discounts, and there are virtually no returns. There is also direct contact with readers, which helps with future marketing. On the other hand, the cost of promoting can eat deeply into each sale, and there are all the worries associated with invoicing, shipping, etc.

Not only can individuals be sold to directly, but libraries, school, and businesses frequently buy by mail.

Subscriptions & Prepublication Sales

Once a publication has been conceived, it is often sold in advance of printing. If it is a serial, subscriptions are solicited. Both prepublication sales and subscriptions generally rely on discounts as incentives to those who order and pay early. This provides a way of estimating how many to print, and it can even pay for the printing in advance. When publishers have sales reps calling on stores, orders are taken months in advance for books not yet in print, but payment is not made until delivery.

Event Sales

All sorts of special occasions and events serve as opportunities to get a publication out. Publishers attend the trade shows appropriate to their publications — everything from international booksellers conventions and shows to county fairs. There are plenty of writers' groups around the country that have regular conferences and will likely be supportive, offering a space for sales. Other professional meetings can be productive, too. Conferences of teachers, for instance, always have a vendors section.

☞ In classroom publishing situations, it's unlikely there will be **BOOK CLUB** possibilities. But with so many super specialized clubs, it could be that your project can find a natural home.

☞ **DIRECT SALES** offer the most flexibility and the greatest opportunities, especially for classroom publishers. That can be seen from the earlier discussion of direct marketing techniques. Sales can be as personal and direct as a visit by some of those involved with the project.

Most projects that involve sales are directed to other students. To get the word out, announcements are made over the intercom, posters put around the school, and notices printed in the school paper. This sort of direct marketing is often seen as a campaign to generate excitement about the publication.

- Phyllis Rude of Anchorage, AK, directs the publication of the annual *Pen of the Panther* by her Mears Junior High students: "Copies are sold for a nominal $1 during lunch periods during the last two weeks of school. Announcements over the intercom, in the school newsletter, and in the hallways **herald the big day** when the book is distributed."

- *Red Alder Trunk*, a magazine for young writers, published in Vancouver, BC, by a homeschooler family, is 22 pages of contributions by writers of all ages. Says parent/publisher Dan Chapman, "The project receives no outside grants or support. It is **subscriber supported** at $12 yearly."

- Carolyn Tragesser of Moscow, ID, says of her junior high project, "We had posters plastered around the school to advertise our sale. ...We

This nationally marketed directory from the students of Bob Hughes in Escondido, CA, uses a simple saddle-stitched binding. The cover is a standard coated stock. All copy is laser print.

NATIONAL FUND RAISING DIRECTORY

IDEAS----SOURCES----ADDRESSES
FOR ANY GROUP THAT DOES FUND RAISING
SCHOOLS--CHURCHES--CLUBS

AMERICA'S ONLY COMPLETE LISTING
OF COMPANIES IN THE
FUND RAISING FIELD. HUNDREDS
OF IDEAS WITH NAMES, ADDRESSES,
AND TELEPHONE NUMBERS OF
EXACTLY WHOM TO CONTACT

PUBLISHED BY THE ORANGE GLEN HIGH SCHOOL
CHAPTER OF THE DISTRIBUTIVE EDUCATION
CLUBS OF AMERICA (DECA)

$5.00

Fund Raising Projects

Sometimes it's possible for a publisher to associate a particular title with someone else's project. Perhaps the publication can be sold by an organization as a way to raise funds.

Direct Mail Sales

Direct mail marketing has already been mentioned, it's worth reemphasizing that this is an excellent way to sell. But only if the mailings are selective and repetitive.

promoted it in school ...We sent out letters to all of the parents of students who had submissions in it and to the staff members. we said, 'If you want to be guaranteed your copy then prepay.' We did that to find out how many to print, and then we doubled that number."

- Carol Lange, of Alexandria, VA, takes another **prepublication sale** approach with students at Thomas Jefferson High School for Science and Technology: "We sell the publications in a package. For $40 they get the yearbook and the spring supplement to the yearbook, the magazine for the arts and sciences, the science journal, and all issues of the newspaper."

- Bob Hughes of Escondido, CA, has a six-year-old project that relies entirely on **direct mail sales**. After discussing advertising, his marketing club publishers plan and carry out a direct mail campaign to all schools in the United States. They include a form letter and an effective flier for their NATIONAL FUND RAISING DIRECTORY.

☞ Many **SCHOOL AND COMMUNITY EVENTS** can be tapped. At these, a simple booth and display will provide plenty of contact with members of the community.

☞ **FUND RAISING PROJECTS** can work two ways: you can use your publication to raise money for itself, or you can associate with some worthy community cause, donating a portion of your sales to it.

☞ If you use **DIRECT MAIL** without bookstore backup, mention that the publication is only available through you.

Careers options: marketing and distribution

Careers are now available in...

Writing
Publishing
Editing
Graphic arts
Photography
Printing
Binding
Bookselling
Marketing
and more...

The striking number of ways publications are promoted and sold indicates a like number of career opportunities. Of course, smaller publishers combine many marketing and sales functions, but large ones employ entire departments devoted to selling. And within these departments there are roles for writers, editors, artists, sales people, direct mail specialists, publicists, and others. Training is often on-the-job, but there are numerous schools with programs in sales and marketing.

Many people involved in selling publications, especially books, come to their jobs through a deep love of literature. They may not be writers or editors, but they enjoy playing important roles in the publishing process. Bookstores hire entry-level clerks, preferring people with some knowledge of books. Traveling sales reps quite often have strong backgrounds in the subjects of the books they sell, i.e., biology, history, political science, or literature.

Publishing seems unusual among industries in how freely people move from one role to another over the course of a career. To give a sense of this, here's the story of Debbie Garman, publicity manager for Timber Press, which specializes in horticultural books.

Debbie got a degree in Latin American studies before becoming a clerk in a B. Dalton bookstore. She moved to a small independent bookstore as its mass market book manager, then to the role of book department manager in a medium-size chain store specializing in office supplies and books. Next, she became a district sales manager for Dell Publishing, working on commission and covering four western states. She traveled a lot, enjoying it for awhile ("I wouldn't have survived as long selling shoes or sardines."), but finally moving on to Crown Publishers in San Francisco. Crown sent her on the road to sell in Northern California, Idaho, and Montana. After a stint doing that, Debbie wanted a job that stayed put and she became the trade book buyer for the Reed College Bookstore in Portland, Oregon, a job she found challenging because of student and faculty pressure to select "politically correct books."

She eventually left that job to become the executive coordinator of the Pacific Northwest Booksellers Association, which allowed her to work from home for the next four years. This job kept her in touch with bookselling, but at too great a distance, so when the publicity manager's position at Timber Press became available, she took it.

Debbie Garman's story is not unusual. It indicates that in the publishing process, one does not have to get locked into choices. There is no penalty for trying new areas. From interviews with Debbie and others, it's safe to say that marketing and distribution are experiencing fewer changes than other areas of publishing. Technology is enhancing jobs rather than eliminating them. Still, anyone thinking of a sales related career ought to have good basic math, language, and computer skills. Debbie recommends the following: retail sales background, good language skills, computer skills (especially desktop publishing), curiosity, and a fascination with books.

Besides staff jobs, some freelance opportunities exist in marketing. Publicists, direct mail specialists, and consultants in all areas commonly have their own businesses and sell their services to several or many publishers. However, most of these folks have acquired solid backgrounds inside the industry before hanging out their independent shingles.

171

Career options: other

Careers are now available in...

Writing
Publishing
Editing
Graphic arts
Photography

Printing
Binding
Bookselling
Marketing
and more...

Working in a world of words and ideas does not have to mean direct employment in writing, publishing, or bookselling. Teachers of all sorts — but especially teachers of writing, English, and journalism — are intimately involved with books and other publications. Those who have gained practical expertise in the field often become teachers of the next generation of computer designers, desktop publishers, graphic artists, printers, and publishers.

Librarians are obviously essential to the whole process, too. They have been important since the first libraries, but never more so than today, when electronic technologies are dramatically changing how we store and retrieve all information.

Other areas that draw on many of the same editorial skills as publishing include advertising and public relations positions in government and industry. Technical skills, such as printing, are widely needed by business and government, while artistic ability can lead to careers that have little to do with publishing or words.

One growing area that serves publishing, graphic arts, and advertising businesses is service bureaus. As we've mentioned, many publishers contract for services they cannot do themselves. This may be because of a lack of expertise, time, expensive equipment — or for some other reason. Service bureaus have emerged to provide a range of design and pre-

press production services — typesetting, scanning, mechanicals, high-resolution film and graphics, publication design, and even writing. Most specialize in a few areas, but they offer excellent opportunities for anyone with strong graphic arts skills and computer savvy. The importance of such "middleman" operations is the result of rapidly changing technologies, which have increased the need for highly skilled technicians using equipment that's too expensive for individual publishers or businesses.

We asked several service bureau owners what they suggest to anyone wishing to enter the field. Rich and Lin Sanders of L.grafix in Portland, Oregon, are themselves examples of the skills service bureaus seek. Lin was trained in the graphic arts and worked in advertising, and Rich worked as a printer and typesetter before they formed their own business. They advise that mechanical drafting is still a good background for prepress work, as are computer design, desktop publishing, and work on high school publications or in the school print shop. They emphasize getting hands on experience. "Don't wait until you've graduated," says Lin. "Apprentice to a printer or a service bureau or a publisher." People skills, they say, are extremely important, and business skills are a real plus.

...you can play with type...you can play with type...you can play with type...you can play with type...you can play with type...you can turn it into crazy shapes...you can play with type...you can play with type...

172

Chapter 7

FUNDING STUDENT PROJECTS

As we've seen, there are projects suited to virtually any budget. In this section we'll consider some of the ways projects can be funded, and we'll look at how several of those we surveyed handled this issue. Frankly, we see too many publishing programs heavily subsidized by the teachers who organize them. Other sources need to be developed. And with that goes convincing administrations on all levels of the value of student publishing, its contributions to literacy, cultural awareness, and the self-esteem of participants.

Ideally, necessary monies would simply be available, but we know that's a dream. Instead, we must organize this aspect of the process just as we do any other.

There are so many positive aspects to classroom publishing that it should be easy to select the most appropriate ones for a given group of prospective supporters. Your list may be even longer, but the following come to mind: literacy, democratic values (freedom and responsibility of the press), cultural development, whole language learning, writing across the curriculum, businesses skills, career training, personal development, research skills, and problem solving.

Just as all student participants must be recognized, giving credit to sponsors is simply good manners.

Parental support

When the classroom publishing project is modest, resulting in one or a few copies of each student's work, the materials at hand will usually do. Even then, though, there can be extraordinary expenses, such as binding materials, copying

Floss to Gloss

☞ *Prairie Winds* is a 12-year-old statewide magazine of the literary and visual arts published by the Black Hills Special Services Cooperative in Spearfish, SD. Unusual in many ways — it publishes both student amateurs and adult professionals as peers — the project has also been unusual in the variety of its funding. It has **SUBSCRIPTIONS, GRANTS, AND GENERAL SALES.** Grants are both public and private. It's been supported by **Citibank** and "jointly by a grant from **South Dakota Arts Council** with funding from the **State Legislature,** the **National Endowment for the Arts,** and the **Bush Foundation** in cooperation with the **Black Hills Special Services Cooperative.**" Sales of a specially commissioned **POSTER** also support the magazine.

☞ *The Claremont Review* of Claremont High School in Victoria, BC, is a perfect bound literary review dedicated to young adult writers, grades 8–12. **PARENTS BOUGHT A LASER PRINTER** and other hardware, even though the publication is not solely for their kids. Bill Stenson, teacher/coeditor, reports that 1,000 copies of the first edition cost $3,300 to print. Money was raised from the **CORPO-**

173

costs, etc. If the school's coffers are empty, the first logical place to turn is parents. But asking individual parents to underwrite materials can be a hardship for some and may cause both parents and students embarrassment. A better approach would be to convince the parent-teachers organization to sponsor the project.

If the project's goal is to print and distribute or sell significant quantities of the publication, the problem changes dramatically. A few dollars here and there is not enough. The need may run to the 100s or 1000s of dollars before anything comes off the press. Some parent groups may be able to afford a large outlay of cash, but most cannot easily do so. It may be that their commitment is to hold fund raising events for this purpose. Or they may form a committee to solicit donations from local businesses and service organizations. Where there is commercial potential for the publications, the initial funding may be viewed as providing seed money, rather than on-going support.

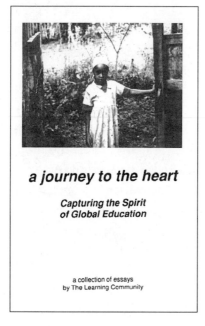

a journey to the heart

Capturing the Spirit
of Global Education

a collection of essays
by The Learning Community

a journey to the heart *was one part of a larger project carried out in 1989–90 by The Learning Community, a special program involving twenty-five students and their teacher, Gary Bacon, in a public high school in Los Altos, California. It was published by Rainbow Bridge of Palo Alto, California.*

Besides raising funds to travel to Kenya and to do this book, the project was able to raise $5,000 extra for service projects while in Africa.

The book is 5 ½" x 8 ½", 136 pages, perfect bound, with a 4-color cover printed on coated stock and finished with a gloss film. Prepress production was handled with a combination of traditional and computer publishing tools, including an IBM compatible computer, a Canon LBP-Mark III Laser Printer, Ventura Publisher page composition software. It was printed offset.

RATE COMMUNITY (recognized in the book), and there were even contributions from some **INDIVIDUALS** whose companies declined to give. **SUBSCRIPTIONS** and — believe it — a cut from certain government supervised **BINGOS** were important revenue sources. After two years of activity, they hope to qualify for a Canada Council **GRANT**.

☛ *Young Voices* is published six times a year in Olympia , WA, providing an outlet for elementary through high school writers. Begun with a **LOAN**, costs are now covered by **ADS** (many), **SUBSCRIPTIONS**, and **GRANTS**. Another sponsorship program invites **INDIVIDUALS, FAMILIES, AND BUSINESSES** to be patrons. The magazine also has a regular, **COMMERCIAL DISTRIBUTOR**.

☛ *Signatures from Big Sky*, the Montana literary/art magazine, is published and **FUNDED BY** the **Montana Association for Gifted & Talented Education**, the **Montana Association of Teachers of English & Language Arts**, and the **Montana Art Education Association**. Support was also garnered from **Liz Claiborne, Artcraft Printers, Montana Office of Public Instruction, Montana Power Company, Montana Magazine**, and the **Great Falls Reading Council**. Their funded budget for 750 copies, plus an ad campaign, was $3,500 in 1992. Other expenses were volunteered by **board members**.

☛ BookWorks, The Academy Elementary School Student Publishing House in Madison, CT, says in their manual on publishing that "**COMMUNITY SUPPORT** for our publishing program has come in many ways. Through the **'Apples for Students'** pro-

Community support

Projects that have strong links with the community stand the best chance of getting its financial support. There are several ways to approach this: donations, in-kind contributions, and loans. And there are a number of groups within most communities who are likely sponsors.

SERVICE CLUBS

Most service clubs are business oriented, so they should readily see the value in sponsoring any project that both enhances literacy and teaches business skills. Those aspects should be emphasized. An interested club can be involved as deeply as it wishes, from simply donating money to giving time and labor. They may take over certain fund raising tasks completely, making their sponsorship an important project of their own.

LOCAL BUSINESSES

Service clubs could be key to involving local businesses, since they draw heavily from that arena for membership. But local enterprises can be contacted directly. Those with some relationship to publishing or public relations should be approached first, but it would be a mistake to limit efforts to them. We recently learned of a school in Boise, ID, that created an "adopt our school" program that involves many business in the immediate area; they contribute cash and both goods and services, when appropriate.

Some projects naturally attract business support. Andrea Mayer's project in Worcester, NY, is an example. Though initial funding came from other sources, THE COMMUNITY AND ITS BUSINESS, touched the lives of many in this small community. With profiles of most of the small businesses in town, project loyalty and cooperation were high. The finished book was presented to the participating businesses in a ceremony at the school, and the book has proved useful to local businesses such as realtors who use it to introduce new people to the community.

gram sponsored by Stop and Shop, a New England grocery chain, we received our computers and laser printer. **Senior citizen volunteers** type our manuscripts through a recently developed town-wide program called STEP: Skills, Talents, Enrichment Program. In addition **parents** help with binding and in the gathering of donated materials."

☞ In Anchorage, Dennis Stovall's program purchased "two new additional... computers last year that were paid for with **PROFITS** from our student newspaper." He also has developed **DONATIONS** and **COMMUNITY SUPPORT**.

☞ Andrea Mayer of Worcester, NY, says her 11th and 12th graders' book, THE COMMUNITY AND ITS BUSINESSES, "was originally stared out of a **GRANT** from the Catskill Regional Teacher Center." The $800 helped set up a publishing center and buy a bookbinding machine.

☞ To fund her first grade publishing company, Charlesmont Publishing, Celeste Stivers wrote a **GRANT** to Baltimore County, her school district, which had a teacher incentive program with $120,000 available. "I did it at the end of the school year and worked on it during the summer," she says. "Timing is important — applying when others might not be applying. I put together a video for the grant, so there was the written part and also the visual. We filmed the teachers. It was like a little show. Ten or twelve people participated in the video and everyone said they would do it [publishing]."

☞ Bill Coate of Madera, CA, is fortunate in having his publishing program included in the **SCHOOL BUDGET**. "It wasn't

Other publications can have similar results. The simple fact that students are so thoroughly engaged — as we've seen they are — in their projects, wins over even reluctant community folks. Some years ago we participated in a project in a destitute mill town that had lost its factory. Kids there faced a bleak future and saw little reason to stay in school. On the streets, they were headed for trouble. The community's elderly were being harassed, and no one was happy. A project was organized to work with a group of kids who'd already slipped through the cracks. Many were barely literate. Most had no writing skills. Few knew how to type. The project was to interview their grandparents' generation (those people they'd been bothering on the streets) about what it had been like dealing with the depression of the 1930s. Local businesses loaned typewriters, cameras, and tape recorders. They donated paper, film, audio tape, pens, and other supplies. Even city government gave support. The result was an astonishing unification of the community, made even more impressive by the acquisition of more than basic skills by the kids. It was a project that not only got support from the community, but supported "community."

We've previously suggested that any businesses related to publishing be contacted as early as possible and invited to participate. Look in the telephone directory for publishers, printers, typesetters, service bureaus, color separators, Velox and PMT services, graphic artists, printers, and binders. Small businesses may have no cash to spare, but many are pleased to come to school to explain their crafts — or they welcome students in their shops, where they can demonstrate their skills. They're also sources for samples, such as color separations, color keys, printed signatures, typesetting, etc.

NATIONAL CORPORATIONS

Many corporations have special funds for supporting community services where they have facilities. Everyone from Xerox to Mervyn's has provided support for student efforts. Sometimes the backing is much needed cash. In other instances, it's in-kind contributions.

In Texas, next to a photocopier plant, a teacher has arranged for student publications to be reproduced on the newest and best of the company's equipment.

The Claremont Review is published twice yearly and is open to submissions from students in grades 8–12 in both Canada and the United States. Initial funding came from a number of sources, including corporate donars, individuals, and a government supervised bingo casino. One thousand copies of the first edition were produced at a cost of $3,300. Subscriptions are also an important source of revenue.

The literary review is 5 ½" x 8 ½" in format, 96 pages, with a four-color cover printed on coated stock and finished with a varnish.

NOTES/IDEAS

USE THESE ISLANDS OF WHITE FOR YOUR ADDITIONS, AND LET US KNOW ABOUT 'EM TOO.

Dennis Stovall's publishing program in Anchorage got needed computers through persistent hustling on his part. After being turned down by several companies, six Kaypro computers arrived at the school.

The fact that a publishing project is part of the curriculum ought to legitimize even first time efforts. Established publications will have samples to show prospective funders. The first step, in either case, is to identify potential donors. Usually, we know who the bigger businesses are because they're so prominent. Our students may well have parents employed with them, which provides a strong hook. But there are probably businesses with a presence regionally or nationally, but not locally, who would support your project if approached with a solid proposal.

To track down likely candidates, the phone book is a beginning, as are any personal contacts or student connections through relatives. Chambers of Commerce have directories. Most states have economic development commissions or departments that compile lists of businesses and industries. Libraries have special directories that cover nations or business types.

Funding with sales

Using sales to fund an appropriate publishing project works best when the publication has a track record and the revenue can be applied to future efforts. However, there are ways to generate cash in advance by selling either subscriptions to a periodical or offering a prepublication special for a book. Both approaches serve additionally as a way of estimating the final press run.

In the chapter on promotion and distribution, sales possibilities were discussed in detail. If your publication will be sold outside the school, consider those options carefully.

PREPUBLICATION SALES

Generally, a prepublication offer has some incentive built into it. It may be a discount, a special edition, a signed copy,

at first. You know, it's amazing how some publicity greases the administrative wheels. We're in rough times now…but they do buy us equipment. For instance, they supplied a Macintosh for me and a Macintosh for each of the other teachers and we have this huge screen. The money that the district spends is pretty much on equipment that could be shifted and used by a lot of other people."

☞ Chris Weber of Portland, OR, got the money to start TREASURES "from an **INHERITANCE** of mine, because I realized we were waiting for non-profit status and I had no real knowledge of grant writing. I spent $10,000 on it. By the second year I had formulated some primitive **GRANT** writing skills. They certainly look primitive to me now. We received somewhere around $22,000 from various organizations. The Collins Foundation was our primary grantor."

☞ Tim Gallagher of the ALBUQUERQUE TRIBUNE, **FUNDS** Nan Elsasser's books, but also provides **MENTORING** for her project and others. "Mainly at the high school and junior high school level," he notes. "Sort of advising. Also giving **AWARDS** to publications — usually weekly or monthly newspapers. At the elementary level we had an interesting experiment last spring where we actually produced a page in our own newspaper with fifth graders. They did it only once, and they were supposed to do it more than that, but the kids are having a hard time keeping it alive.

"I go into the classrooms about once a semester. We've had a lot of fun talking with them about ethics in journalism: actual situations you get into, decisions you have to make. There's also been a lot of an invitation to a publication party, or a bonus item. With student publications, that may not be necessary. But it's important to make it clear to those who buy early when they can expect delivery and that you intend to use their cash in the meanwhile. Prepublication sales can begin quite early and go through several stages, each of which can be seen as a promotional effort that will help even after the publication is available. The stages can be a series of decreasing discounts, so that those buying earliest benefit the most.

Obviously, students, parents, and faculty are prime prospects for prepublication sales. The next likely group includes anyone interested in the subject. This is especially true if the publication has a strong, unifying theme. For instance, if the project involves research into local history, there were probably many people interviewed who would like a copy. Of course, in some projects, those who provided important information will be rewarded with free copies, but most will still be glad to buy one.

SUBSCRIPTIONS

In the world of serials — even those that are infrequent — subscriptions serve the same function as prepublication sales of books: you have money in advance and know roughly how many copies to print. Subscriptions are solicited through direct sales techniques, usually with well organized subscription drives directed to the targeted audience. The incentive to subscribe is normally a lower price per issue than if it were purchased singly — plus there are convenience and guaranteed delivery, often before the publication is available to anyone else.

Fund raising events

Using events to raise money for worthy projects is a time honored tradition, though with publications it may make more sense to sell them. However, this is an excellent way to involve parents in project support. And it's a way to get funds from people who won't buy the publication. The

practical advice too, about what kind of job they're doing on their paper. Usually I get called if they're having any type of a crisis. We've hired a number of them to help in the sports and features area.

"Nan came and saw us and she was looking for people to underwrite the cost of the books. The project really gets to the heart of fighting illiteracy, and once she explained the project to us…**NEWSPAPERS** tend to make a lot of money, and when they do, I think one of the things they ought to do with their profits is put them back into making us a nation of readers. Nan's books cost $300–$400 to print each time, so it costs $1,000 per year. Newspaper groups [such as the American Society of Newspaper Editors] have **FOUNDATIONS** just for literacy.

"I believe that free press and free speech in America still really belong to the people and part of the job of the guardians of the free press is to affect the rest of the populace with that desire to keep things free in this country. Keep us talking to each other. Winston Churchill said that the biggest enemy of a tyrant is a free press. Part of our role is to keep young people aware of just how important these freedoms are."

☞ David Schaafsma, whose project was CORRIDORS in Detroit, puts it succinctly: "Some of the people got really excited hearing about the kinds of things that these kids were doing. I found that I could look like a **FUNDING GENIUS**, because it was such an obviously worthwhile project to do."

☞ A fine example of a statewide publication supported by grants is the annual book of student writing (POPPIES, SUNFLOWERS, BLUEBELLS AND BEGONIAS) sponsored by the range of events and activities is virtually endless — from bake sales to carnivals to raffles. If you've gotten the backing of a club or organization, this may be the means of choice.

Loans

Businesses depend on loans and lines of credit to develop and market new products. A well conceived classroom publishing project that holds a clear potential to repay the money ought to be able to get off the ground with a loan. Loans can be arranged through a variety of sources. We've heard of them being made to projects by local school districts, local businesspeople, teachers, and banks. Depending upon the lender, interest rates can vary from zero to whatever the market will bear. Be sure to include the cost of using the borrowed money in you calculations.

Grants & gifts

Both private and public sources for grants are worth pursuing. Be aware, though, that they often require lengthy application processes and give funds only at certain times of the year. Check with organizations, arts agencies at all levels, and foundations on their granting programs. Many libraries can direct you to lists of grantors, and your state arts commission should be able to provide a list of likely donors. Since grants take so much time, contact grantors early and request not only the application forms and guidelines but a list of previously funded projects. This will help you tailor you approach to each and maximize your chances. You will also find that most grantors are willing to walk you through the application process, telling you what to emphasize.

It's generally the case that grantors would rather provide start up money than constant support. So, the more your grant request looks like a one-time approach, the better it will be received. It's also usual for only a portion of the requested money to be granted, which means that you should not depend on getting the full amount. Instead, ask for a little more than you need and expect less.

Montana Artists in the Schools program. The cost to produce 850 copies was $5.30 each, which was supported by the participating schools, the Montana Arts Council, the Montana State Legislature, and the National Endowment for the Arts.

NOTES/IDEAS _____

USE THESE ISLANDS OF WHITE FOR YOUR ADDITIONS, AND LET US KNOW ABOUT 'EM TOO.

179

Besides grants, donations from individuals can be solicited. Alumni are approachable, if you have access to them. And the business support mentioned above is similar to a grant.

Other funding

Imagination is the only limit on the possibilities. Unfortunately our society has a literacy problem. Fortunately there's serious interest at the moment in improving the situation. That attention can benefit us in our efforts to establish and fund publishing programs in the schools.

We've seen how a variety of projects have been funded or have gotten in-kind support. One method we haven't discussed is the sale of advertising in publications or the resale of mail order merchandise — other books, t-shirts, etc.

High school newspapers sell space, and it's possible to integrate advertising into some other publications, such as literary magazines. It is even possible to develop the sort of discrete advertising that public broadcasting has long been noted for, where sponsors get a modest mention or the display of their logos somewhere in the book or on its cover. This notification may be key to getting support from some sources.

NOTES/IDEAS _____

USE THESE ISLANDS OF WHITE FOR YOUR ADDITIONS, AND LET US KNOW ABOUT 'EM TOO.

Chapter 8

LEGAL & SOCIAL ISSUES OF PUBLISHING

Publishing is a real world activity, just like teaching. And it must fit into the broader scheme of things to succeed — even if its role is iconoclastic. Publishing and the law have a long, intimate relationship in our society. While we prize freedom of speech, we also value individual privacy and freedom from unwarranted public abuse, and these dance around one another in constant motion and tension. The line between legitimate free expression and libelous abuse is fuzzy. But it's important to understand the essential distinctions.

Publishing also involves the ownership and control of intellectual property — the rights of the writers and the rights of the publishers, which are also often a source of tension. But here, the line is more clear. The copyright law is (except for a couple of notable sections) explicit, and most writers work with contracts that state the rights and obligations of all parties. An overview of copyright law is useful to anyone publishing anything.

Related to these issues, but also standing on its own as a major problem in a free society, is censorship. What is society's right to control what citizens may read, view, or publish? Constitutional guarantees not withstanding, censorship is common.

Libel & slander

Libel and slander are areas of law that have grown in importance recently. The difference between them is that libel is published and slander is orally communicated. Here's a short definition:

A statement is libelous if it is false and if it is broadcast or printed so that the person mentioned is held up to public ridicule or contempt, or if the false statement has the effect of injuring the person in his or her business or occupation.

The responsibility to know the truth rests with the writer and publisher, so it's not a defense that one is only repeating what was heard or read elsewhere. Of course, if someone consents to having material published about him- or herself, he or she takes the chance that it won't be pleasant. The consent does not have to be written and signed. Someone allowing an interview for publication has granted the writer the right to quote in context.

But none of this is meant to keep any of us from expressing opinions, though the line dividing opinion from fact is also fuzzy. Just be sure to state the facts on which your opinion is based. Remember that word: FACTS.

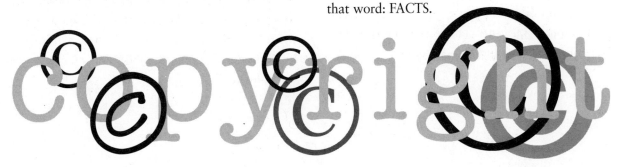

Privacy

Privacy, and who has it, is one of the fundamental questions of libel. For instance, just because a mayor and an English teacher are both public employees does not mean that both are public. The teacher is a non-public official, as would be a former mayor.

Still, one can become public, and thus open to exposure by the press, if he or she holds such an important and powerful position that a court would deem them "public figures" for all purposes (Jay Leno, for instance). And an individual can make him- or herself a "public figure" voluntarily by leaping into the midst of an important and public controversy with the intent of affecting the outcome (for instance, a militant racist who campaigns against equal rights).

The key difference between libel and invasion of privacy is that in the former an individual's reputation and character are at stake and in the latter an individual's feelings and peace of mind are violated. Only living people have a right to privacy — not the deceased and not public organizations or corporations.

Among the acts that might constitute invasion are use of another's name or likeness for commercial purposes, publicizing parts of someone's private life that most people would find offensive, attempted fictionalization of someone's private life that fails to conceal their identity, and being intrusive with regard to another's privacy or personal affairs.

Note, however, that if someone does something in public and is caught at it by the camera or the reporter, there is no invasion of privacy.

All of these issues relate to why, when photographing individuals or private property for use in a publication or for other commercial purposes, it is imperative to get a signed model release.

Copyright

Copyright refers to the ownership of artistic or intellectual properties — books, drawings, paintings, musical compositions, etc. But more than ownership is covered by copyright law; it is possible for the creator of a work to grant a license to its use, and that license, or right, can be total or partial. In fact, rights may be divided almost infinitely, usually through contractual agreements.

THE LAW & CONVENTIONS

U.S. copyright law is made by Congress, which may change it as circumstances warrant. The most recent major change in the law went into effect January 1, 1978, but there have been changes as recently as 1988, when the U.S. joined the Bern Convention. The Bern Convention is the standard for most of the world. The day-to-day custodian is the Library of Congress, which keeps records of rights (though not all) and archives copyrighted materials.

The actual registration of copyright is now optional. But registration allows anyone whose copyright has been infringed to use the courts to seek justice. Either way, the creator of copyrightable material is protected from the moment his or her work is saved in a tangible form, be that on paper, audio tape, video tape, computer disk, or any other medium. It does not have to be published to be copyrighted.

When something is published, the formal notice of copyright is not required, but it seems a good idea to remind others. It should include the word "copyright," its abbreviation "copr." or the © symbol followed by the first year of publication, and the name of the owner.

WHAT CANNOT BE COPYRIGHTED

There is no copyright on ideas, nor on facts. Both belong to everyone, and all that copyright can protect is their unique presentation. But beware of lifting someone's story, because its plot and sequence may be unique and copyrighted. Which isn't to say that two people at opposite ends of the country, without contact, can't create nearly identical stories. If they do, neither has infringed on the rights of the other, but if someone copies, it's theft.

Titles and forms are a couple more things that can't be copyrighted. People frequently devise complex forms and publish them believing the copyright on the publication covers the forms. In fact, the only thing copyrighted is the unique expression that might be written on the forms as explanation, etc. Titles, or the words or phrases they employ, are often too generic to be owned by anyone.

There are what amount to exceptions to the above, but not under copyright law. Unique ideas can be well protected by trademarks, patents, and similar laws of commerce. Taking the title of some famous book that's still protected by copyright might be viewed as expropriation of the fame or value of someone else's name (the other author's), and that's invasion of privacy.

THE GRANT OF RIGHTS

Before 1978, protection was 28 years from publication with the right to renew for another 28. After 1978, previously renewed material received another 29 years for a possible total of 75. If it hadn't yet been renewed, it received a renewal of 47 for a total of 75. And for work created since 1978, a copyright is good, with few exceptions, for the creator's lifetime plus 50 years. The exceptions are pseudonymous or anonymous creations and "works for hire," which are protected 75 years from publication or 100 years from creation (whichever is shorter).

Once copyright has expired, the work is in the public domain. That's the case for anything published more than 56 years before January 1, 1978. The creator of copyrightable material may choose, at any time, to place it in the public domain.

The importance of ownership and the need to protect it cannot be overemphasized, since it is so easy to steal intellectual property without even thinking of it as theft. How many times have we seen a copyrighted cartoon reproduced in a newsletter, almost always without permission? How many times have we photocopied extensively from a book and passed it around to colleagues or to students without considering it a violation of someone's rights? Certainly without thinking ourselves dishonest or thieves?

183

RIGHT OF FAIR USE

There are occasions when selective use of published material is allowed, particularly for educational purposes or for quotation in review. But such uses, coming under the "Right of Fair Use" clause of the copyright law, were never intended to allow any copying that might take the place of the use of the original or deny a sale of the original by its publisher.

The text of the law is ambiguous, which is unfortunate. When quoting for educational purposes, a good rule is to request permission when the total amount to be quoted from throughout the work of another is greater than a few paragraphs or, in a very large work, a few pages. If the intended use is commercial, other than for a book review, even a line or two may require permission and the right to quote may have to be purchased from the copyright owner.

WRITER OR WORK FOR HIRE

This is a special category that includes anything written by someone specifically in the employ of another who, in the course of that employment, creates copyrightable work. The copyright belongs to the employer. This is also the case when an author, by contract, agrees to be a "writer for hire" and to grant all rights to the contractor.

AVOIDING COPYRIGHT PROBLEMS

Classroom publishers, no matter their age, are bound by the same rules. Part of teaching young writers and publishers about their craft is to give them a full understanding of their rights and respon-

sibilities. Many classroom publishing projects, including some of those reviewed for this book, contain unpermitted material — illustrations and reprints of copyrighted works for which there were no permissions. For the most part, this was probably innocent infringement. Neither teachers nor students knew they were stealing, but there's no qualitative difference between shoplifting and using someone's words or art without permission.

Unless we are aware of what constitutes fair use and what infringes on the rights of others, we cannot teach our students to act consciously and honestly — and to treat the work of others as they would have their own treated.

FIGHTING CENSORSHIP by Winifred Conkling

From "The Big Chill," Teacher Magazine, November/December 1991. Reprinted by permission.

Journalism advisers have long been the champions of students' First Amendment rights though they often acknowledge that censorship decisions boil down to difficult judgement calls by administrators. When teachers believe their student publications have been improperly censored, they should keep the following tips in mind:

• Always comply with direct orders from the principal or school board. Obey all school rules. Several federal courts have refused to hear free speech cases brought by students who failed to follow administrators' demands.

• Ask the administration to state in writing exactly what is objectionable about the censored material. In many cases involving the student press, the administration's objection is based on an article's viewpoint, which is not an acceptable ground for censorship.

• Review the censored material and determine whether it is "unprotected." By definition, unprotected speech is not covered by the First Amendment and can be censored. The most common cat-

egories of unprotected speech in student publications are obscenity, libel, invasion of privacy, and material that causes a "substantial disruption of school activities."

• Discuss the issue with the principal or censor. if the talks prove fruitless, take the case to the superintendent or the school board. These attempts to settle the dispute are critical; many courts won't hear a case unless all available administrative means of resolution have been exhausted.

• If all discussions fail to resolve the matter, a lawsuit is an option. For additional information on filing a suit and a list of First Amendment lawyers who may take on the case free of charge, contact the Student Press Law Center at (202) 466-5242.

FOR MORE INFORMATION

The following associations provide services and support to journalism advisers and students:

• Columbia Scholastic Press Association, Box 11,

Continued on page 185

Censorship

From the discussions of libel, slander, and invasion of privacy it should be clear that there are legal and ethical limits on what one person may say or write about another. It might sometimes seem to be censorship, but such restrictions are attempts to ensure the greater rights of citizens rather than restrict them. The real issues of censorship arise elsewhere.

The imposition of someone else's values on anyone by denying the right to read or publish material that offends that other person (or group) is censorship. In a society that includes so many groups and individuals with differing religious and moral values — and which guarantees each-the right free exercise of those beliefs — setting "appropriate" or "consensual" limits on publishing or speech is always treading on thin ice. But along with the right to use an unpopular form of expression goes the right to not read or view something that offends.

We hold as ideal to democracy the free exchange of ideas, which means that even unpopular ones have a right to be heard.

Censors generally see themselves as guardians of right. The problem is that they believe they have the only correct definition of "right." In order to ensure our freedoms, courts have tried to set limits on what

Continued from page 184

Central Mail Room, Columbia University, New York, NY 10027; (212) 280-3311. Membership: $79 per school publication. Fee includes a critique of the publication, a subscription to the quarterly magazine *The Student Press Review,* and eligibility for competitions and awards.

• First Amendment Congress, University of Colorado at Denver, 1445 Market St., Suite 320, Denver, CO 80202; (303) 820-5688. Journalism advisers can receive the free quarterly newsletter *First Amendment Congress* by contacting the organization. FAC also offers the *Education for Freedom* journalism curriculum guide for either K–6 or 6–12 programs. Each guide costs $25.

• Journalism Education Association, Kansas State University, 103 Kedzie Hall, Manhattan, KS 66506; (913) 532-5532. Membership: $35 for teachers and advisers. Fee includes subscriptions to the quarterly magazine *Communication: Journalism Education Today,* the quarterly newsletter *NewsWire,* and three issues of the *Student Press Law Center Report.* Members also receive consultation services on the JEA hot line and discounts on books, reports, and other journalism publications.

• National Scholastic Press Association, University of Minnesota, Rarig Center, Room 620, 330 21st Ave., S., Minneapolis, MN 55455; (612) 625-8335. Membership: $69 per publication. Fee includes publication critique, consultation service, conventions for students and advisers, and a subscription to the quarterly magazine *Trends in High School Media.*

• Quill and Scroll Society, Department of Journalism & Communications, University of Iowa, Iowa City, IA 52242; (319) 335-5796. Lifetime school charter: $30; membership: $10 for teachers and students. Members receive the quarterly magazine *Quill and Scroll,* publication and resource lists, and eligibility for student awards, competitions and scholarships.

• Student Press Law Center, Suite 504, 1735 Eye St., N.W., Washington, DC 20006; (202) 466-5242. Membership: $15. Members receive *SPLC Report,* published three times a year, and free legal services. SPLC provides telephone consultations on media law, offers advice on using freedom-of-information laws, and files legal briefs on behalf of student journalists.

may or may not be censored. The ambiguous result is a test based on "community standards" and "redeeming social significance." Since those are always changing, so is what may be censored. But that's when censorship reaches the courts. Far more often, it takes place with little or no fanfare.

To be honest, we all censor all the time. We just do it for ourselves by making selections. That's no problem unless it means we're close-minded and unwilling to consider new or different ideas. Still, that's up to each of us. It's when we start making choices for others that things get sticky.

Parents are expected to select what their children read. Teachers and librarians constantly choose what students or patrons will have access to. Bookstores decide what to stock. Theaters select the films to be shown. And every choice of what to include is a choice to exclude something else. There's no way around doing this, but it's the underlying criteria that decide whether a choice is censorship or not.

The truly nasty thing about censoring ideas is that it is an act of momentary power that by its very exercise grants the right to someone even more powerful to censor the first censor. And in every case, the censor, by denying the rights of others admits the weakness of his or her ideas to win over others through discussion or persuasion.

USE THESE ISLANDS OF WHITE FOR YOUR ADDITIONS, AND LET US KNOW ABOUT 'EM TOO.

Section 3

Resources

This section contains valuable reference material. The annotated bibliography includes selected publications on most aspects of publishing. You are sure to add others. And we'd appreciate hearing from you when you discover some especially useful source.

There are lists of publishers, events, and organizations that we hope will abet your classroom efforts. Because career information in publishing is generally scattered, we tried to gather much of it here. You will find college and university programs in publishing, printing, and related crafts. Of course,

writing is at the beginning of the publishing process, and we could have filled the entire book with schools that offer basic writing courses, but we didn't — they're relatively easy to find. We have, however, included graduate programs.

Not so well known are outlets devoted to writing by youth. We've listed some you may already know. Others, we hope, will be welcome additions.

While we've compiled some deep lists, none is exhaustive. There may be resources near you that make more sense than those we've included. Use our lists as starting points.

Contests

Byline
Student Page Contests
PO Box 130596
Edmond, OK 73013
This monthly magazine for writers has a regular feature called "The Student Page" which offers writing contests (prose and poetry) on themes, publication for the winners, and occasional articles to help students improve skills. Write for the yearly list of themes, fees, and prizes. Students in grades 1–12 may enter.

CREATIVE WITH WORDS PUBLICATIONS (CWW)
Brigitta Geltgrich, Editor and Publisher
PO Box 223226
Carmel, CA 93922
Children's manuscripts (prose and poetry) are accepted year-round for possible inclusion in this annual anthology devoted to furthering creative writing in children and furthering folkloristic tales (tall tales, fairy tales, etc.). Send an SASE for detailed contributor's guidelines, including information on an annual poetry contest.

Cricket
PO Box 300
Peru, IL 61354
This monthly magazine for children sponsors monthly contests for young writers and artists. The usual age limit is 14, but occasionally an "alumni" category is added with no upper age limit. Entries must follow specific rules and themes described on the "Cricket League" page of the magazine. Categories include story, poetry, art, and photography. Teachers may write to request contest entry forms for multiple student submissions. First prize winners' work is published. Other prize winners' names are listed. Examples of contest themes: a Thanksgiving Day story, a drawing of the fairy godparent you'd like to have.

Little Green Creative Arts Project
c/o Sebastian International
6109 DeSoto Ave.
Woodland Hills, CA 91367
A hair products company sponsors an annual international children's art and writing competition with a "save the environment" focus every January through May. Children draw and paint pictures, or write stories and poems that express fears, hopes, or ideas about the environment. Local winners are entered into nationwide judging. Five 1992 winners won trips for two to the Brazilian rain forest; a grand prize winner won a $5000 savings bond.

National Written & Illustrated By... Awards Contest
Landmark Editions, Inc.
PO Box 4469
Kansas City, MO 64127
Landmark sponsors an annual competition for student writers (ages 6 to 9, 10 to 13, and 14 to 19) which results in publishing contracts for the winning students. Contest winners are treated to an all expense paid trip to Kansas City, where they work with Landmark on final production of their books. Later, there are annual author royalties and college scholarships for the students. Books may be on any subject, in any genre. Deadline for entries is May 1.
www.landmarkeditions.com

Education

PUBLISHING PROGRAMS

Book Publishing Institute
Howard University Press
1240 Randolph St. NE
Washington, DC 20017
202-806-4935
Summer publishing institute

Denver Publishing Institute
University of Denver
2075 S University Blvd #D-114
Denver, CO 80210
303-871-2570
Summer publishing institute

Folio Publishing Weeks
Six River Bend
PO Box 4949
Stamford, CT 06907-0949
203-358-9900
Various conferences focusing on magazine, directory, and book publishing

Magazine Career Institute
Graduate School of Journalism
Columbia University
New York, NY 10027
212-854-4150
Magazine seminars

NYU Center for Publishing
New York University
48 Cooper Square, Rm 108
New York, NY 10003-9903
800-FIND-NYU
Summer publishing institutes and continuing education courses

Pace University Graduate Publishing Program
The Information Center
1 Pace Plaza
New York, NY 10038-1502
212-346-1417
Master's programs on publishing books, magazines, and videos, including summer programs

Publishing Program
University of Chicago
Office of Continuing Education
5835 S Kimbark Ave.
Chicago, IL 60637
312-702-1723
Continuing publishing courses, including summer sessions

Radcliffe Publishing Procedure
Radcliffe College
77 Brattle St.
Cambridge, MA 02138
617-495-8678
Summer course on publishing magazines and books

Stanford Professional Publishing
Bowman Alumni House
Stanford University

Stanford, CA 94305-4005
415-725-1083
Summer institute on book and magazine publishing

Vassar College Institute of Publishing and Writing
PO Box 300
Poughkeepsie, NY 12601
914-452-7000
Annual summer conference

PRINTING DEGREES

ALABAMA
Alabama Agricultural and Mechanical University

ARKANSAS
Arkansas State University

CALIFORNIA
City College of San Francisco
Compton Community College
Fullerton College
Los Angeles Trade-Technical College
Modesto Junior College
Pasadena City College
Sacramento City College
San Joaquin Delta College
Santa Monica College

IDAHO
Lewis-Clark State College

ILLINOIS
Triton College

INDIANA
Ball State University
Vincennes University

KANSAS
Allen County Community College
Garden City Community College
Pittsburg State University

KENTUCKY
Eastern Kentucky University

MASSACHUSETTS
Springfield Technical Community College

MICHIGAN
Ferris State University
Macomb Community College
Western Michigan University

MISSISSIPPI
Mississippi Valley State University

NEBRASKA
Central Community College–Hastings Campus

NEW YORK
Rochester Institute of Technology

NORTH CAROLINA
Chowan College
East Carolina University

OHIO
Bowling Green State University

OREGON
Portland Community College

PENNSYLVANIA
Beaver College
Drexel University

SOUTH DAKOTA
South Dakota State University

TEXAS
Austin Community College
East Texas State University
Texas Southern University

UTAH
Salt Lake Community College

WASHINGTON
Clark College
Spokane Community College

WEST VIRGINIA
Fairmont State College
West Virginia Institute of Technology

WISCONSIN
Fox Valley Technical Institute
Madison Area Technical College
Milwaukee Area Technical College
Western Wisconsin Technical College

GRADUATE WRITING PROGRAMS

ALABAMA
Auburn University

ALASKA
University of Alaska–Anchorage
University of Alaska–Fairbanks

ARIZONA
Arizona State University
Northern Arizona University
University of Arizona

CALIFORNIA
California State Univ–Fresno
California State Univ–Long Beach
Chapman College
Mills College
New College of California
San Diego State University
San Francisco State University
University of California–Irvine
University of Southern California

COLORADO
Colorado State University
The Naropa Institute
University of Denver

CONNECTICUT
University of Connecticut

DELAWARE
University of Delaware

189

DISTRICT OF COLUMBIA
The American University

FLORIDA
Florida Institute of Technology
Florida International University
Florida State University
The University of Florida

GEORGIA
Georgia State University

HAWAII
University of Hawaii–Manoa

ILLINOIS
Columbia College–Chicago
Illinois State University
University of Illinois at Chicago

INDIANA
Indiana University
Purdue University

IOWA
Iowa State University
Maharishi International University
University of Iowa

KANSAS
Kansas State University
University of Kansas
Wichita State University

KENTUCKY
Morehead State University
Western Kentucky University

LOUISIANA
McNeese State University
University of New Orleans

MAINE
University of Maine at Orono

MARYLAND
The Johns Hopkins University
University of Maryland at College Park

MASSACHUSETTS
Boston University
Emerson College
University of Massachusetts
University of Massachusetts–Dartmouth

MICHIGAN
Michigan State University
Northern Michigan University
University of Michigan
Western Michigan University

MINNESOTA
Mankato State University
University of Minnesota

MISSISSIPPI
Mississippi State University
University of Mississippi

MISSOURI
Northeast Missouri State University
Southwest Missouri State University
University of Missouri–Kansas City
Washington University

MONTANA
University of Montana

NEBRASKA
University of Nebraska–Lincoln

NEVADA
University of Nevada–Las Vegas

NEW HAMPSHIRE
University of New Hampshire

NEW JERSEY
Rutgers University–Camden

NEW MEXICO
New Mexico State University
University of New Mexico

NEW YORK
Brooklyn College/CUNY
Columbia University
Cornell University
Hofstra University
Lehman College
New York University
Sarah Lawrence College
State University of New York–Albany
Syracuse University

NORTH CAROLINA
East Carolina University
University of North Carolina–Greensboro

NORTH DAKOTA
University of North Dakota

OHIO
Antioch University
Bowling Green State University
Case Western Reserve
Cleveland State University
Miami University
Ohio State University
University of Cincinnati
Wright State University

OKLAHOMA
Central State University
Oklahoma State University
University of Oklahoma

OREGON
Portland State University
University of Oregon

PENNSYLVANIA
Bucknell University
Penn State University
Temple University
University of Pittsburgh

SOUTH CAROLINA
University of South Carolina

SOUTH DAKOTA
University of South Dakota

TENNESSEE
Austin Peay State University
Memphis State University
University of Tennessee–Chattanooga
University of Tennessee–Knoxville

Markets for Young Writers

Bear Essential News for Kids
Garrett Communications, Inc.
209 E. Baseline Rd., Suite E-203
Tempe, AZ 85383
Bear Essential News for Kids is a free monthly newspaper for kids and their families. Five editions serve Arizona and Southern California. It offers many opportunities for student writers, photographers, and artists. Cub reporters represent their schools, submitting stories. There are poetry and art sections, plus a monthly artwork competition. For more information, read the paper.

Boys' Life
Magazine Division - Boy Scouts of America
PO Box 152079
Irving, TX 75015-2079
The popular magazine for boys 8 to 18 is written primarily by adults, but has a few opportunities for student writers. The "Reader's Page" invites student contributions and pays $25 for those which are published. The "Think & Grin" feature takes children's jokes.

Chickadee
56 The Esplanade
Suite 306
Toronto, ONT M5E1A7
This magazine for children ages 3–9 focuses on nature and science. It's published by the Young Naturalist Foundation ten times a year. Children's drawings, letters, jokes, and photos are featured in the "Chirp" section. For information, write to the magazine at 255 Great Arrow Ave., Buffalo, NY 14207-3082.

The Claremont Review
4980 Wesley Road
Victoria, BC V8Y 1Y9
Here's a new high quality literary review, published twice a year, showcasing the poetry and prose of young adult writers, grades 8–12. The editors welcome submissions from any young writers, not just Canadians. Published authors receive a copy of the review. Write for submission information.

Cobblestone Publishing, Inc.
Editorial Department
7 School St.
Peterborough, NH 03458
This company publishes four magazines for young people: *Cobblestone, Faces, Calliope,* and *Odyssey.* Most of the content is written by professional writers. *Faces* runs a page of young people's letters and drawings. The "Dear Ebenezer" department in *Cobblestone* invites children's writing and art submissions. Look for copies of the magazines at your school or library.

Creative Kids
PO Box 6448
Mobile, AL 36660
This publication, edited by adults, is written by children ages 5–18. Uses cartoons, reviews, songs, poems, articles, puzzles, photographs, art-work, comic strips, interviews, activities, editorials, and plays. Send an SASE for detailed contributor's guidelines. For subscriptions or a sample copy ($3), write to the magazine at PO Box 637, 100 Pine Ave., Holmes, PA 19043.

CREATIVE WITH WORDS PUBLICATIONS (CWW)
Brigitta Geltgrich, Editor and Publisher
PO Box 223226
Carmel, CA 93922
Children's manuscripts (prose and poetry) are accepted year-round for possible inclusion in this annual anthology devoted to furthering creative writing in children and furthering folkloristic tales (tall tales, fairy tales, etc.). Send an SASE for detailed guidelines, including information on an annual poetry contest.

Highlights for Children
803 Church St.
Honesdale, PA 18431
This reading and activities magazine for children, published ten times a year, accepts children's stories, poems, riddles, jokes, and drawings. Send an SASE for guidelines. Read the magazine for notices of special topics children can illustrate or write about.

Merlyn's Pen
PO Box 1058
East Greenwich, RI 02818
A national magazine of student writing, published four times during the school year, requests writing and art from students in grades 7–10. Uses short stories, science fiction, movie, book and music reviews, essays, poems, parodies, photos, drawings, and cartoons. Submission guidelines appear in the magazine.

Prairie Winds
Kathy Huse-Wika, Project Director
208 E. Colorado Blvd.
Spearfish, ND 57783
Prairies Winds, a twice-yearly magazine of literary and visual arts, publishes work by South Dakota students (K–12), as well as by teachers and professional writers and artists. Write for guidelines and information on the annual Young Writers Conference.

Ranger Rick
National Wildlife Federation
1400–16th St.
Washington D.C. 20036-2266
National Wildlife Federation's monthly for kids prints "only a tiny fraction "of submissions received. Has a letters column.

Read
Weekly Reader Corporation
245 Long Hill Rd.
Middletown, CT 06457
Most of the material in this periodical for junior and senior high school students is written by staff or adapted from other sources "In Your Own Write" invites student letters, prose, and poetry. Look for instructions in the magazine concerning submissions.

Rethinking Schools
1001 E. Keefe Ave.
Milwaukee, WI 53212
A teacher's journal requests students, parents, and teachers send young people's poetry, prose, and artwork for its student page. The editors prefer drawings in pencil or black ink. Please enclose age, school, and phone number with submissions.

Signatures From Big Sky
c/o Shirley M. Olson
928 4th Ave.
Laurel, MT 59044
Three education groups founded this annual Montana student literary/art publication in 1991. Work may be in any genre. Deadline is Feb. 1 for spring publication. Submissions are made to 14 teachers (K-12) throughout the state who are listed inside the publication. The magazine is distributed to all Montana school libraries.

Skipping Stones
PO Box 3939
Eugene, OR 97403-0939
This quarterly non-profit children's magazine encourages cooperation, creativity, ecological stewardship, and celebration of cultural and linguistic diversity. Much of the writing and artwork is done by children and young adults from the United States and other countries. The magazine is especially interested in young people's stories about their ethnic heritage. Write for information on submission guidelines.

STONE SOUP
PO Box 83
Santa Cruz, CA 95063
STONE SOUP is the oldest magazine devoted exclusively to children's writing and art. Children through age 13 are encouraged to submit stories, poems, book reviews, and art. Contributors whose work is accepted for publication are paid. Send an SASE for submission requirements. Sample copy for $4.

'TEEN
Rhyme & Reason
PO Box 3341
Hollywood, CA 90028
'TEEN publishes original poetry by young people on its monthly "Rhyme and Reason" page. For details on submission requirements, look at this page in a copy of *'TEEN*.

Voices
SEVENTEEN Magazine
850 Third Ave.
New York, NY 10022
"Voices" is *SEVENTEEN* Magazine's section that presents original material from writers 21-years-old and under. Types of material include first person narratives, opinion essays, reflective essays about personal decisions and relationships, and light or funny pieces. Writers are paid $50 to $150. Send an SASE for guidelines.

Writing!
Weekly Reader Corporation
60 Revere Drive
Northbrook, IL 60062-1563
This children's magazine about writing, published monthly through the school year, welcomes student contributions of fiction, nonfiction, poetry, etc. Areas for student contributions include a "Student Writing Department" and "Reader's Choice," a section of book reviews. The "Write In" section uses questions from students (who receive $25 each) about the process of writing. Read the magazine for an understanding of editors' needs and information on writing contests the magazine sponsors.

Young Voices
PO Box 2321
Olympia, WA 98507
Stories, articles, essays, poems, and drawings by elementary through high school students are published six times a year. Material used is paid for. Guidelines for contributors are listed in the magazine.

Registrations

GGX Associates
11 Middle Neck Road
Great Neck, NY 11021
516-487-6370
Bar codes

International Standard Book Numbering Agency
R.R. Bowker/Martindale-Hubbell
121 Chanlon Road
New Providence, NJ 07974
800-521-8110
Contact the ISBN Agency to obtain an ISBN (International Standard Book Number). Request a "Title Output Information Request Form," and a "User's Manual." The charge is $100.

Landy & Associates
Marc Landy
1049 Sudden Valley #156-P
Bellingham, WA 98226
206-647-7494
Bar codes

Library of Congress
CIP Office
Washington, DC 20540
To receive information regarding Library of Congress Catalog Card Numbers, write to the CIP Office and ask for "Procedures for Securing Preassigned Library of Congress Catalog Card Numbers" and their "Request for Preassignment of LCC Number" application (Form 607-7).

Library of Congress
Register of Copyrights
Washington, DC 20559
Write to the Register of Copyrights; request three copies of Form
TX (for registering books) and copies of Circular R1, Copyright
Basics, and Circular R2, Publications of the Copyright Office.

Precision Photography Inc.
1150 North Tustin Avenue
Anaheim, CA 92807
714-632-9000
Bar codes

Reviewers for Children's Books

ALA Booklist
Up Front: Advance Reviews
50 East Huron Street
Chicago, IL 60611
312-944-6780

Horn Book Magazine
Anita Silvey
Park Square Building, 41 Beacon Street
Boston, MA 02108
800-325-1170

Kirkus Reviews
Advance Information
200 Park Ave. South
New York, NY 10003
212-777-4554

Kliatt Young Adult Paperback Book Guide
Doris Hiatt
425 Watertown Street
Newton, MA 02158
617-965-4666

Library Journal
Nora Rawlinson
249 West 17th Street
New York, NY 10011
212-645-0067

School Library Journal
Trevelyn Jones
247 West 17th Street
New York, NY 10011
212-463-6759

Miscellaneous

Interlochen Center for the Arts
PO Box 199
Interlochen, MI 49643
A summer creative writing program that offers students individ-
ualized apprenticeship opportunities in poetry, fiction, nonfiction, and screenwriting. The program includes workshops with
professional writers and an opportunity for students to submit
their best work for national competition and publication.

Multicultural Publishers Exchange
PO Box 9869
Madison, WI 53715
A unique resource for teachers involved in multicultural classroom publishing: a newsletter with a focus on the growing
multicultural segment of the publishing industry. Published six
times a year, it has news and information on independent book
publishers of color, new titles, book fairs, and writing competitions, plus a bulletin board of announcements. Write for the
MPE catalog of 350 titles by and about African, Asian, Pacific
Islander, Latino, and Native American people.

Oregon Writing Festival
c/o Julie Stewart
Gresham High School
1200 N. Main St.
Gresham, OR 97030
The Oregon Department of Education and the Oregon Council
of Teachers of English sponsor this annual one-day spring
conference to encourage the efforts of students and teachers to
improve writing. Students in grade 1-12 are welcome; districts
decide which students will attend. Students have an opportunity
to hear from well-known writers and to participate in writing
workshops. Contact your state's department of education for
information on similar programs in your state.

A Selected Bibliography

ACP/NSPA Magazine Guidebook
620 Rarig Center — University of Minnesota
330 21st Avenue South
Minneapolis, MN 55455
This guidebook to high school and college magazine journalism,
available by mail order, offers students and teachers guidelines
for planning and producing magazines with examples of some of
the best in the U.S.

Adler, Elizabeth W. *Print That Works: The First Step-by-Step
Guide that Integrates Writing, Design, and Marketing.* Palo Alto,
CA: Bull Publishing, 1990. Comprehensive. For anyone involved
in the publication of flyers, reports, newsletters, catalogs, books,
and more. Substantial focus on desktop publishing.

Aliki. *How a Book Is Made.* New York, NY: HarperTrophy, 1988.
A children's book on the making of a picture book — from an
idea in the author's mind right on through printing and promo-

tion. Delightful four-color illustrations of nattily attired cats as the book production team. A good book for anyone wanting a quick overview of book production.

Applebaum, Judith, and Nancy Evans. *How to Get Happily Published*. New York, NY: New American Library, 1982. The authors bring decades of publishing experience to this book meant for any writer. Agents, book contracts, editors, vanity presses, and self-publishing are among the topics covered.

Author Aid/Research. *Literary Agents of North America Marketplace*. New York: Author Aid Associates, biennial. Essential reference for writers who use or are considering using an agent, listing hundreds of U.S. and Canadian literary agencies and their specialties, policies, services, etc.

Balkin, Richard. *How to Understand & Negotiate a Book Contract or Magazine Agreement*. Cincinnati, OH: Writer's Digest Books, 1985. A literary agent provides help for negotiating profitable contracts by yourself, or in tandem with an agent or lawyer. Advice on "bargaining chips," specific negotiating processes for different types of publishers, and much more.

Barker, Malcolm E. *Book Design & Production for the Small Publisher*. San Francisco, CA: Londonborn Publications, 1990. A non-intimidating book on book design for the novice and the more experienced book designer/publisher as well. Barker shows methods used by professional designers and also explains why they're used and how they can be adapted to your own needs.

Beach, Mark, Steve Shepro, and Ken Russon. *Getting It Printed*. Portland, OR: Coast to Coast Books, 1986. How to work with printers and graphic arts services to assure quality, stay on schedule, and control costs is the focus of this comprehensive handbook. Printing papers and ink, typesetting, printing methods, and much more are discussed.

Bjelland, Harley. *The Write Stuff: Learn How to Write Better Right Now With the Approach That Combines Creativity and Computer Logic*. Hawthorne, NJ: The Career Press, 1991.

Blundell, William E. *The Art and Craft of Feature Writing*. New York: New American Library, 1988. A Wall Street Journal writer and seminar leader emphasizes storytelling techniques in a step-by-step how-to guide.

Bly, Robert W. *The Copywriter's Handbook*. New York, NY: Dodd, Mead & Company, 1985. How to write copy that sells — from print ads to catalogs, direct mail to radio or TV commercials — is the focus of this book written for everyone who writes or approves copy.

Brady, Philip. *Using Type Right*. Cincinnati, OH: North Light Books, 1988. A reference guide with 121 rules for placing type on the page, successfully and effectively. Tips for better design, working with typesetters and printers, avoiding costly mistakes.

Bunnin, Brad, and Peter Beren. *The Writer's Legal Companion*. Reading, MA: Addison-Wesley Publishing, 1988. A readable reference on all aspects of publishing law, from copyrights and libel to the obscure clauses in magazine and book publishing contracts. Advice, too, on the business of publishing, including marketing and selling books.

Burack, A. S., editor. *Writing Suspense and Mystery Fiction*. Boston, MA: The Writer, 1977. Thirty mystery and suspense novelists and short story writers discuss techniques. The book includes "A Layman's Guide to Law and the Courts" and "Glossary of Legal Terms" prepared by the American Bar Association.

Burgett, Gordon. *How to Sell More Than 75% of Your Freelance Writing*. Rocklin, CA: Prima Publishing & Communications, 1990. Many beginning writers think that 90 percent of their success in selling their writing is talent related. Burgett says most success comes from successfully selling ideas to editors. He tells how to avoid beginners' mistakes and how to maximize your results as a freelancer.

___. *The Travel Writer's Guide*. Rocklin, CA: Prima Publishing, 1991. The author, a successful travel writer and writing teacher, covers all the important topics, from marketing to tax deductions, for novice and veteran travel writers.

Carpenter, Lisa ed. *Children's Writer's & Illustrator's Market*. Cincinnati, OH: Writer's Digest Book Club, Hundreds of markets for children's writing (from preschoolers to teenagers) are listed in this annual guide.

Case, Patricia Ann. *How to Write Your Autobiography: Preserving Your Family Heritage*. Santa Barbara, CA: Woodbridge Press, 1977. A teacher offers step-by-step guidelines for readers of any age to write a clear narrative of their place in family history. The resulting book can be a one-of-a-kind contribution to family unity and continuity. The focus is on following a writing outline, rather than on book production.

Cool, Lisa Collier. *How to Write Irresistible Query Letters*. Cincinnati, OH: Writer's Digest Books, 1987. A successful freelance writer and literary agent offers practical advice on how to craft persuasive letters that will sell your article and book proposals to editors.

Copperud, Roy H. *American Usage and Style: The Consensus*. New York: Van Nostrand Reinhold, 1980. Copperud helps writers attain greater language precision, avoid misspellings and grammatical errors, and set the proper tone with this book. He offers a consensus of style and usage by comparing the judgment of leading authorities and the definitions of seven current dictionaries.

Daniel, Lois. *How to Write Your Own Life Story*. Chicago, IL: Chicago Review Press, 1980. A writing teacher provides a step-by-step guide to autobiography for the non-professional writer, including a list of topics, tips for jogging your memory, advice on research and on publishing pieces of your work.

Devine, Joe. *Commas Are Our Friends*. Seattle, WA: Green Stone Publications, 1989. A writer, educator, and humorist provides a humorous, painless twist to grammar and punctuation in this book designed to serve as a refresher course.

Dowling, LuAnne, and Jane Evanson. *Writing Articles: A Guide to Publishing in Your Profession*. Dubuque, IA: Kendall/Hunt Publishing, 1990. Two educators offer a step-by-step guide for the process of organizing, writing, and revising articles for publication in professional journals and magazines.

Emerich, Jean (compiled by). *Proper Noun Speller*. Los Angeles, CA: QuikRef Publishing, 1990. Spell correctly the operas, mountain ranges, political leaders' names, and brand names you're searching for with the help of this 15,000 entry reference book. A handy book covering a vast number of subject categories.

Franklin, Jon. *Writing for Story*. New York, NY: New American Library, 1986. A Pulitzer Prize-winning journalist shares tips, tools, and techniques for the new nonfiction, combining the readability and excitement of fiction with the best of expository prose.

Fulton, Len, editor. *International Directory of Little Magazines and Small Presses*. Paradise, CA: Dustbooks, annual. Used as the standard reference worldwide by writers, librarians, students and the publishing industry, this annual includes subject and regional indexes as well as more than 4,500 detailed market listings.

Gardner, John. *On Becoming a Novelist*. New York, NY: Harper & Row, 1983. Writer's block, revision, and rejection — major tests of a novelist's will and spirit — are among the topics addressed by novelist Gardner in this book completed just before his death. Believing that novelists are self-made, he provides practical suggestions, exercises, and encouragement.

Gibaldi, Joseph, and Walter S. Achtert. *MLA Handbook: For Writers of Research Papers, Theses, and Dissertations (student edition)*. New York, NY: Modern Language Association, 1990. This standard reference book on the mechanics and format of research papers is based upon practices required by college teachers throughout the U.S. and Canada. Topics include using the library, outlining and writing, punctuation and capitalization, and formal manuscript preparation.

Goldberg, Natalie. *Wild Mind: Living the Writer's Life*. New York, NY: Bantam Books, 1990. Writer, poet, and writing teacher Natalie Goldberg offers compassionate, practical, often humorous advice on bringing new life to your writing, overcoming procrastination and writer's block, and learning self-acceptance. She has exercises to get your pen moving. Along the way, she tells some delightful stories.

___. *Writing Down the Bones: Freeing the Writer Within*. Boston, MA: Shambhala, 1986. "Dive into absurdity and write. Take chances. You will succeed if you are fearless of failure," advises Natalie Goldberg in this book meant to take the fear out of writing and encourage the flow of words to paper. Personal, easy-to-read, a small gem for writers.

Gosney, Michael, John Odam, and Jim Schmal. *The Gray Book: Designing in Black & White on Your Computer*. Chapel Hill, NC: Ventana Press, 1990. Three leading educators in the field of desktop publishing design show and tell how to create stunning pages in black, white, and the shades of gray in between.

Henderson, Kathy. *Market Guide for Young Writers*. Sandusky, MI: Echo Communications, 1990. This is the original "how to get published" guide for young writers, now in its third edition. It includes advice for submitting work, profiles of published young writers, and information on more than 150 markets and contests for writers ages 8 to 18.

___. *Market Guide for Young Artists and Photographers*. Crozet, VA: Betterway Publications, 1990. Here are marketing tips for kids, from age eight through the teens, plus submission guidelines for more than 100 market opportunities and contests. Also here are profiles of successful young artists and photographers and adult professionals who work with creative young people.

Huddle, David. *The Writing Habit: Essays*. Salt Lake City, UT: Peregrine Smith Books, 1991. Writing instructor Huddle addresses topics that range from how to balance writing and "having a life" to how to improve your style.

Klauser, Henriette Anne. *Writing on Both Sides of the Brain: Breakthrough Techniques for People Who Write*. San Francisco, CA: Harper & Row, 1986. Psychological insights and writing exercises from an upbeat writing instructor help readers tap into their creative powers.

Kremer, John, editor. *Directory of Book Printers 1991 Edition*. Fairfield, IA: Ad-Lib Publications, 1991. This guide lists 782 printers of book, catalogs, magazines, and other publications. It also has helpful information on selecting a printer, requesting quotations, and saving money on your book printing bill.

Kubis, Pat, and Bob Howland. *The Complete Guide to Writing Fiction and Nonfiction: And Getting It Published*. Englewood Cliffs, NJ: Prentice Hall, 1990. This guidebook covers both the craft and the business of writing for publication. A detailed section examines how the publishing industry works.

Kuswa, Webster. *Sell Copy*. Cincinnati, OH: Writer's Digest Books, 1979. How to write, sell, and buy good copy, from scripts to direct mail, is the focus of this book. Lots of tips for freelancers on a wide range of markets.

Lee, Linda. *How to Write and Sell Romance Novels: A Step-by-Step Guide*. Edmonds, WA: Heartsong Press, 1988. Romance writer Linda Lee presents techniques, writing exercises, and a process for moving your idea along to a finished manuscript ready to sell.

Levoy, Gregg. *This Business of Writing*. Cincinnati, OH: Writer's Digest Books, 1992. Levoy, a fulltime freelance writer, has practical advice for building a successful writing career of any kind. Included are expert tips from other writers.

McCormick, Mona. *The Fiction Writer's Research Handbook*. New York, NY: New American Library, 1988. This reference book is designed specifically for fiction writers, listing many specific sources and telling how to use libraries, special and private collections, and computers for research.

Melton, David .*Written & Illustrated By....* Kansas City, MO: Landmark Editions, Inc., A detailed teachers' manual that offers step-by-step instructions for teaching students how to write, illustrate and bind original books. There are lesson plans, over 200 illustrations, and suggested adaptations for use at all grade levels, K through college. Useful for teachers whose students plan to enter the annual Landmark Written & Illustrated By...Awards Contest.

Mullins, Carolyn J. *The Complete Manuscript Preparation Style Guide*. Englewood Cliffs, NJ: Prentice-Hall, 1982. A technical writer offers guidelines for preparing manuscripts in all major styles, plus instructions for theses, plays, poems, and other writing. There are tips, too, on running a manuscript typing service, on copyright and permission rules, etc.

Mystery Writers of America. *Mystery Writer's Handbook*. Cincinnati, OH: Writer's Digest Books, 1984. Masters of mystery writing offer their thoughts on the craft as well as tips on the business of mystery writing.

Nelson, Roy Paul. *Publication Design*. Dubuque, IA: Wm. C. Brown Publishers, 1991. An overview of publication forms and their designs, with a rich assortment of examples, by a highly regarded journalism professor.

Pachter, Marc, editor. *Telling Lives: the Biographer's Art*. Philadelphia, PA: University of Pennsylvania Press, 1981. Seven of the most honored contemporary biographers, including Barbara Tuchman and Justin Kaplan, interpret the art of biography in this collection of essays.

Perret, Gene. *Comedy Writing Workbook*. New York, NY: Sterling Publishing, 1990. Getting serious about comedy, one of Bob Hope's top writers provides practical exercises for sharpening comedy skills. He covers one-liners and monologues, anecdotes, even cartoon captions, and shares secrets of comedy celebrities.

Perry, Carol Rosenbloom. *The Fine Art of Technical Writing*. Hillsboro, Oregon: Blue Heron Publishing, Inc., 1991. Here is a practical, non-specialized book for writing technical or scientific publications, theses, term papers, and business reports. The author debunks the notion that writing about "dry" subject matter is mechanical.

Polking, Kirk, Joan Bloss, and Colleen Cannon, editors. *Writer's Encyclopedia*. Cincinnati, OH: Writer's Digest Books, 1983. This comprehensive reference on writing defines hundreds of terms writers need to know, provides writing instruction, and more. A good book for writers, editors, poets, students, and teachers.

Poynter, Dan. *Publishing Short-Run Books: How to Paste Up and Reproduce Books Instantly Using Your Quick Print Shop*. Santa Barbara, CA: Para Publishing, 1988. Poynter tells how to produce books quickly and inexpensively at your local quick print shop, bypassing graphics arts shops and commercial printers. This method is a good option for publishers wanting to test market a book, for family histories, private poetry printings, etc.

___. *The Self-Publishing Manual: How to Write, Print & Sell Your Own Book*. Santa Barbara, CA: Para Publishing, 1986. Authoritative guide for anyone interested in self-publishing. Poynter covers it all, from the "why" of self-publishing (more money, more control, etc.) to the "how" of printing, book promotion and distribution.

Poynter, Dan, and Mindy Bingham. *Is There a Book Inside You? A Step-by-Step Plan for Writing Your Book*. Santa Barbara, CA: Para Publishing, 1991. Here's a combined how-to and reference book written for both the novice and the experienced writer. Learn how to pick your topic, write the book, evaluate your publishing options, and get the help you need.

Rico, Gabriele Lusser. *Writing the Natural Way*. Los Angeles, CA: J. P. Tarcher, 1983. A writing instructor shares techniques she's developed for releasing creative potential and triggering dormant language capabilities within the right brain. Her purpose: to turn the task of writing into the joy of writing.

Rivers, William L. *Finding Facts*. Englewood Cliffs, NJ: Prentice-Hall, 1975. A guidebook for anyone who does research, with advice on conducting interviews, training your eye and mind to observe, and using reference sources effectively.

Ross, Marilyn, and Tom Ross. *Marketing Your Books*. Buena Vista, CO: Communication Creativity, 1989. Self-publishing experts Marilyn and Tom Ross share their marketing secrets, from "at home" radio interviews to public speaking, book club sales to serial rights sales.

Ross, Tom, and Marilyn Ross. *The Complete Guide to Self-Publishing*. Cincinnati, OH: Writer's Digest Book, 1985. "Everything you need to know to write, publish, promote, and sell your own book" is the subtitle of this book. Anyone interested in self-publishing will find valuable, detailed information.

___. *How-to-Make Big Profits Publishing City & Regional Books*. Buena Vista, CO: Communication Creativity, 1987. This book addresses starting your own business - on a minimal budget - writing, publishing, and selling tourist guides, local field guides, directories or magazines.

Sanford, Bruce W. *Sanford's Synopsis of Libel & Privacy*. New York, NY: Pharos Books/Scripps Howard, 1991. A lawyer offers 36 pages of valuable tips and advice for reporters and editors seeking to avoid lawyers, lawsuits, and the law of libel.

Sawyer, Richard. *How to Write Biographies and Company Histories*. Missoula, MT: Mountain Press Publishing, 1989. This detailed guide describes how a writer can make a profitable business from writing biographies and company histories.

Sears, Peter. *Gonna Bake Me a Rainbow Poem: A Student Guide to Writing Poetry*. New York, NY: Scholastic, 1990. Poet and teacher Sears offers instruction and examples of students' poetry to enable any student to write poetry. He discusses various types of poems: love, humor, fantasy and more.

Selling, Bernard. *Writing From Within: A Unique Guide to Writing Your Life's Stories*. Claremont, CA: Hunter House, 1990. Writing instructor Selling guides writers, non-writers and teachers through the process of tapping into self-awareness and creating vivid, polished self-portraits. Examples of student writing are included.

Sitarz, Daniel. *The Desktop Publisher's Legal Handbook*. Carbondale, IL: Nova Publishing, 1989. A lawyer/publisher offers practical advice on how to recognize and successfully avoid legal problems in publishing: copyright, libel and defamation of character, subsidiary publication rights, and more.

Smith, C. Zoe , Ph.D., Ed. *Teacher's Guide to Intensive Journalistic Writing Courses*. Princeton, NJ: Dow Jones Newspaper Fund, 1991. High school teachers involved in the development of Intensive Journalistic Writing have contributed course outlines and lesson plans to this guidebook. The book can be used along with the *Teacher's Guide for Advanced Placement Courses in English Language and Composition*, published by the College Board, in preparing students to take the Advanced Placement examination in English Language and Composition.

Stovall, Dennis, and Linny Stovall, editors. *Writer's Northwest Handbook*, 4th edition. Hillsboro, OR: Media Weavers, Blue Heron Publishing, 1991. Published every two years, this regional guide offers 3,000 market and resource listings, plus 50 articles and writing tips. Particularly useful is the section for young writers and potential markets.

Straczynski, J. Michael. *The Complete Book of Scriptwriting*. Cincinnati, OH: Writer's Digest Books, 1982. A successful scriptwriter presents essential information for understanding and breaking into dramatic scriptwriting for TV, radio, film, and theater.

Strunk, William Jr, and E. B. White. *The Elements of Style*. New York: MacMillan Publishing, 1979. The classic little book (92 pages), now in a third revised edition, covers language usage rule, principles of composition, and style.

Thomas, Frank P. *How to Write the Story of Your Life*. Cincinnati, OH: Writer's Digest Books, 1984. Thomas puts concepts from his adult education classes into a book. He offers writing and organizing tips, ideas for reproducing your work and getting published, plus writing samples.

Ueland, Brenda. *If You Want To Write*. St. Paul, MN: Graywolf Press, 1987. This classic on writing and the creative process, was first published in 1938. Ueland, who published six million words in her 93 years, infused her writing with sassiness and a spirit of independence and joy.

Williams, Joseph M. *Style: Toward Clarity and Grace*. Chicago, IL: University of Chicago Press , 1990. In this trade edition of Williams' best-selling textbook, the author helps experienced writers improve any kind of prose, from a short memorandum to a lengthy report, proposal, or article. The author is a professor of English and linguistics. The textbook edition, with exercises, is published by Scott, Foresman and Company.

Williams, Thomas A. , Ph. D. *How to Publish Your Poetry: The First-Ever Marketing Manual and Success Guide for Poets*. Washington, NC: Venture Press, 1991. Successful poets knows how to sell as well as to write, says Williams. The business side of being a poet — from poetry readings to publishing and promoting your work — is the focus of this practical guide.

Writer's Digest Books. *Writer's Market: Where & How To Sell What You Write.* Cincinnati, OH: Writer's Digest Books, 1992. This annual guide to more than 4000 magazine and book publishing markets, provides contact names and addresses, tips on editorial needs, pay rates and submission requirements. Tips on marketing yourself and interviews with writers, editors and agents are also included.

Wyndham, Lee. *Writing for Children and Teenagers.* Cincinnati, OH: Writer's Digest Book Club, Valuable advice is offered for success in the children's literature market, including help on working with book packagers.

Yudkin, Marcia. *Freelance Writing for Magazines and Newspapers: Breaking In Without Selling Out.* New York, NY: Harper & Row, Publishers, 1988. Some books on freelance writing lure readers with promises of fame and/or wealth. Yudkin wants to see freelancers succeed, too, but her focus is on helping people communicate ideas and skills through periodicals that will reach audiences they respect. A thoughtful, practical approach.

Zinsser, William K. *On Writing Well: An Informal Guide to Writing Nonfiction.* New York, NY: Harper & Row, 1980. Considered a classic on writing, this book is full of excellent advice for any writer, beginner or professional. A seasoned writer, editor, and writing instructor, Zinsser has added advice on sports writing, writing in your job, humor writing, jargon, sexism, and more in this second edition.

GLOSSARY

AA. Author alteration; this abbreviation is used to indicate changes or corrections made by the author after type has been set or the page composed, usually on a **galley proof**.

Acetate. Flexible transparent plastic sheet used to make overlays.

Acid-free papers. Most papers manufactured since the late 1800s contain an acid which eventually causes the paper to become yellow and brittle. Many library collections have been endangered because of this, and recently manufacturers are changing their methods and producing papers that have acceptable levels of pH and are acid-free. These papers should last several hundred years. *Also see* **pH**.

Against the grain. To work at right angles to the direction of the paper's grain. When printing is done so that the spine runs against the grain, the pages will be more difficult to fold and may have a tendency to deform or to break the binding because of expansion and contraction due to changing humidity. *Also see* **grain** and **with the grain**.

Agent. Business representative for writers or artists. Also called a *Literary Agent* or *Artist's Agent*.

Airbrush. Small ink sprayer used by graphic artists for retouching photos and creating illustrations.

Aligning numerals. Now referred to as **modern numerals,** these are numbers that are the same height as the capital letters of a typeface, i.e., ABCD1234567890EFG. Non-aligning numbers have ascenders and descenders like lowercase letters, i.e., abcd1234567890efg.

Alley. Space between columns of type on a page, it is also sometimes called a column **gutter**.

Alphabet length. The length of a complete lowercase alphabet (a-z) of a typeface will usually vary from one typeface to another because the widths of the individual letters are designed to be different. It is useful to know the alphabet length when doing **copyfitting** or selecting a typeface for a project.

Arabic numerals. 1, 2, 3, 4, 5, 6, 7, 8, 9, 0. *See also* **roman numerals.**

Art director. Person who supervises the creation and preparation of copy provided to printers.

Artboard. Also called a **mechanical**.

Artwork. Print-ready mechanicals, including type, graphics, and photographs.

Ascenders. The parts of lowercase letters extending above their x-height. These are the loops and strokes of the letters b, d, f, h, k, l, and t. *Also see* **descenders**.

ASCII. This acronym stands for American Standard Code for Information Interchange, a standard for communication between computers.

Back matter. This part of a book follows the main body of text and can include appendices, bibliography, glossaries, index, and colophons

Bar code. A computer readable symbol of thick and thin lines containing information about a product. There are many bar code formats, but books use one called **Bookland EAN** to encode the ISBN and price. Bookland is an imaginary country throughout the world to identify books, and EAN stands for European Article Number. *Also see* **ISBN**.

Base line. The imaginary line running under each a line of type and touching the bottoms of letters without descenders. *Also see* **ascenders** and **descenders**.

Basic size. The standard paper size in each grade used to calculate basis weight. Book papers are usually cut to 25" x 38". Cover papers are sized 20" x 26".

Basis weight. Weight in pounds of one ream (500 sheets) of a particular grade cut to its **basic size**. *Also see* **grammage**.

Bibliography. A list of books, periodicals, and other references specific to the information in a book or other publication.

Bind. Hold together pages or signatures and their covers with glue, wire, thread, or other fasteners.

Binder's board. Stiff paperboard designed for the covers of case bound books.

Bindery. Business or section of a printing plant that collates, trimming, folds, gathers, binds, and otherwise finishes a book or other bound publication.

Blanket cylinder. Press cylinder on which the offset blanket is held.

Blanket. The thick rubber sheet on the blanket cylinder of an offset press that transfers ink from the printing plate to the paper.

Bleed. Printing that extends beyond the trim point of a sheet or page. Images can bleed off one, two, three, or four edges.

Blind folio. A page number is a **folio**. A blind folio is one that for some intentional reason does not appear on the page. For instance, a number seldom if ever appear on a title page, even though that page may be counted in the numbering.

Blow up. A photographic enlargement is a blow up.

Blueline, blues, or blueline proof. These are proofs made by a printer directly from the negatives or plates before printing, to provide a final check. They are usually printed on a specially coated photographic paper that shows all images in a light blue. *Also see* **proof.**

Board. Another name for **artboard** or **mechanical**.

Body copy. Copy set in text type, as opposed to headlines or other special type formats.

Bond paper. A grade of paper generally used for writing, typing, printing, and photocopying.

Book paper. This paper grade is used for printing books, magazines, and similar publications. It may also be called **text paper.** Book papers include a broad range of weights, finishes, and colors.

Bookbinder. A person who operates a bindery.

Brightness. This refers to how much light a particular type of paper reflects.

Bulk. Paper thickness, or bulk, is expressed in thousandths of an inch or pages per inch (**ppi**). *Also see* **caliper**.

Bullet. An ornamental dot used for emphasis.

Burn. In modern printing, burn means to expose blueline paper, printing plates, or other photosensitive media to light.

Burnish. Usually done with a special burnishing tool, but also with any smooth, hard object, burnishing refers to smoothing and sealing parts of a layout to a mechanical. The term is also used to describe the application of press-on letters to paper.

Burst perfect bind. A high quality method of perfect binding in which the spines of signatures are notched and hot glue is forced in before the cover is applied. *Also see* **perfect bind.**

Butt fit. Colors fitted edge to edge with only fractional overlap. This gives the appearance of a tight butt with the overlap ensuring that no line appears between colors.

Butt. To fit together edge to edge, without overlap.

C1S. Paper that is coated on one side. This is commonly used in heavier weights as cover stock for perfect bound books.

C2S. Paper that is coated on two sides. Unlike C1S, C2S is rarely used for perfect bound covers because it is difficult to get glue to adhere to the coating.

Caliper. This refers to paper thickness of paper in thousandths of an inch, and the term comes from the caliper used to measure it.

Callout. Generally, text used as an illustration by taking it from the body of copy and giving it special treatment, i.e., boxing it or setting it in larger or italic type.

Camera-ready copy. Artboards or mechanicals, with all halftones, type, etc., in place, ready to be photographed for platemaking according to the requirements of the printer.

Cap height. Height of a typeface's capital letters. *Also see* **x-height**.

Caption. Descriptive text accompanying a picture.

Case bind. To bind by gluing signatures to a case made of binder's board or similar stiff material. The outside is general finished with fabric, plastic, or leather. Case bound books are also referred to as hardcover or cloth bound.

Center marks. Lines on a mechanical, negative, plate, or press sheet indicating the center of a layout.

Centered. Unjustified lines of type with the middle of each line at the mid line of the column.

Character count. The number of characters in a pica, inch, line, column, or page varies with each typeface. In order to fit copy, it is important to know both the character count (including spaces between words) and the **alphabet length**.

Character set. A term referring to the specific assortment of letters, numerals, punctuation, special spaces, and symbols available in a typeface.

Character. Any letter, numeral, symbol, punctuation mark, or space.

Characters per pica (cpp). For a specific size and style of typeface, the number of character fitting into a 1-pica space. Along with **character count** and **alphabet length**, cpp is useful in copyfitting.

CIP data. Cataloging In Publication data — a program of the Library of Congress (and some other national libraries) to standardize cataloging information for books by providing the publisher with pre-assigned information that can be printed on the reverse of the title page. CIP data can also be gotten from independent services.

Cleat bind. Another term for *side stitch binding*.

Clip art. Illustrations printed on white, glossy paper or available on computer disk that can be used without license in layouts and designs.

Coarse screen. Halftone screen with a ruling of less than 133 lines per inch.

Coated paper. Coated papers may have finishes ranging from high gloss to matte. While prices vary for similar papers with different coatings or gloss, the important consideration is the use to which it will be put. For instance, high resolution photos may require a glossier paper.

Coated paper. Refers to paper coated with enamel or clay during manufacture to improve ink holdout and smoothness — especially important in the reproduction of photos, fine drawings, or small text.

Collate. To assemble sheets or signatures into proper order.

Colophon. Once the trademark of a publisher or printer, today it most often lists those who designed and produced the book, along with related information such as the choices of paper and typefaces.

Color (referring to type). When looked at from a slight distance, or squinted at, a page appears not as individual words but as a block that is more or less gray. If it appears too black, the type is too densely set and more space is probably needed between lines (leading) or characters (tracking), and vice versa.

Color bar. This is the strip of colors printed outside the crop marks of a press sheet to evaluate ink density.

Color key. This is an color proof comprised of overlays of the four colors.

Color matching systems. Any of a variety of standard systems of numbered ink swatches used to specify color.

Color process printing. The same as **4-color process printing.**

Color separation. Four-color printing (yellow, magenta, cyan, and black) is the method used to reproduce natural colors on paper. Each color ink is applied from a different plate, and the component colors must be first separated either mechanically or electronically into halftone negatives before this can be done.

Color swatch. An ink color sample. *Also see* **color matching systems**.

Comb binding. The use of a flexible plastic comb whose teeth are inserted through holes in a stack of paper.

Compose. To set type or to create complete, computer generated artwork.

Comprehensive dummy (comp). A simulation of a complete printed piece.

Condensed type. A typeface that has been by design or artificial means made narrower. *Also see* **expanded type.**

Continuous-tone image. An image, such as a photograph, in which the tones range from white to black, with grays in between. *Also see* **halftone** and **line drawing.**

Contrast. The gradations in tones between white and black in continuous-tone images, whether the changes are gradual or abrupt.

199

Copy. All written material needing to be edited or typeset. Also, all material that will be printed, including words and illustrations.

Copyedit. To edit a manuscript or piece of copy before typesetting. *Also see* **proofread.**

Copyfitting. Determining how much text will fit a given number of pages or how many pages will be required for a given amount of copy.

Copyright. Ownership of intellectual property by its author, photographer, or artist, or by the publisher purchasing a license to all or part of the rights.

Copywriter. Someone who writes advertising copy.

Cover stock. Paper designed for the covers of perfect bound books or for the dust jackets of case bound books.

cpp. *See* **characters per pica.**

Creep. Tendency of the middle pages of a folded signature to extend beyond those outside.

Cromalin. DuPont's trade name for a color proof printed on one page.

Crop marks. The lines at the corners of an image indicating the outside edges or the areas to be cropped (eliminated).

Cropping. Eliminating unwanted areas of a photograph or illustration. It is done to make a graphic fit the layout or improve the look.

Crossover. Type or graphics that extends across the gutter to the opposite page.

Descenders. The parts of lowercase letters extending below their baseline. These are the loops and strokes of the letters g, j, p, q, and y. *Also see* **ascenders.**

Desktop publishing. A term coined by Paul Brainerd of Aldus Corporation, developer of PageMaker software, to describe electronic typesetting and page composition on microcomputers. A more accurate phrase would now be *electronic prepress.*

Digital typography. Forming characters electronically, generally with a laser, by creating tightly spaced dots on either paper or photosensitive media. The more dots (and the smaller) per inch, the higher the resolution of the type.

Dingbat. Special type used for emphasis or ornamentation.

Display initial. The large letter used at the beginning of a paragraph or chapter. A **drop cap** descends into the text below. A **raised cap** stands on the baseline of the first line of text and ascends into the white space above.

Display type. Type used for headlines and titles. It is usually larger than the text type and may be a separate typeface.

Dot gain. The effect of ink being absorbed by paper and spreading to an area slightly larger than that indicated on the mechanical or negative. Dot gain varies with the type of paper and the saturation of the ink. It should be taken into consideration when fine type or lines are used on such absorbent papers as newsprint.

Drilling. Boring holes in paper so sheets fit over the posts of loose-leaf binders or allow the insertion of the teeth of plastic combs, spiral bindings, or other mechanical fasteners.

Drop folio. A folio is a page number. When it is placed on the bottom of a page, it is a drop folio.

Drop out. The elimination of halftone dots or fine lines because of overexposure while making the negative or printing plate.

Dull finish. A paper finish that reflects little light, as opposed to **gloss finish.** *Also see* **matte finish.**

Dummy. A preliminary layout showing the elements to be included in their approximate positions. Sometime this is a sketch, and it may be a miniature version of an entire book.

Duotone. A halftone printed in two colors to achieve the effect of greater depth. Two negatives are used, one for each color. The usual combinations are black and gray, blue and black, and black and brown.

Dust jacket. The paper cover that is wrapped around a **case bound** book. Meant to protect the book's cover material, it is now both an artistic devise and a sales tool.

Dylux. DuPont's trade name for photosensitive paper used for bluelines.

Electronic imaging. Computerized creation or assembly of an image from existing images or computer scans.

Electronic page composition. Creation of camera-ready, fully composed pages of text and graphics on a computer. *Also see* **desktop publishing.**

Electronic photo retouching. Enhancing or correcting a scanned photograph on a computer.

Em dash. A punctuation mark used to indicate a break in a thought or in the structure of a sentence. It can also be used to indicate missing material in a sentence. You have the choice of leaving or not leaving a space before and after an em dash. *See also* **en dash.**

Em space. A space equal in width to (1) the size of a capital M in the type being used or (2) the point size of the type. It is used as punctuation to show missing text or a break in sentence flow similar to parentheses. *Also see* **en space.**

En dash. A punctuation mark that is half the width of an **em dash.** It is used to link items such as dates, i.e., 1921–45.

En space. A space that is half the width of an em. *Also see* **em space.**

Endpapers. Also called *end sheets* and *end leaves*, these are the heavy papers glued to inside back and front covers of case bound books. They serve to attach the book block to the case, and they are often decorative, as well.

Epilogue. The opposite of a **prologue** (which introduces), the epilogue summarizes or concludes.

Errata slip. Errata is Latin for errors. When mistakes are discovered after a book or periodical has been printed, a loose page called an errata slip is sometimes inserted to correct them.

Estimate. This is a projected price of a printing job based on the customer's original specifications. It is also called a *quote.*

Excerpt. Part of another text included in a document.

Expanded type. A typeface expanded in width, either electronically or by design. *Also see* **Condensed type.**

F&Gs. These are folded and gathered signatures of a book, not yet bound.

Family of type. The several styles of a typeface are a family. These might include some or all of the following: roman, italic, bold, semibold, ornamental, swash, etc. Each style has an obvious family relationship, but like brothers and sisters, can be quite different in many ways.

Film lamination. This is one protective coating commonly used on book covers to enhance durability or for artistic effect. The two most common films, which are applied as a thin sheet after printing, are gloss and matte.

Fine screen. A halftone screen of 150 lines or more per inch.

Finish size. This is the final, trimmed size of a publication after all bindery work.

Finishing. Used to describe all bindery work.

Flood varnish. A protective coating frequently used on cover stock. *Also see* **spot varnish.**

Flood. This means to totally cover a sheet of paper with ink or varnish.

Flush cover. A flush cover is trimmed to the same size as the pages of a publication.

Flush left. Type aligned vertically on the left side of a column.

Flush right. Type aligned vertically on the right side of a column.

Foil stamping. A die is used to stamp and emboss text or design, often on the spine or front cover of a case bound book.

Folio. A page number is called a folio.

Font. A complete character set for one size of one typeface is a font. Though font is often used interchangeably with **typeface,** they are not the same.

Footers. Text placed at the bottom of each page as a recurring element, generally including a folio and information such as book title, chapter title, or author's name. *Also see* **running heads.**

Foreword. Usually written by a person other than a book's author, the foreword is the first item in the front matter. A **preface** is a written by a book's author. *Also see* **front matter.**

Format. As a noun, this refers to the organization and style of a publication or one of its parts. As a verb, it is the act of giving the publication, a part of a publication, or only type, its organization and style.

Four-color process (4-process color). A printing method using the four process colors of ink (cyan, magenta, yellow, and black, or CMYK) to reproduce color artwork such as photographs or illustrations.

Front matter. The first section of a book, always preceding the main body of text, and including the half title page, title page, frontispiece, copyright page, foreword, preface, introduction, table of contents, and so forth.

Frontispiece. A frontispiece is either an illustration facing the title page or the page facing the title page itself.

Galley or galley proof. A proof, or finished sample, of typeset text, which was originally made by inking hand-set metal type while it was still in the tray (galley) used for composition and pressing a sheet of paper directly on it. *Also see* **proofreader.**

Gang. Pieces are ganged when two or more are printed at the same time on each sheet of paper. It also refers to grouping other things, such as photos, for some part of the process.

Gather. Signatures are gathered into the proper order for binding.

GBC binding. A trade name for plastic comb binding.

Generation. This term refers to how close an image is to the original, which is the first generation, i.e., the original camera-ready copy for this page. The second generation is made from the original, i.e., the negative shot from the original. The third generation is made from the second generation, i.e., the printing plate made from the negative. The fourth generation is made from the third, i.e., the printed type you are reading. As a rule, the fewer generations between original and final, the higher the quality.

Gloss. A finish on paper, ink, or varnish that reflects a lot of light. *Also see* **matte.**

Glossary. You are reading a glossary, which is a list of definitions of words used in a particular publication or related to its subject.

Grade. There are seven major grades of paper, each having a variety of weights, colors, contents, and finishes. The seven are uncoated book, coated book, text, cover, bond, board, and specialty.

Grain long. Paper is grain long when its fibers run parallel to the longer dimension.

Grain short. Paper is grain short when its fibers are parallel to the shorter dimension.

Grain. When paper is manufactured, the flow of the pulp onto special screens causes the fibers to line up in one direction, called the grain. Paper will fold or tear more easily in the direction of the grain. A simple test is to take a small square of paper, moisten it on one side, then watch how it curls — the grain will be in the direction of the trough of the curl. The grain direction is important to good book construction, where grain should run in the same direction as the spine. When binding is done against the grain (sometimes called *cross grain*), pages may pucker or open poorly. This is because, as humidity changes, paper expands and contracts more across the grain than with it. *Also see* **with the grain** and **against the grain.**

Grammage. Most of the world, except the U.S., calculates the **basis weight** of paper by measuring the number of grams per square meter. *Also see* **basis weight.**

Graphic arts. Inclusively, the arts, crafts, and professions involved in designing for print and printing.

Graphic designer. A graphic designer creates designs for printed matter and may also plan or coordinate the production of them.

Graphics. Visual elements, including illustrations, photographs, and sometimes type, that are part of a printed whole.

Gray scale. A printed scale of values ranging in tone from white to black indicating percentages of black.

Greeked type. Greeked type is a substitute for real text comprised of meaningless words that reflect the frequency of letters in normal English. It is used to simulate the look of a layout or for estimating the amount of text for copyfitting.

Grid. Grids are a common tool in organizing a layout by providing uniform, proportionally spaced guides.

Groundwood paper. Papers made from chemically treated ground wood fibers, generally represented by newsprint and other cheap papers.

Gutter. The space between pages at the binding — the margin closest to the binding — is the most common definition, but gutter is also used to refer to the space between any two columns of text. *Also see* **alley.**

Hairline. A very thin space or line about 1/100 of an inch.

Half title page. A page with only the title of a book; usually the first page.

Halftone screen. A piece of film with a grid of lines that breaks light into dots as it passes through. Halftone screens are available in a variety of patterns (round, square, vertical, horizontal, diagonal, etc.) and fineness. They are selected according to the desired effect and the best resolution of the printer to be used.

Halftone. A halftone is created by photographing an illustration or a photograph through a halftone screen that breaks the image into dots which give the illusion of shades of gray when they are printed.

Hanging Indentation. Hanging indentation means that the first line of a paragraph begins flush left and the rest of the paragraph is indented.

Hard copy. Copy that is written or printed on paper.

Hard cover. A **case bound** book.

Headbands. Strips of braided thread applied at the top or bottom of the spine of a case bound book for reinforcement or decoration.

Hickey. An imperfection in printing in heavily inked areas, often caused by a bubble in the ink. *Also see* **pickey.**

High contrast. This means there are few if any shades of gray, with mostly black or white.

High-bulk paper. This is paper manufactured to be relatively thick (higher *ppi*) for its basis weight. It is usually more textured, rougher, or toothy.

Image area. This is the area inside the margins of a page or a mechanical where ink can be applied, including the text area and any other graphics, headers, footers, etc.

Imposition. This is the placement of pages on mechanicals so they will appear in proper order when the printed signatures are folded.

Imprint. An imprint is the name a publisher uses for its line of books or for one specific line of books.

Introduction. This is the last part of the front matter and introduces a publication's subject. *Also see* **foreword** and **preface.**

ISBN. The International Standard Book Number is a ten digit code with a prefix identifying the publisher and country of publication and a suffix assigned to a specific edition of a book (a book with both hard and soft bound editions would use a separate number for each). The numbers are administered by a voluntary international organization with an administrative organization handling assignments in each country. The ISBN U.S. Agency is administered by the R. R. Bowker Company in New Jersey. The number is used by libraries and bookstores to locate publishers and books and to organize inventory. It should appear on the copyright page or the reverse side of the title page and on the back cover.

ISSN. The International Standard Serial Number is assigned by the Library of Congress in Washington, DC, to periodicals. It serves a similar function to the **ISBN.**

Italics. The slanting type used for each glossary entry in this book, and frequently used for emphasis in publications, italic type is one style in a family of typefaces. It was first designed to save space. *Also see* **roman type,** which is what you are now reading.

Jog. To shake or vibrate a stack of pages in order to straighten or align them, either by hand or machine.

Justified type. Type that has all lines (except indented first lines of paragraphs and short last line) vertically aligned on both right and left margins. *Also see* **ragged type.**

Kerning. Kerning is adjusting the space between certain letter pairs which normally seem to be too far apart or too close.

Keylines. A lines or boxes showing the exact size and location of artwork. Keyline is also used another term for *mechanical.*

Laminate. As a verb, it means to adhere materials to each other, such as plastic film to cover paper, or different papers into paperboard. As a noun, it refers to materials that have been laminated.

Landscape. A format for a page or publication that is wider than it is tall. Also called a *horizontal format. Also see* **portrait.**

Laser printing. This is a method of imaging that uses a laser beam to place dots representing type or graphics either directly on a photosensitive material (RC paper or negative film) or as electrical charges on a transfer drum that then applies the image as a toner powder to paper. The resolution of laser printers ranges from less than 300 dpi (dot per inch) to 5,000 dpi. The type you are reading was imaged by laser at around 1,200 dpi.

Layout. A layout is a drawing of a design showing the placement, sizes, and intended colors of copy for a publication.

LCCN. The Library of Congress Catalog Number is a unique number assigned to a book by the Library of Congress, which catalogs and archives all publications submitted to it. The LCCN is usually printed on the copyright page.

Leader. A row of dots or other characters used to connect elements separated across a page, as in a table of some sort.

Leading. Pronounced *ledding,* this refers to the space between lines of type, expressed in points. It comes from the days of handset type when thin strips of lead were used to space lines apart.

Legend. This usually refers to tables or lists of symbols and definitions used in a chart or on a map**.**

Legibility. This is the clarity of type and how easily it can be recognized by the eye of the reader. Legibility depends upon type size, type style, letterspacing, line length, paper texture, paper color, and various subjective factors. *Also see* **readability.**

Letterpress. A letterpress prints directly from the raised surfaces of type or engravings.

Letterspacing. This is the amount space between letters, which is important to *legibility, readability,* and *copyfitting. Also see* **kerning, tracking,** and **leading.**

Ligature. Two or three letters that, because of their design, look better when printed as one character that better integrates them. The letters ff, fi, fl, ffi, ffl form ligatures in many typefaces. On computer publishing systems, these characters must generally be entered using special key combinations.

Light table or box. A table or box with glass surface evenly lit from below. Light showing through the paper makes layout of mechanicals easier.

Line drawing or copy. Elements to be printed that have no halftones and are simply high contrast.

Line measure or length. This is the length of a line of type. *Also see* **copyfitting.**

Lines per inch. The measure of halftone screen density or resolution.

Linotype. The trade name for a machine manufactured by Megenthaler that sets lines of metal type. These are now rarely used, having been replaced by photo- or laser-imagesetters.

Lowercase. Small letters, as opposed to **uppercase** or capital letters, are so called because when type was hand-set it was stored in wooden cases, with sections for different letter, symbols, and spaces. Capital letters were in one case and small letters in another. When setting type, typesetters placed the tray with the capitals above the other, thus uppercase and lowercase letters.

Magenta. One of the four process colors (CMYK) also called as process red.

Margin. The space around the borders or outside the print area of a page.

Mark up. To write instructions on copy or proofs telling a typesetter or author how to correct or change it.

Mask out. To cover part of the artwork so it is not included on the negative or plate.

Matte finish. Slightly dull finish, as opposed to glossy.

Matte ink or varnish. Ink or varnish that appears dull when dry.

Matte laminate. A dull finished plastic film applied to heavy papers, such as cover stock.

Measure. The length of a line of type is a measure. *Also see* **line measure or length.**

Mechanical binding. A binding that uses metal rings, posts, plastic combs, wire spirals, or other special fasteners.

Mechanical separation. A mechanical with a separate overlay for each color.

Mechanicals. Camera-ready artboards on which all text, graphics, photos, and other elements to be printed have been mounted in place for printing.

Medium screen. A halftone screen with 133 to 150 lines per inch.

Mimeograph. Printing using a plastic stencil mounted on a rotating ink drum.

Model release. A form granting commercial use of a photograph that includes a recognizable individual or private property. The necessity of a release is dictated by the circumstance under which the photo was taken, and a legal guide to publishing should be consulted for the rules and exceptions.

Moiré pattern. In halftones and other screened images, a moiré pattern occurs when different screens are applied to each other or are not correctly aligned.

Monospacing. An alphabet in which all letters are of equal width is monospaced. The best example is type from an old manual typewriter. *Also see* **proportional spacing.**

Mounting board. Thick, smooth paper used to paste up copy for mechanicals.

Negative. An image on paper or film in which the black and white of the original are reverse. *Also see* **positive.**

Non-aligning or old style numerals. Numbers with ascenders and descenders similar to lowercase letters, i.e., abcd1234569890efgh. *Also see* **aligning numerals.**

Non-image area. Area of mechanical that will not print.

Non-photographable or non-reproducing blue. A light blue color that does not photograph and which may be used to write instructions on material that will be photographed, such as copy, photos, etc..

Notch binding. A book binding where the spine edge of the gathered signatures is scored with diagonal notches into which glue is forced to create the bind.

Offset printing. Lithographic printing in which ink is transferred from a printing plate on one cylinder to a rubber blanket on another, and then is applied to paper.

Opacity. A paper quality indicating how resistant it is to having print on the other side show through.

Opaque. Meaning that light does not flow through, i.e., not translucent or transparent. Used as a verb, it means to cover or block out.

Optical character reader (OCR). This usually refers to a combination of computer hardware, character recognition software, and a scanner.

Orphan. A single line of a paragraph left on the bottom of a page with the rest on the next page is called an orphan. *Also see* **widow.**

Overlay. A piece of transparent or translucent material, such as plastic or tissue, attached to cover a mechanical.

Pad binding. A simple binding made by applying glue along one edge of a stack of sheets.

Page proof. A page completely formatted. *Also see* **proof.**

Pages per inch (ppi). A measure of the thickness of paper for a bound publication in which each sheet counts as two pages. This measure must be known so the spine width of the cover will be correct.

Paste-up. To affix copy to mounting boards with hot wax, glue, or other adhesives. Also, another term for **mechanical.**

PE. A notation for printer's error used during proofreading.

Perfect bind. A book binding where the spines of the gathered signatures are planed off, roughed, and glued to the cover.

Perfecting press. A printing press that prints both sides of the paper in one pass.

pH. A symbol for acidity or alkalinity using a scale of O to 14, where 7 is neutral. Numbers less than 7 indicate an acid; numbers greater than 7 indicate a base (alkaline). *Also see* **acid-free paper.**

Photocopy. Printing by transferring images electrostatically and using a fine toner powder that is heat-fused to the paper.

Photosensitive. Any material, including paper, film, and printing plates of metal or plastic, that has been coated with light-sensitive chemicals — chemicals that react differently when exposed to different amounts of light.

Photostat. A photograph of line copy and halftones, generally to achieve a desired enlargement or reduction, and also called a stat, PMT, or Velox.

Phototypesetting. Setting type by projecting light through outlines of characters onto photosensitive paper. This method is rapidly being replaced by digital or laser imagesetting.

Pica. A typesetting measure equal to 1/6 of an inch or 12 points.

Pickey. A loose paper fiber or other piece of dust, coating, or lint that lifts from an inked surface to leave an imperfection. *Also see* **hickey.**

Plate cylinder. Cylinder of an offset press on which the printing plate is mounted.

Plate. *See* **Printing plate**.

Plugging. When printing ink fills in around halftone dots, or fine details, including the open spaces (counterweights) of some letters, such as *e* and *a*. This can be caused by overinking or by using a paper which is too absorbent to handle fine lines and small space. *Also see* **dot gain.**

PMS. The abbreviation for *Pantone Matching System*, a standard set of numbered ink colors used in printing.

PMT. The abbreviation for *photomechanical transfer*. A screened photo of a piece of art, generally reduced or enlarged. *Also see* **photostat** and **Velox.**

Point. In typesetting, a measure equal to 1/72 of an inch or 1/12 of a pica. The sizes of typefaces are expressed in points, as is the associated **leading**: type set 10/12 (or 10 on 12) is type 10 points high with two points of lead (space) added between lines.

Portrait. A format where the page, publication, or element is taller than wide. *Also see* **landscape.**

Position Stat. A **photostat** used to indicate which picture is to be placed and how it is to be cropped. *Also see* **cropping.**

Positive. An image on paper or film in which the black and white areas are the same as on the original. *Also see* **negative.**

PPI. *See* **pages per inch.**

Preface. A section of the front matter written by the author. *Also see* **foreword** and **front matter.**

Preparation or prep. All layout, stripping, camera-work (halftones, etc.), paste-up, and platemaking done before printing begins.

Prepress. Another term for **preparation.**

Press check. Examination of **press proofs** pulled before the actual production run is allowed.

Press proof. An actual copy or proof made on the press with the plates, paper, and ink specified for the print run.

Printing plate. In offset lithography, the surface holding the image to be printed. It may be made of a variety of materials, from papers to metals.

Process blue. Another term for **cyan** (**C**MYK), one of the colors used in 4-color process printing.

Process colors. The colors used in 4-color process printing: yellow, magenta, cyan, and black (CMYK).

Process red. Another term for **magenta** (C**M**YK), one of the colors used in 4-color process printing.

Prologue. A book's introduction and part of the **front matter.** *Also see* **epilogue.**

Proof. A test sheet of the actual printed piece used to find mistakes or problems so they can be corrected before the run is finally printed. *Also see* **galley** and **blueline.**

Proofread. This means to check a **proof** for mistakes in writing, typesetting, or composition.

Proofreader's marks. A set of standard symbols and abbreviations for marking up manuscripts and proofs. Most dictionaries and style manuals include charts of proofreader marks.

Proofreader. A person who reads the **proof** taken from the composed type looking for mistakes.

Proportional scale or wheel. A mechanical device for calculating the percent that an image must be enlarged or reduced for inclusion in a mechanical.

Proportional spacing. When letters of a character set use space in proportion to their individual widths. *Also see* **monospacing.**

Pulp. The mixture of fibers and water from which mills make paper. Fibers can be from a number of sources, including ground wood, cotton, linen, hemp, flax, and papyrus.

Ragged right or left. This means to set type so that one edge is justified vertically, leaving lines of uneven length. A more common term is *unjustified* to denote ragged right type.

RC paper. Resin-coated, photosensitive paper for typesetting and PMTs.

Readability. This is a subjective measure of how easily the printed words can be read. It is related to **legibility**

Ream. 500 sheets of paper.

Recto. In a publication of more than two pages, this is a right-hand page, from the Latin for *right*. *Also see* **verso.**

Register marks. Cross-hairs on the edges of mechanicals and negatives that serve as guides.

Register. To properly position artwork, negatives, or printing.

Request for quote (rfq). A set of specifications sent to a printer asking for a bid on a job.

Reversed type. Type printed as white against a darker background.

Right reading. Copy that can be read normally, from left to right.

Rights. The ownership of or license to use creative work or intellectual property. *Also see* **copyrights.**

River. A visible pattern of white space running like a river down a block of text.

Roman type. Type is not italic. Put another way, type that is upright (not slanted).

Roman numerals. Numbers as written by the Romans using letters of the alphabet — i, ii, iii, iv, v, x, c, etc. or I, II, III, IV, V, X, C, etc. *Also see* **Arabic numerals.**

Rubylith. A trade name for red film used for masking on **mechanicals**.

Rules. Straight lines of any thickness, generally given in points or fractions of points.

Runaround. Type conforming to the outline of a graphic element, usually with a specified offset from its borders.

Running head(er) or foot(er). Information at the top or bottom of every page of a publication. Also simply called **headers** or **footers**.

Saddle stitching. Saddle stitching is a simple binding where sheets are stapled together on the fold at the, as is often done with smaller publications such as booklets, magazines, and brochures.

Sans serif. This term refers to a typeface without serifs, which are those small strokes at the start and finish of the main letter strokes. They are remnants of the origin of type in handwriting, especially calligraphy. The typeface you are reading is san serifs. Sans serif types are almost all linear, with uniform strokes and geometric curves. Because they have so little variation in shape, they are rarely used for large blocks of text, or where reading long passages is important, because they get boring and hard for the eye to follow. They're quite economical in terms of space and generally set well at smaller sizes, so they are often used in directories, like phone books, are for captions, catalogs — or in larger sizes for headlines and titles of publications where the body type is **roman.**

Scaling. The means to enlarge or reduce some graphic element by a specified percentage to fit in a layout or a mechanical.

Scanner. This is an electronic device, now usually computerized, used to capture an image from which to make color separations, halftones, or to scale and place images directly by way of a page composition computer program. Scanners are also used in combination with optical character readers (OCRs) to translate text on paper to computer readable formats that can be edited with word processors. Scanners are available in a broad range of resolutions and prices.

Score. To make a shallow cut or dent in paper so it will fold more easily.

Serif. This refers to typefaces with letter strokes whose widths vary and which are begun or ended with a slight calligraphic flourish. *Also see* **sans serif** for more discussion**.**

Screen density. The number of lines per inch in a halftone screen determining the resolution of the halftone image and ink coverage when printed.

Screen tint. Use of a halftone screen to create a percentage shade, such as gray, of an ink in printing.

Screen. Piece of film with dots or lines of uniform frequency (density) and various shapes, used to make halftone photos or plates. *Also see* **halftone screen.**

Self-cover. This means using the same paper for both cover and inside of a publication so that all can be printed at once. It's used on many catalogs and magazines and, of course, on all newspapers.

Set solid. Refers to type set without extra space (**leading**) between the lines.

Sew. Use thread to bind signatures together at their spines.

Sheetfed press. A sheetfed press prints from cut sheets of paper, rather than from a roll. *Also see* **web press.**

Show through. This is when the print one side of paper can be seen on the other. *Also see* **opacity.**

Side sewing. Similar to **side stitching**, this is the process of using heavy thread to sew through stacked pages along the spine edge.

Side stitching. The method of book binding in which the pages are trimmed on all four sides and bound with metal staples near the spine.

Signature (sig). A signature is a group of pages printed on one sheet of paper and arranged so that, when folded and trimmed, the pages will appear in the correct order. The number of pages per signature depends on the size of the sheet and the size of the finished page. A single sheet with one page on each side is a 2-page signature; if two pages are printed on each side, it's a 4-page signature. For most work, there are 8, 12, 16, 24, or 32 pages per signature.

Small capitals or caps. In more sophisticated typefaces, these are specially designed uppercase letters that are slightly taller than the x-height of the lowercase characters, i.e., AAaBBbXxx. Today, they are often generated by computers by simply using a smaller version of the face's uppercase letters.

Smyth sewn. Refers to one method of binding by sewing the pages of signatures together with thread and gluing them to the cover, which is usually a case, but may be a paper cover.

Soft copy. As opposed to hard copy, this text is stored in computer memory or on tapes or disks.

Softcover. A book bound without a case, and usually referring to **perfect bound** books.

Spec sheet. A page of specifications for a project or a part of a project.

Spec type. To determine the specifications for the type to be used..

Specifications. These are instruction for either all or part of a project setting out precisely how things will be done, such as the typefaces, line measures, page sizes, and ink colors.

Spine. The edge of a signature or publication at which it is bound.

Spiral binding. A mechanical method of binding using a spiral of wire or plastic wound through punched or drilled holes.

Spirit duplicating. A printing method that uses a fluid to dissolve some of the ink from a paper plate on a cylinder (drum) to make each impression.

Spot varnish. A coating applied like ink either to protect a paper surface or as an element of art. It may be applied to the entire sheet or only to certain spots, and it may have a number of finishes, from high gloss to very dull matte. *Also see* **flood varnish.**

spread. Abbreviation of *two-page spread*, or *double-page spread* — two pages seen side by side. In designing a book you should consider the two pages as one unit, not as two separate units. **stat.** *Also see* **photostat.**

Stet. This is **proofreader's mark** or copy editor's mark used to reverse a correction and meaning "let it stand."

Stock. Printers refer to paper as stock.

Stripper. An individual who strips (assembles) negatives or other elements into a mechanical for making a negative or a printing plate.

Stripping. The job of assembling negatives into mechanicals in preparation for making printing plates, stripping is more and more being done by computer as part of complete electronic prepress production.

TE. Stands for Typesetter's Error. *Also see* **PE.**

Text or body type. A typeface selected for the major copy of a publication.

Thumbnail. This is either a miniature printed version or a rough sketch of a proposed page layout.

Trap. When one ink is used butted against or completely enclosed by another, a trap is used to slightly overlap the adjacent inks, ensuring that no line of unprinted paper is visible between the colors.

Trim marks. As the name suggests, these are lines on a mechanical, negative, plate, or press sheet showing where to trim edges from paper or where to cut smaller sheets out of larger after printing. *Also see* **crop marks.**

Trim size. This is the specified finished size of a publication. Some common trim sizes are 5 1/2" x 8 1/2", 6" x 9", 7" x 10", 8 1/2" x 11", and 11" x 17". It is useful to understand that trimming will rarely be exactly to these dimensions, so they are best thought of as nominal sizes (sizes in name only). Trim obviously has to be enough to remove any crop marks, which means that crops drawn at the specified trim size will guarantee that the actual finished size will be smaller.

Type family. *See* **family of type.**

Type size. This is the height of an alphabet in a typeface, from the bottom of its descenders to the top of its ascenders. It is expressed in points. *Also see* **points.**

Type style. Italic, extended, condensed, light, bold, heavy, book, semibold and other variations of a typeface that are part of a family of type.

Typeface. A set of designed characters — letters, numbers, symbols, spaces, and punctuation — with strong commonality.

Typesetter. A typesetter sets type, which is done in a variety of ways, either mechanical, photographic, or electronic. A typesetting machine is also called a typesetter.

Typo. A typographical error.

Typography. This is the technical art of typesetting and making larger decisions concerning the selection of typefaces for particular publications.

Ultraviolet coating (uv). Ultraviolet coatings are so called because ultraviolet lights are used to dry (cure) the liquid applied to printed paper to enhance or protect it. Finishes vary from matte to gloss.

Uppercase. Capital letters. *Also see* **lowercase** for more discussion of these terms.

Unjustified. This has the same meaning as **ragged right or left**.

UV coating. *See* **ultraviolet coating**.

Varnish. Varnish, which may provide finishes and effects, is liquid applied to enhance or protect printed matter, especially cover. *Also see* **flood varnish** and **ultraviolet coating.**

Velox. A type of Kodak photographic paper used for screened positives to be positioned on a **mechanical,** it adds one **generation** between the original and the printed version. *Also see* **PMT** and **photostat.**

Verso. This refers to a left-hand page in a publication of more than two pages. It's from the Latin verb for "to keep turning." *Also see* **recto.**

Vertical justification. This means to make sure that adjacent columns of text are aligned at top and bottom. It is done by adjusting space (**leading**) between lines of type.

Web press. An offset press that prints from a roll of paper.

Web. A roll of printing paper is a web.

Weight (of type). A description of how light or dark, thin or bold, a typeface appears. The number of weights in a family of type varies from one to several. *Also see* **family of type** and **type style.**

Weight (of paper). See **basis weight**.

White space. This refers to areas without images on the page. It is considered in publication design as an essential element of good composition.

Widow. A widow is a short line ending a paragraph that appears alone at the top of the next page or column. It also is used to denote an extremely short last line, usually a lone word or word part, in any paragraph. *Also see* **orphan.**

Window. A precise area on a layout which is left opaque so that it will be a solid transparent image on the negative, allowing easy positioning (stripping) of a **halftone.**

Wire-O binding. A mechanical binding using double loops of wire and otherwise similar to spiral binding.

With the grain. Parallel to the grain direction of paper. *Also see* **against the grain** and **grain.**

Word spacing. The amount of space between words is originally set by the type designer, along with character spacing, but it is generally adjustable, and almost always will be changed when type is fully justified.

Wrong reading. This refers to an image on a positive print or negative that is backwards compared to the original.

X-height. This is one of the important and basic measures of a typeface. It refers to the height of the body of a letter, without descenders and ascenders, using the letter x as the base.

INDEX